A REPUBLIC,
IF YOU CAN KEEP IT

A REPUBLIC, IF YOU CAN KEEP IT

NEIL M. GORSUCH

with

JANE NITZE *and*
DAVID FEDER

———

CROWN
FORUM

NEW YORK

Published in the United States by Crown Forum,
an imprint of Random House, a division of
Penguin Random House LLC, New York.

crownpublishing.com

CROWN FORUM with colophon is a registered trademark
of Penguin Random House LLC.

Photo credits are located on page 329.

LIBRARY OF CONGRESS CATALOGING-IN-PUBLICATION DATA
NAMES: Gorsuch, Neil M. (Neil McGill), 1967– author.
TITLE: A republic, if you can keep It / Neil Gorsuch.
DESCRIPTION: New York : Crown Forum, 2019. | Includes
bibliographical references and index.
IDENTIFIERS: LCCN 2019012484 | ISBN 9780525576785 (hardback) |
9780525576792 (ebook)
SUBJECTS: LCSH: Law—United States. | Judicial process—United States. |
BISAC: BIOGRAPHY & AUTOBIOGRAPHY / Lawyers & Judges. |
POLITICAL SCIENCE / Government / Judicial Branch. |
BIOGRAPHY & AUTOBIOGRAPHY / Political.
CLASSIFICATION: LCC KF213 .G67 2019 | DDC 349.73—dc23
LC record available at https://lccn.loc.gov/2019012484

Printed in the United States of America

2 4 6 8 9 7 5 3 1

FIRST EDITION

For Louise, Emma, and Belinda

CONTENTS

3.

THE JUDGE'S TOOLS

4.

THE ART OF JUDGING

5.

TOWARD JUSTICE FOR ALL

6.

ON ETHICS AND THE GOOD LIFE

—

7.

FROM JUDGE TO JUSTICE

—

A REPUBLIC,
IF YOU CAN KEEP IT

INTRODUCTION

O N A BEAUTIFUL AUTUMN AFTERNOON IN 2016, I found myself sitting outside enjoying lunch with a friend. In kind tones, he told me that he thought it was a shame I hadn't made then-candidate Donald Trump's publicly announced list of potential Supreme Court nominees. No matter, I replied: I was very happy with my job as a federal circuit judge and loved my life in Colorado. Soon enough the conversation moved on, a lazy meal ended, and we said our goodbyes. But before I managed to walk a block, my phone buzzed. It was a text from my lunch companion: A new, second list just came out and I had to see it.

Looking back, I can see that this moment marked the beginning of the end of my life as I had known it. It wasn't so obvious at the time. Even as the election neared, the polls reported that candidate Trump had little chance of becoming President Trump. What's more, my friends told me, the second list was just a courtesy or maybe for show and only the first list mattered; so even if the polls proved wrong, there was no way I'd wind up the nominee. All that sounded about right to me.

It came as a surprise, then, when I received a call two months later asking me to come to Washington to interview with the Vice President–elect. And it was an even greater surprise when, soon after that, the President-elect asked me to visit him in New York for a second interview.

The shock still hadn't worn off when I found myself sitting with my wife, Louise, in the White House on January 31, 2017. I could hardly believe that later in the evening the President would announce to the nation his intention to nominate me to the Supreme Court. The formal nomination would be transmitted to the Senate first thing the next day, February 1, on what would have been my father's eightieth birthday. It was a lot to take in.

Not just for me, but for my family too. Earlier in the day, the President tweeted: "Getting ready to deliver a VERY IMPORTANT DECISION! 8:00 P.M." The media knew the decision concerned the Supreme Court pick but had no idea who the nominee would be. Television commentators speculated all day. Meanwhile, I sat quietly in the Lincoln Bedroom working on my remarks for the evening's announcement. The President had offered me that historic spot as an office for the day. Knowing that Louise was born and raised in England, he gave her the use of the bedroom across the hall typically reserved for Queen Elizabeth and once occupied by Winston Churchill. Finding a little time late in the day, Louise rang her father back in England to tell him the news, but before she could say anything my father-in-law interjected that he had stayed up to watch the announcement. He had seen all the reporting, and he was sure that a friend of mine was about to get the nod. Louise replied that she was *pretty* sure I was the pick. No, he countered, the other fellow was caught on television just now driving toward Washington, and the newscasters were sure it was him. My father-in-law wasn't even convinced when Louise told him that we had slipped through the White House kitchen entrance and were now in the Lincoln Bedroom. Maybe the real nominee was in a room down the hall?

To be fair to my father-in-law, I was almost as surprised as he was that I was busy preparing for a nationally televised appearance in the White House. Only days earlier, I was happily living on a quiet country road called Lookout Ridge outside Niwot, Colorado, a little town named for a great Arapaho chief. Yes, I had written hundreds of judicial decisions over the last decade, sitting on an appellate court that serves about 20 percent of the continental United States. But few people outside of legal circles knew who I was.

That life was now over. Our trip to Washington was enough to convince me of that. Two young White House lawyers, Mike and James, had arrived at our home on the Sunday afternoon before the scheduled Thursday evening announcement of my nomination with the task of accompanying Louise and me to the nation's capital. I was out mowing the lawn and asked the pair to join us for our usual Sunday dinner of chicken curry. They accepted and, after our meal together, headed off to a local hotel with plans to return the next morning to collect us for the flight.

Except at some point Monday morning the President told the media that he would be making his nomination on Tuesday instead of Thursday. Eager to break the news of the President's pick before he could make his own announcement, reporters quickly descended on all of the homes of the prospective nominees, and satellite dishes, cameras, microphones, and lawn chairs soon crowded the end of our street.

Mike and James, wearing suits and ties (not exactly standard attire in the Colorado countryside), approached the frenzy in their rental car and immediately realized that if they continued to our home they would be spotted. To avoid that, and after more than a few abandoned plans—including a run to the local superstore for casual clothes—the lawyers called to ask: Would Louise and I please hike a mile through the prairie, away from the reporters' camp? They promised to pick us up at a trailhead. It may have sounded good to them, but the prospect of lugging my wife's suitcase through brush seemed like a bad idea to me.

Instead, Louise and I decided to ask a neighbor to drive us out. The reporters had already seen his car come and go a few times and maybe they wouldn't notice—and, even if they did, it seemed to beat the alternative. Our neighbor, a dear friend, enthusiastically agreed.

As we got into his car he said, "You know, Neil, I have a better idea. There's another way out." That was news to me. We had lived in our home for years, and while there were plenty of hiking trails and horse paths, there were no other roads out of the neighborhood. My friend pointed to a path that led from the back of a neighbor's house to a nearby commercial barn and said he had managed to drive it before. "I grew up in Iran during the revolution, and I learned a thing or two there," he continued. "And I would *never* buy a house with only one escape route."

So I fled my house—and, temporarily, the spotlight—by way of a bumpy farm track. My neighbor and I came to call our experience the Escape from Lookout Ridge. In retrospect, it wasn't an "escape" at all. That drive threw me face first into the topsy-turvy world of modern-day Supreme Court confirmation battles.

THIS BOOK WAS BORN of that confirmation process, though it is not about it. A decade earlier, the Senate had confirmed my judicial nomination to the Tenth Circuit by a voice vote, without opposition, and with the support of both of my home state's senators, one a Democrat and the other a Republican. My hearing had lasted about fifteen minutes. This time around was different. As the months-long process unfolded, I heard people speak about the law and my decades in the profession in ways I didn't recognize. Some suggested that as a judge I "liked" one group of persons or "disliked" another. In an effort to prove their point, they would sometimes single out a case where I had ruled for or against a particular kind of person but overlook plenty of cases where I had ruled the other way. Often, too, they would fail to engage the critical legal or factual reasons for the different outcomes. Others insisted that I promise to overrule certain decisions they disagreed with or reaffirm ones they preferred.

By the end of it all, I came to realize that some today perceive a judge to be just like a politician who can and must promise (and then deliver) policy outcomes that favor certain groups. They see the job of a judge as less about following the law and facts wherever they lead and more about doing whatever it takes to "help" this group or "stop" that policy. And it struck me: It's one thing to worry some judges *might* aggrandize their personal preferences over a faithful adherence to the law; but it's another thing to think judges *should* behave like that.

The idea that judges do—and should—allow their policy preferences to determine their legal rulings was foreign to my experience in the law. The judges I admired as a lawyer and those I have come to cherish as colleagues know that Lady Justice is portrayed with a blindfold for a reason. These judges strive every day to ensure that their decisions aren't based on which persons or groups they happen to like or what policies they happen to prefer. They don't pretend to be philosopher-kings with the right or ability to pronounce judgment on all of society's problems. They never boast that they can foresee all the (often unintended) consequences of their decisions, let alone accurately calculate the optimal social policy outcome. They don't seek favor or fear condemnation but recognize instead that the judge's job is only to apply the law's terms as faithfully as possible.

As the process unfolded, I came to worry that our civic understanding about these things—about the Constitution and the proper role of the judge under it—may be slipping away. At our founding the people fought a revolution for the right not to be ruled by a monarch or any other unelected elite, judges included. They wanted to rule themselves. They knew the right of self-government promised many gifts. The right to chart our own destiny as a people. To speak our minds, work as we wish, exercise our own faiths or none at all, pursue happiness as we see it, and secure a more promising future for our children. And to do all this in a culture that cherishes differences and aspires to assure equal treatment under written law.

The framers also knew that with a republic comes responsibility. Self-government is a hard business and republics have a checkered record in the court of history: Often they flicker brightly only to dim quickly. To succeed where so many others had failed, the framers understood that our republic needs citizens who know how their government works—and who are capable of, and interested in, participating in its administration. We won't always agree about the right policies for the day. That's to be expected, even treasured. After all, the capacity to express, debate, and test all ideas is part of what makes a republic strong. But to have any chance we must be able to listen as well as speak, to learn as well as teach, and to tolerate as well as expect tolerance. This republic belongs to us all—and it is up to all of us to keep it. I think that's what Benjamin Franklin was getting at when he spoke publicly after he emerged from the Constitutional Convention. A passerby asked what kind of government the delegates intended to propose, and Franklin reportedly replied: "A republic, *if you can keep it.*"

My hope in writing this book is to contribute to a revival of interest in the Constitution of the framers' design and the judge's role in it. The founders studied history and sought to learn from the problems and build on the successes of past governments, and the written Constitution they designed has secured our freedoms and allowed us to govern ourselves for two centuries while winning countless imitators across the globe. Every one of us who shares this inheritance must understand the great gift we've received—not least because every generation must take its turn shepherding the government of and by the people, and every generation must do its part to ensure that its blessings are passed safely to those who follow. Many wonderful people and groups, like the National Constitution Center, iCivics, and Colonial Williamsburg, are hard at work promoting greater understanding and appreciation of our Constitution. My effort here doesn't pretend to be as encyclopedic as theirs. Nor is this book intended for academics. It is intended for citizens interested in introductory and personal reflections on our Constitution, its separation of powers, and some of the challenges we face in preserving and protecting our republic today. It doesn't contain all the answers or respond to every criticism. Instead, the reflections found here represent just a sampling of the speeches, articles, essays, and judicial opinions I've offered over the course of my thirty-year life in the law on some of the subjects I care most about. In one sense, too, I am today just in the early part of a new journey, having taken my current job only recently. So in that way, as well, this book represents more of a starting than an ending point.

FOR ME, ANY REFLECTION on our Constitution has to begin with an appreciation of its design. Of course, the Bill of Rights is vital: It promises the right to free speech, free exercise of religion, and so many other essential liberties. The Reconstruction Amendments and their promises of equal protection of the laws and due process are foundational too. But without limits on the powers of government, the promises of individual rights contained in these provisions are just that: promises.

Our founders knew that the surest protections of human freedom and the rule of law come not from written assurances of liberty but from sound structures. As James Madison put it, men are not angels and the value of their promises depends on structures to enforce them. To protect the rights of the people, the founders designed a Constitution that cedes to the central government only certain limited and enumerated powers that are, in turn, carefully separated and balanced. To the people's representatives in Congress, the framers gave the power to make new laws restricting liberty—but at the same time they insisted that our representatives follow a deliberate and difficult process designed to achieve broad consensus before any new law might emerge. To ensure that the laws able to survive this careful process are vigorously enforced, the framers gave the power to execute the law to a single president rather than trust management-by-committee—but they also sought to ensure that the president could never arrogate the power to make laws or judge persons under them. Finally, to guarantee that all persons, regardless of their popularity or prestige, would enjoy the benefit of the laws when disputes arise, the framers created an independent judiciary—but they insisted, too, that judges insulated from democratic processes must have no role in lawmaking and should be counterbalanced with juries composed of the people.

In all these ways, the framers recognized that each branch had not only a virtue to offer but also a vice to guard against. When this design is respected, liberty is protected and the rule of law advanced. But when the executive or judiciary claims the power to write new legislation, or when the legislature or executive assumes the power to adjudicate cases, or when some other blurring of the lines occurs, liberty and the rule of law are placed at risk. Nor are these hypothetical worries or problems of the distant past. Later in the book, I share some everyday cases I encountered in my time as a judge where

overlooking the structural protections of our Constitution had profound consequences for real people in our own time.

The design of our founders doesn't just disperse power; it also
has implications for how power should be exercised in each branch.
Take the judicial branch. When it comes to the business of judging,
our separation of powers makes clear that a judge's task is not to
pursue his own policy vision for the country, whether in the name of
some political creed, social science theory, or any other consideration extrinsic to the law. Nor is it to pretend to represent (or bend
to) popular will. The task of making new legislation is assigned elsewhere. As Alexander Hamilton put it, a judge's job is to exercise
"merely judgment," not "FORCE [or] WILL." A judge should apply
the Constitution or a congressional statute as it *is*, not as he thinks it
should be.

How is a judge to go about that job? For me, respect for the separation of powers implies originalism in the application of the Constitution and textualism in the interpretation of statutes. These tools
have served as the dominant methods for interpreting legal texts for
most of our history—and for good reason. Each seeks to ensure that
judges honor the law as adopted by the people's representatives, and
each offers neutral (nonpolitical, nonpersonal) principles for judges
to follow to ascertain its meaning. Rather than guess about unspo-
ken purposes hidden in the hearts of legislators or rework the law to
meet the judge's estimation of what an "evolving" or "maturing"
society should look like, an originalist and a textualist will study
dictionary definitions, rules of grammar, and the historical context,
all to determine what the law meant to the people when their representatives adopted it.

Now, sticking to the law's original meaning doesn't always make
a judge popular or majorities happy. There are times when a faithful
application of the law means that a friendless party will win and the
sympathetic side will lose. That can be a hard thing for many people
to swallow, and a hard thing for a judge too. But sticking to the law's
terms is the very reason we have independent judges: not to favor
certain groups or guarantee particular outcomes, but to ensure that
all persons enjoy the benefit of equal treatment under existing law as
adopted by the people and their representatives.

Still, this tells only half the story. While our constitutional republic may be the greatest the world has known, that is no license to ignore its shortcomings. Some I've alluded to already and many are discussed in the chapters that follow. What happens to our experiment in self-government when we have such difficulty talking with and learning from one another in civil discussion? How can a self-governing people rule themselves if so many do not understand how our government works or the limits on its powers? How can we expect our own rights to be protected if we are not willing to respect the rights of others in return?

For judges and lawyers there are other questions, too, that maybe hit even closer to home. Why is it that cases in our civil justice system today drag on for so long, and the fees pile up so high, that many people cannot afford to bring good claims to court and others are forced to settle bad ones? How is it that in our criminal justice system the laws have grown so numerous that a prosecutor can often enough choose his defendant first and find the crime later? Over the years, I've worked on and written about challenges like these. I don't begin to claim to have all the answers, but I am sure we cannot ignore the questions.

WHY DO THE IDEAS found in these chapters matter to me? Each of us has a story and reasons to be grateful for this nation, its many blessings, and why we are drawn to its service. My story has its roots in the American West and is the product of the people there.

I grew up a short bike ride away from my grandparents, who did as much to shape me as anyone. My paternal grandfather, John, grew up in Denver when it was a small cow town. One of my favorite photos shows him and his brother on a mule in the middle of a dusty Denver road that's now a busy boulevard. He worked his way through college as a trolley car driver, started his own law firm, and served as president of the Denver Bar Association. He cared deeply about his community and he showed it, whether it was by serving charities or lending his efforts to the National War Labor Board in World War II or to fair housing efforts in growing Denver in the years that followed. He loved his family and practical jokes too. He had a terrible voice but loved to sing. By his example, he taught me to care about my community, work hard, and make the time we have here count—and to be sure to laugh a lot along the way.

My maternal grandfather, Joe, grew up on the wrong side of town, in a poor Irish and Italian neighborhood. His father died of tuberculosis before he was born and Joe helped support his mother and sister while still a child, working as a red cap at Denver's Union Station. But he never complained. He was a man of great faith—maybe the greatest faith of anyone I've known. Looking back, he even said that God was kind for taking his father so soon, because if his father had lived any longer he and his whole family likely would have died from the disease. The nuns must have seen something promising in Joe because they arranged his scholarship to college. He became a surgeon but was never above kneeling at a bedside to pray with his patients. His nickname growing up was Tuffy, and he was tough indeed. He loved this country and the opportunities it had given him, and he loved leading quizzes for his many grandchildren, asking them to name all the states, state capitals, and presidents.

My grandmothers were strong women. They had to be. John's wife, Freda, was a Colorado rancher's daughter. Joe's wife, Dorothy, grew up in small-town Nebraska. Freda was fiercely independent and probably a better athlete than her husband. She helped teach me to fish. Her family came to the West as immigrants and built a small lodge, the Wolf Hotel, at a railway stop in Saratoga, Wyoming. The hotel stands today, with family photos on display in the restaurant. Her brothers ran the family ranch in northern Colorado. Their little log cabin remained there for many years with my father's childish handprints visible in the cement outside. Dorothy raised seven children, including six strong women, in a small home. She made sure each got the best education they could: all attended college. She saw some of her daughters die before she passed, but she never lost her faith. She adored long family road trips through the Southwest and Mexico; she'd picnic by the roadside and say the rosary with her husband aloud on the drive. She and Joe even ventured all the way to the Panama Canal before the era of superhighways, sometimes driving their car down dry riverbeds, just to see if they could make it. Dry as the West is, we all knew to bring an umbrella to her summer-

time mountain picnics: Dorothy had an uncanny knack for attract-
ing unwelcomed rain.

My parents learned from their parents and I learned from them
both. My father served in the U.S. Army and then followed his father
into the law, but his real joy came from the outdoors. He loved camping, hunting, and skiing, but fishing most of all. He'd take my
brother, sister, and me on camping and fishing trips in the mountains
in his ancient army surplus canvas tent that never kept its water-
proofing. Frost and rain became familiar friends. Even a slight breeze
would knock over that old tent, and we learned to sleep with the
canvas on our faces. He loved practical jokes too. I will never forget
his reaction when he went to fill his coffeepot with water early one
morning in camp, bleary-eyed, only to find that my brother had invited a garter snake to spend the night inside. I don't think I ever saw
him move so fast or jump so far. Maybe his favorite day ever was
when he hooked a huge trout but the dog started to get tangled in the
line. Dad had two bad choices: keep going and likely lose the fish to
the dog's excitement, or put down the rod and rush to put the dog in
the car and likely lose the fish while the line went slack. He chose the
second option. Miraculously, the fish was still on the line when he
returned and he managed to reel it in. That fish still hangs in his
old fishing cabin, but the car didn't fare so well. In his excitement,
the dog chewed through all of the upholstery on the side facing
the river, sending tufts of cushioning everywhere. It took my father
years to get the car fixed. I still don't know whether he waited so long
because of his frugality or because he liked the memory so much.
Maybe both.

My mother was brilliant and a feminist before feminism. Born in
Casper, Wyoming, she graduated from the University of Colorado at
nineteen and its law school at twenty-two. That was a time when almost no women went to law school. She studied and taught in India
as a Fulbright Scholar and went to work as the first female lawyer in
the Denver District Attorney's Office. There, she helped start a program to pursue deadbeat dads who had failed to pay child support,
long before efforts like that were routine. Her idea of daycare often
meant me tagging along. She never stopped moving. When she ran
for the Colorado state legislature, where she was soon voted the

outstanding freshman legislator, she wore out countless pairs of shoes walking the entire district again and again. As kids, we just had to keep up. Later, she served as the first female administrator of the Environmental Protection Agency in Washington.

I will never forget introducing Louise to the family. We met during my time in England studying for a doctorate. When I asked her to marry me and move to the United States, I knew it was a lot to ask of her. But Louise was up for the adventure, coming from a family of fearless British bulldogs. Her grandmother grew up in India and remembers watching a tiger run through a neighbor's home chasing the family dog. Louise's grandfather served as a British pilot until he was killed in World War II. Louise's great-uncle also served as a highly decorated pilot, even if he was also often in trouble—including for flying his superior's plane without permission (charges were reconsidered when it came out that he managed to take down a German plane in the process), and for flying his entire squadron under Sydney Harbour Bridge to celebrate V-J Day. Louise's other great-uncle was a paratrooper, a hero of the Battle of Arnhem, who helped lead men stranded in German-occupied territory safely across enemy lines. When Louise flew to Denver to meet the family for the first time, my father thought it would be a nice surprise to invite over much of our enormous Colorado family and some friends too. Maybe a hundred people greeted her at the house as she arrived jet-lagged from her transatlantic flight. I was afraid she might just turn around.

She didn't and she fell in love with the West. We raised two girls along with chickens, a goat, horses, a rabbit, dogs, cats, mice, and more in our home on the prairie. When I went to court to hear cases as a judge, she often went to sort cattle with cowboys. She loves the marvelous incongruities of the West today. The annual cattle drive that closes down the busiest street in downtown Denver for a parade. The stock shows where young 4-H members like our daughters primp their barn animals with hairdryers for display. The prize bull who gets to spend a day in a temporary pen in the lobby of the fanciest hotel in town—all right next to families gathered for an afternoon tea that Louise says is as good as any in England. Seeing all this through her eyes made me love my home—and her—all the more. We shared the wonder of the national parks of Wyoming and Colorado. The proud traditions and sad history of the Native American tribes in New Mexico and Oklahoma. The Great Salt Lake and the Mormons' inspirational migration against all the odds and much prejudice. The grit and resilience of the Kansas farmer and the state's bloody civil war history.

The West is close to our hearts. So are those we have worked and shared our lives with there. The Tenth Circuit is a highly diverse court, with judges of enormously varied and interesting backgrounds. They live in the mountains and on the flats, near the border and in great cities; they come from fancy law schools and local ones; and no fewer than three women have served as our chief judge. The court is also rightly regarded as maybe the most collegial federal circuit in the country. Judges work hard but are never hard on one another. During the confirmation process, some of my colleagues, seeing me on television in Washington and knowing I had caught pneumonia from all the travel back and forth, said I looked too skinny. So they sent a huge basket of food to fatten me up, "with love from your Obama-appointed colleagues." That's the Tenth Circuit.

Louise and I loved sharing the West with my law clerks too. Some were native to the area, but others came from far-flung places. They joined us on ski trips and hikes, and most every year a trip to the rodeo. I hired clerks who demonstrated not just intelligence but interest in public service and in the West. They helped me on cases that you don't often see in other parts of the country. Cases about the rights of Indian tribes and the assaults on their sovereign lands. Cases about renewable energy, the use of national parks and other public lands, and fights over western gold: water. The clerks became a family to Louise and me.

THESE DAYS I SOMETIMES find myself thinking back a quarter century to a day when, as a law clerk, I was walking with my boss, Justice Byron White, along the ground-floor hallway of the Supreme Court. As we passed portrait after portrait of former justices, he asked me how many of them I could name. As much as I wanted to impress the boss, I admitted the answer was about half. The justice surprised me when he said, "Me too. We'll all be forgotten soon enough."

At the time, I didn't realize what he was telling me. Justice White was not just one of the most famous men of his day but one of the most impressive. He was a World War II hero. The highest-paid professional football player of his day. A Rhodes Scholar. Before joining the bench, he served as John Kennedy's deputy attorney general and helped desegregate southern schools. He never cared a fig when others criticized him—as many did, harshly and often, sometimes for supposedly "straying" from results they expected of him, and at other times for doing exactly what they knew he would do. How could anyone forget him? It seemed to me impossible.

Justice White's portrait now hangs in the hallway with the others. Every time I walk by I see visitors standing before it wondering who he was. The truth is, Justice White was right and we are all forgotten soon enough. But with the passage of time I've come to see that this is exactly as it should be. In our conversation all those years ago, Justice White wasn't so much lamenting a loss as speaking a truth he warmly embraced. He knew that joy in life comes from something greater than satisfying our own needs and wants. That this raucous republic is among history's greatest experiments. And that, at the end of it all, the most any of us who believe in its cause can hope for is that we have done, each in our own small ways, what we could in its service.

1.

"A REPUBLIC, IF YOU CAN KEEP IT"

WHEN YOU START A NEW JOB, YOUR FRIENDS AND family inevitably ask, "Is it what you expected?" The answer to that question is usually a mix of yes and no. It certainly has been for me.

The "no" part is pretty obvious. After all, no one can really expect or prepare for the job of Supreme Court justice. To serve the American people on our highest court is a humbling responsibility. In our history, only 114 men and women have done so.

The "yes" part may be a little less obvious. But in many ways the people and place are happily familiar. A surprising number of the Court's employees still remember me from my days as a law clerk years ago—and all have gone out of their way to offer me a warm welcome. It is an honor to work with such dedicated public servants.

As it happens, too, three of the justices who served on the Court back then were still serving when I returned. Justice Anthony Kennedy, for whom I clerked, is rightly regarded in our profession as a model of civility and judicial temperament. It was a special joy to be able to work by his side again—and apparently the first time a law clerk and his former boss had the chance. When I was serving as Justice White's law clerk, he retired and Justice Ruth Bader Ginsburg was appointed to serve as his successor. I remember the day my old boss passed along to his new colleague his law clerk manual, just in case she'd find it helpful in setting up her office. Shortly after my confirmation, Justice Ginsburg returned that same document to me, along with many helpful updates she had added over the years. That was quite a moment for me. I also have a distinct memory from my time as a law clerk of watching Justice Clarence Thomas walk from his chambers to the Justices' Conference Room to discuss cases. He was lugging a rolling book cart filled with briefs and binders and papers, his booming laugh filling the hallways. Fast-forward and, on one of my first days as a justice, I'm walking to the Conference Room to discuss cases, and what do I see? Justice Thomas, with his book cart filled with briefs and binders and papers, and his same booming laugh.

More than all that, though, my new day job is a little like the one I shared for many years with wonderful colleagues on the court of appeals. Now, as then, the days are filled with reading briefs, listening to the arguments of lawyers, studying the law in solitude, and engaging with colleagues and law clerks. Each court, too, bears rites and rituals that serve to remind us of the seriousness of our common enterprise and the humanity of each person in it. When we conferred on cases at the Tenth Circuit, inevitably someone would volunteer to bring coffee, mugs would be passed around, and before getting down to the business of discussing cases we'd begin by asking after one another's families. When a new member joined the court, we convened in a retreat to welcome the new judge, answer questions, express our support, and reflect on our aspirations as colleagues. Every other year, we gathered in conferences with the lawyers who regularly appeared before us to discuss the state of the circuit, along the way coming to appreciate one another more fully not just as professionals but as persons.

At the Supreme Court, the rituals are different but the point is the same. We eat lunch together regularly and share experiences and laughs along the way (Justice Stephen Breyer seems to possess an endless reservoir of knock-knock jokes). We flip burgers together at the Court's annual picnic and celebrate birthdays and the holidays with song (always enthusiastically if not always melodically). We welcome employees' children in our chambers for trick-or-treating as they parade costumed around the building. Every justice at some point in the year sits down for lunch with the law clerks of every other justice. And whenever we gather for work, no matter how stressful the moment, each justice shakes the hand of every other justice. That practice dates back to the late nineteenth century and may seem a small gesture, but those thirty-six handshakes can break the ice and lead to kind words or a personal story. More recently, Justice William Rehnquist introduced an end-of-term party in which our law clerks put on a skit whose primary purpose seems to be to rib each of the justices good-naturedly. When he wrote to Chief Justice Warren Burger proposing the idea, Justice Rehnquist reportedly quipped, "I should think we could have a very enjoyable evening out of it"—and we do. At the gathering, there's also a contest where the law clerks try their hand at trivia questions about the Court, its cases, and its history. In front of all the Court's employees, the Chief Justice grills the clerks with questions like "What phrase is inscribed on the *back* of the Supreme Court Building?" ("Justice the Guardian of Liberty") and "Where and when did the first meeting of the Supreme Court take place?" (The Royal Exchange in New York City in February 1790). Simple traditions like these help renew our mutual respect and affection even, and especially, when we are unable to agree on the work at hand. They help ensure, too, that as a Court we never lose sight of our shared history.

My worry is that in our country today we sometimes overlook the importance of these kinds of bonds and traditions, and of the appreciation for civility and civics they instill. The problem can be summed up in a few numbers. According to polling by the Woodrow Wilson National Fellowship Foundation, 60 percent of Americans would flunk the U.S. citizenship test. In fact, it seems only one state— Vermont—has a majority of people who could pass it (and even then, many only with a D). Polling by the Annenberg Public Policy Center suggests that half of Americans don't know that freedom of speech is protected by the First Amendment. And, yes, according to a survey by the American Council of Trustees and Alumni, it seems about 10 percent believe Judith Sheindlin serves on the Supreme Court. You may know her better as Judge Judy. Meanwhile, a recent study, Civility in America, indicates that nearly three-quarters of Americans believe the country is suffering from a crisis in civility. A quarter have reported enduring cyberbullying or incivility online. About the same percentage have transferred children to different schools because of incivility. At the same time, other people are actually calling for an *end* to civility. They say that civility is a coward's virtue and that more anger is needed—that the stakes are too high and the ends justify the means.

But a government of and by the people rests on the belief that the people should and can govern themselves—and do so in peace, with mutual respect. For all that to work, the people must have some idea how their own government operates—its essential structure and promises, what it was intended to do and prohibited from doing. We must, as well, be able to talk to one another respectfully; debate and compromise; and strive to live together tolerantly. As Lincoln put it in far more trying times, "We must not be enemies. Though passion may have strained, it must not break our bonds of affection." History teaches what happens when societies fail to pass on civic understandings and come to disdain civility: Civilization crumbles. Europe in the twentieth century had people, too, who, seeking to remake the social order in the vision of their ideology, thought the stakes of the day were too high to tolerate discourse and dissent. They also believed the ends justified the means, and it didn't end well.

None of this means, of course, that we are destined for the same path. The essential goodness of the American people is a profound reservoir of strength, and this nation has overcome much graver challenges time and again. But we should never ignore the fact that republics have a mixed record in the history books. Our blessings cannot be taken for granted and need constant tending. As Franklin said, we have been given a republic, *if* we can keep it. During my first year in office, I decided to make the challenges we face when it comes to civics and civility the focus of my public appearances. The two speeches that follow are examples.

PASSING THE TORCH

———

Soon after my appointment to the Court, I was asked to speak to students and teachers at the William J. Hughes Center for Public Policy at Stockton University. The center is named for a friend and former congressman and it seeks to nurture interest in public service. Before turning to discuss civics and civility, I was asked to offer a few observations about my transition to the Court. Over the course of my first year, I gave versions of this talk to many groups; what follows represents where the speech stood by the year's end.

THEY SAY IT'S THE EVERYDAY THINGS THAT MATTER MOST. SO when I recently moved my office from Denver to Washington, I spent a little time thinking about what I wanted on the walls. Unsurprisingly, my office bears personal reminders of family, friends, and my home in Colorado. But professionally, I wondered, who did I want looking down on me and who did I want to look up to every day?

For starters, I knew that I wanted a reminder of the man who preceded me on the Court, Antonin Scalia. Maybe above all, I admire his intellectual humility. He didn't claim the right to rule the country based on his personal preferences about how society should "evolve." Bring him evidence about what the written words on the pages of the law books mean—evidence from the law's text, structure, and history—and you could win his vote. I hope that my approach to judging on the Court will share at least that much in common with his. And, as it turns out, I wound up with a pretty unusual reminder of the man. Some years ago on a hunting trip, Justice Scalia bagged an enormous elk that he proudly displayed in his office at the Court—even going so far as to name him Leroy. Leroy is so huge that, after the justice passed, it seems he was destined to become homeless, much too much for anyone's living room wall. And then someone got the idea that Leroy might make an unusual welcome-to-the-neighborhood gift for me. So it was that I was invited to a Scalia law clerk reunion at the Court and the great elk was rolled out and duly presented. And the truth is, I am delighted to share space with Leroy because it happens that we share a few things in common: We are both native Coloradans. Neither of us will ever forget Justice Scalia. And we've both been crated and jumbled across the country to serve out our remaining time on display at the Supreme Court of the United States.

I never went hunting with Justice Scalia, but a few years ago I did fly-fish with him. It's a sport I've loved since I was a child growing up in Colorado. The peace and time in nature are for me restorative. When you're in the Rockies, your mind tends not to wander elsewhere. But I soon came to learn that, while we might hold similar views on judging, Justice Scalia and I held very different views about fishing. Where I would suggest, say, gently unfurling a line in the direction of a rising trout, Justice Scalia preferred another approach: lashing the stream with the enthusiasm of a son of Queens. When I pointed to a spot likely to harbor trout, instead of stalking slowly in that direction he would storm over in his waders, look around, and then exclaim, "But you said there would be fish here!" As indeed there had been. . . .

Leroy is joined in my new chambers by other reminders. One is a portrait of Justice John Marshall Harlan. The first Justice Harlan was born in Kentucky in 1833, served in the Union Army during the Civil War, and then sat as an associate justice on the Supreme Court from 1877 until he died in 1911—nearly thirty-four years, one of the longest tenures in the Court's history. Justice Harlan was often called the Great Dissenter. And that's a title he *earned*. His most important dissent came, of course, in *Plessy v. Ferguson*. We rightly remember *Plessy* as a stain on the Supreme Court's history. There, the Court upheld state-imposed racial segregation. Only Justice Harlan refused to sign the Court's opinion. Now, Harlan came from a family of slave owners and at one point he'd been a pro-slavery politician. But when as a judge he was charged with interpreting the Fourteenth Amendment, he correctly identified its original public meaning, recognizing that the segregation of African-Americans is *not* the equal protection of the laws. His dissent likely did not win him many friends back in Kentucky, and his portrait depicts a dispirited man; no doubt following the written law in the face of great public pressure is sometimes a lonely business. But some of Justice Harlan's words still sing today. Like these: that "in view of the Constitution, in the eye of the law, there is in this country no superior, dominant, ruling class of citizens. There is no caste here. Our Constitution is color-blind, and neither knows nor tolerates classes among citizens. . . . The humblest is the peer of the most powerful."

Powerful words. They made an impression on me the first time I read them as a student, and they stick with me today. Indeed, the promise of equal treatment under law may be the most radical promise in all our laws—or in the history of law. And Justice Harlan's words—that under our Constitution "[t]he humblest is the peer of the most powerful"—echo the oath federal judges must take before assuming the bench. It's an oath dating all the way back to the Judiciary Act of 1789 in which each of us pledges to "administer justice without respect to persons, and do equal right to the poor and to the rich" alike. That ancient oath and Justice Harlan serve for me as a reminder of those vital commitments.

If Justice Harlan is a reminder of my duties to the Reconstruction Amendments and the judicial oath, another portrait in my chambers—of James Madison—serves as a reminder of my obligation to the original Constitution and to the separate and constitutionally prescribed oath judges take to "support and defend the Constitution of the United States" and to "bear true faith and allegiance to the same." Now, Madison was a bit of an overachiever when it came to the Constitution. He arrived in Philadelphia for the Constitutional Convention about three weeks early and used that time to wrangle up support for his Virginia Plan, which became the backbone of the Constitution. But he wasn't done yet. Madison also took the lead in drafting the first ten amendments to the Constitution, what we know as the Bill of Rights. Add to this the fact that, when he died in 1836, he was the last surviving signer of the Constitution. And that's not all. One of the amendments he had proposed along with the ten that became the Bill of Rights hung around until it was finally ratified as the Twenty-seventh Amendment in 1992 (more on that in a moment). So it is that Madison was the Father of the Constitution, Father of its first amendments, and Father of its most recent amendment. Today, we enjoy a robust debate about what a judge's duty to the Constitution entails. But to me, originalism supplies much of the answer. Originalism is simply the idea that when interpreting the Constitution, we should look to text and history and how the document was understood at the time of its ratification. For your constitutional rights should not be subject to judicial revision. They should mean the same today as they did then and they should never be diminished by courts or judges. Madison is there to remind me of that.

A final reminder in my office is a bust of Byron White. The Supreme Court's curator found it in a storage unit and I asked if I might display it in my office because it holds a special memory. One day during my stint as a law clerk to the justice, the artist who had prepared the bust came to chambers to present a soft clay model for the justice's approval before the final bronze casting. The artist was very nervous: He had worked hard and the model was fragile. He spent a great deal of time carefully unwrapping it and getting everything just right before the justice could take a peek. Finally, he called us in. The justice was clearly impressed. But there was one problem, he said: His nose hadn't been that straight since the 1930s. So he walked over and pushed his thumb into the soft clay bridge of the nose. I thought the artist was going to have a heart attack. But the artist survived and so did the dent on the nose in the final bronze (if maybe with a little later artistic improvement). For me, this memory is a reminder of what Byron White knew and lived: that while this is an important job, it is only a job and we are only imperfect people. So do the best you can, but never take yourself too seriously.

To be sure, some people these days like to magnify the work of the Court in dramatic ways. When many write or speak of the Court's decisions, they tend to focus on disagreements. I guess conflict generates clicks and clicks generate money. But that can paint a misleading picture. Sure, we disagree sometimes on the hardest cases in our whole country. But professional disagreements are expected in our line of work, and they are not the same thing as personal ones. Besides, it's not unusual for 40 percent of cases a term, or even more, to be decided unanimously. And that's no small thing. It takes mutual respect and a lot of plain hard work to get nine people, appointed by five different presidents over a span of almost thirty years and from across the country, to agree on the outcome of hard cases. And even when we do disagree, it seems to me that should be not only expected but sometimes even celebrated. After all, the whole point of having nine justices is to bring different ideas to the table and ensure their careful and thorough testing.

THAT ALSO BEARS ON the matters I would like to discuss with you today: civics and civility. Each serves a vital role in sustaining our republic, a nation established on the idea that the government exists to serve the people—not the other way around. In a time when despots ruled much of the world, our founders chose to believe that the people could govern themselves prudently, without destroying the civil liberties their ancestors had won, and without subjecting political minorities to arbitrary power. It was a revolutionary idea. So much so that when the Constitutional Convention proposed ordaining the Constitution in the name of "We the People," Patrick Henry objected. Who was it, he asked, that "authorized them to speak the language of 'We the People,' instead of 'We the States'?" Madison replied that "[t]he existing system has been derived from the . . . authority of the legislatures of the states; whereas, this is derived from the superior power of the people" themselves.

Many across the world thought this bold experiment in self-government was bound to fail, and the founders themselves recognized it would hardly prove self-perpetuating. They knew the cold truth that keeping a republic depends on certain very special conditions. And maybe highest on the list is that the people themselves know how their government works and are able and willing to participate in its administration. Monarchies and oligarchies have no need for widespread civic education. A ruling elite can learn the business of government from their predecessors easily enough. But in our republic the ruling class is supposed to be the whole of the American people. And for us to govern ourselves wisely, every generation has to learn the business of government and what values our republic was designed to serve and then commit themselves to participating in its operation. Even before the Constitution was created, the Northwest Ordinance declared that "[r]eligion, morality, and knowledge, being necessary to good government and the happiness of mankind, schools and the means of education shall forever be encouraged." For us, civic education and engagement are not just ideals; they are indispensable. As Jefferson put it, "If a nation expects to be ignorant and free . . . it expects what never was and never will be."

Some of this is pretty self-evident. You need to know about politicians, their views, and how they compare with others in order to elect representatives who will speak for you. You need to know, as well, about your rights in order to enforce them. You're more likely to speak your mind freely if you know that the First Amendment protects freedom of speech. You're more likely to protest the police rifling through your papers if you know the government cannot conduct unreasonable searches. You're more likely to worship as you choose if you know your prayers are protected against government interference.

But if we are to be a self-governing people, we need to know not just our rights but the structures that protect them. Our government is one of limited and separated powers, a design deliberately chosen to secure the promise of self-rule and our liberties and to prevent the accumulation of power in too few hands. Yet, according to Annenberg, today it seems only about a quarter of Americans can name the three branches of government. Approximately a third cannot name *any* branch. Many do not know *why* the founders established this separation of powers or *how* it protects their liberties. Civic education is no longer a central part of the curriculum in many of our public schools.

Now, I'll admit that sometimes ignorance is rational. For a boy growing up in Colorado it paid to know a lot about hiking and nothing about surfing. But I just don't know how a government of and by the people can be sustained if we do not understand its basic structures, what powers we have granted the government and which ones we have reserved—and who does and doesn't possess the constitutional authority to make new laws to govern us, to execute those laws, and to judge us under them. What happens to democratic accountability, civic responsibility, and so much more when we lose sight of those things and the reasons for them?

Consider an example. Say a statutory interpretation case yields a result you think stupid. How tempting is it to throw up your hands and blame the judge? But in our system of separated powers, the judge's job is to enforce the laws as the legislature writes them. Of course, if the law offends the Constitution a judge may strike it down. But there's nothing in the Constitution that forbids the people's representatives from adopting stupid laws. In a government by the people, it is *our* responsibility as a people to ensure that our representatives enact wise laws. When we lose sight of that, we weaken the habit of self-government.

The challenge when it comes to civics, though, isn't limited to *education* but extends to *engagement*. Someone has to run the zoo. How can we expect good government if we don't have good men and women willing to run it? Who is going to ensure that the executive branch is faithfully administering the laws? Or that the people's disputes can be resolved fairly and impartially? Or that the laws are altered to reflect the people's changing preferences? Many young people today, it seems, harbor little interest in serving in government. Some may see it as distasteful or view other avenues as more lucrative. Others may be worried about living under the microscope, with a light shined on their every mistake. Still others may consider the process of government unimportant. According to a recent study by Harvard and University of Melbourne political scientists, only about 30 percent of U.S. millennials agree that it's "essential . . . to live in a democracy." Many say they see themselves as global citizens instead. I admire the sentiment to the extent that it signals an interest and a concern for all human persons. But I worry when it signals a disinterest in our own government's affairs. As a global citizen, after all, who do you expect to protect your "unalienable Rights"? Where will you go to complain when you are denied the "Blessings of liberty"?

Keeping our republic depends not just on passing knowledge to the next generation; it depends on able young people willing to take on the challenge—and accept the sacrifices—of self-government. Remember John Adams's warning to his son: "Public business my son, must always be done by somebody.—it will be done by somebody or other—If wise men decline it others will not: if honest men refuse it, others will not." Take to heart, too, the words of Teddy Roosevelt:

> It is not the critic who counts; not the man who points out how the strong man stumbles, or where the doer of deeds could have done them better. The credit belongs to the man who is actually in the arena, whose face is marred by dust and sweat and blood; who strives valiantly; who errs, who comes short again and again, because there is no effort without error and shortcoming; but who does actually strive to do the deeds; who knows great enthusiasms, the great devotions; who spends himself in a worthy cause; who at the best knows in the end the triumph of high achievement, and who at-the worst, if he fails, at least fails while daring greatly, so that his place shall never be with those cold and timid souls who neither know victory nor defeat.

To those who doubt the effort is worth it, let me share with you the story of Gregory Watson (with the help of reporting from Matt Largey). Back in 1982, Gregory Watson was a nineteen-year-old sophomore at the University of Texas. As part of a course on the government he was required to write a research paper. So off to the library he went, where he started browsing books on the Constitution. "I'll never forget this as long as I live," he said. "I pull out a book that has within it a chapter of amendments that Congress has sent to the state legislatures, but which not enough state legislatures approved in order to become part of the Constitution. And this one just jumped right out at me."

The unratified amendment that jumped out was one first proposed by James Madison alongside what eventually became the Bill of Rights: "No law, varying the compensation for the services of the Senators and Representatives, shall take effect, until an election of Representatives shall have intervened." In other words, Congress can't vote itself an immediate pay raise, only one for the next Congress, so the people have a chance in an intervening election to pass judgment on the idea and their representatives who supported it. While the amendment had failed to secure the required assent of three-quarters of states, it had been ratified by a few. Watson ended up writing a paper about the amendment, arguing something that no doubt sounded audacious: The amendment could still be ratified. His professor wasn't buying it, though—she gave the paper a C.

That might have been one of the most consequential Cs ever awarded. It spurred Watson to prove his professor wrong. "I thought right then and there," he said, that "I'm going to get that thing ratified." A constitutional guerrilla campaign followed. Watson wrote letters to members of Congress asking for help with their home state legislatures. Most of the responses were negative; many didn't bother to reply at all. But, eventually, a senator from Maine passed the idea to a friend back home and, in 1983, the state ratified the amendment. That emboldened Watson; he started thinking "this can actually be done." He began writing letters to every state legislator he thought might help. Before long, his campaign started to pick up steam with several states ratifying the amendment every year. Finally, in 1992—a decade after writing that fateful paper—the requisite three-quarters of states ratified the amendment, so more than two hundred years after Madison wrote it, the Twenty-seventh Amendment finally passed. And about that C? The professor came around. On March 1, 2017, she filed paperwork to officially change Watson's grade to an A.

When asked why he did it, Watson offered words that should inspire us all: "I wanted to demonstrate that one extremely dedicated, extremely . . . energetic person could push this through. I think I demonstrated that." I think he did too. Who knows? You might be the next Gregory Watson. You might not amend the Constitution, but there's plenty you can do to make a difference. Vote. Work on a political campaign. Fight for an issue you care about. Or maybe run for office your-self. Never doubt what can be done by one person of goodwill.

CIVIC EDUCATION AND ENGAGEMENT, though, represent only one of the preconditions to securing our republic. As Justice Kennedy likes to point out, the word "civics" springs from the same Latin root as the word "civility." And both are essential elements of civilization. Just consider the First Amendment's guarantees of free speech, free press, and free assembly. Those rights ensure that Americans can generally say anything they want, for more or less any reason they want. But most rights bear a corresponding responsibility. And to be worthy of our freedoms, we all have to adopt certain civic habits that enable others to enjoy them too. When it comes to the First Amend-ment, for example, that means tolerating those who don't agree with us, or whose ideas upset us; giving others the benefit of the doubt about their motives; listening and engaging with the merits of their ideas rather than dismissing them because of our own preconcep-tions about the speaker or topic.

Naturally, this can be hard and no one's perfect. We all make mis-takes. But I worry that, just as we face a civics crisis in this country today, we face a civility crisis too. According to a study called Civility in America, nearly 70 percent of Americans believe the country has a "major civility problem." Nearly 60 percent say they pay less atten-tion to politics today because of its incivility and admit that it deters them from becoming more engaged in public service. More than half think civility in our country is likely to decline even further.

These figures should concern us all. Without civility, the bonds of friendship in our communities dissolve, tolerance dissipates, and the pressure to impose order and uniformity through public and private coercion mounts. In a very real way, self-governance turns on our treating each other as equals—as persons, with the courtesy and re-spect each person deserves—even when we vigorously disagree. Our capacity for civility is, in this way, no less than a sign of our commit-ment to human equality and, in turn, democratic self-government. Alexis de Tocqueville—the great observer of early American society—

understood this connection. "The manners of the Americans," he wrote, "are . . . the real cause which renders that people . . . able to support a democratic government."

While we're talking about the founding and civility, too, it might do to recall a bit about the education of George Washington. He deliberately cultivated habits of civility at a young age—habits that no doubt later helped him be effective in leading our new nation. As a teenager, we're told, he copied by hand the 110 "Rules of Civility & Decent Behavior in Company and Conversation," written by the Jesuits in 1595. Many of these rules remain as true as ever. Take Rule 86: "In Disputes, be not So Desirous to Overcome as not to give Liberty to each one to deliver his Opinion[.]" Some are pretty funny too. Like Rule 12: "[B]edew no man's face with your Spittle, by approaching too near him when you Speak."

Maybe they're pretty old-school, but these rules remain no less important now than when young George scrawled them down as a homework assignment. As the historian Richard Brookhiser has said:

> [M]odern manners in the western world were originally aristocratic. [The word] "Courtesy" [for example] meant behavior appropriate to a court. . . . Without realizing it, the Jesuits who wrote them, and the young man who copied them, were outlining and absorbing a system of courtesy appropriate to equals and near-equals. . . . When the company for whom the decent behavior was to be performed expanded to the nation, Washington was ready.

In no small measure, the character of our nation—which left such a deep impression on Tocqueville—was shaped by the character of Washington. Our next generation of leaders must be as ready as he was.

To be ready today, I might suggest a simpler set of rules than the old Jesuits offered. These are a few that Mother Teresa proposed:

> If you do good, people may accuse you of selfish, ulterior motives. Do good anyway.

If you are successful, you will win false friends and true enemies. Succeed anyway.

The good you do today will be forgotten tomorrow. Do good anyway. . . .

Give the world the best you have and you'll get kicked in the teeth. Give the world the best you've got anyway.

The challenges we face today when it comes to civics and civility, essential ingredients to civilization, are real and all around us. History offers daunting lessons about how difficult civic understanding and civility are to win, and how easy they are to lose. But I am an optimist. We should never lose sight that we live with remarkable success in a richly diverse nation and that Americans have time and again risen resiliently to meet so many grave challenges: from our unlikely success in the Revolution to defending our infant republic in the War of 1812, from the preservation of the Union in the Civil War to the efforts of our civil rights movement to realize the Declaration of Independence's promise that all men are created equal.

Sometimes, of course, the cynic in all of us gets the upper hand. Sometimes it's hard to see the way forward for all the trials that lie so squarely before us. But when you find yourself in doubt, I encourage you to remember this story from G. K. Chesterton. Chesterton noted that an ordinary man, asked "on the spur of the moment" to explain "why he prefer[red] civilization to savagery," likely "would look wildly round at object after object, and would only be able to answer vaguely, 'Why, there is that bookcase . . . and the coals in the coal-scuttle . . . and pianos . . . and policemen.'" But, as Chesterton reminds us, there is sometimes wisdom in a stuttering reply. Sometimes the virtues of civilization are too numerous to count, almost so obvious as to be too obvious to see. If asked to explain them, it's hard to know where to begin.

The same is true of our constitutionally governed republic. We may not always notice them, but what the Constitution calls our "Blessings of liberty" are everywhere around us. They are what allow more than three hundred million of us to go about our daily lives, each in our ways, mostly in peace. Really, it is one of the great wonders in world history. But if those blessings are to endure, it falls to each of us to do what we can to preserve and pass down civic understanding and the virtues of civility. To help prepare those who follow for the high and humbling responsibility of preserving our Constitution, the greatest charter of human freedom the world has ever known. Soon enough the torch will pass to their hands.

WELCOME TO
NEW CITIZENS

———

Not long after my appointment to the Court, I was invited to the Ninth Circuit judges' conference. Before we get to work on judicial matters at a conference like that, everyone sings the national anthem and says the Pledge of Allegiance, and sometimes there's a welcome ceremony for new citizens. It's a special part of the conference, a reminder to us of the wonder of our country and some of the reasons why we do what we do. When my colleagues asked me to welcome the new citizens at their conference, I was honored. In this short talk, I sought to capture what Louise's naturalization meant to me and my family—and to honor the same choice the new citizens and their families gathered that day had made.

I REMEMBER HEARING THE OATH YOU JUST TOOK MANY YEARS ago when my wife became a naturalized citizen. And I remember thinking back then: The oath is so short, only 140 words, but the words are powerful ones. When you finish them, you leave behind one identity and take on a new one. You join a new community of people—one spanning a vast continent, from all faiths, from all ethnicities, from all walks of life. The path to taking the oath almost always involves sacrifices and hard choices too. Some of you may have put yourselves in danger to arrive here. Others may have served in our armed forces. Some of you have traveled long distances and left friends and family behind. Today, we honor what you have done and the choices you have made and we welcome you as our fellow citizens. We are honored that you have chosen to help us in writing the next chapter of our country's story, and I am grateful for the chance to share a few words with you.

It seems to me that one thing that's so unusual about the oath you've taken and the country you've joined is the fact that we are a nation of immigrants. The United States does not have a shared common culture in the classic sense. We do not have the many centuries of shared heritage that exists in, say, China or England. Instead, America is largely bound together by ideas. And the truth is, some of those ideas are hard and entail real challenges for all of us.

Take the idea found in the very first sentence of the Constitution. The Constitution's preamble says that "We the People" "ordain and establish this Constitution" in order to "secure the Blessings of Liberty to ourselves and our Posterity." It is no small thing that the founders claimed our new government was formed by "We the People." They didn't say the government was formed by the Continental Army or the Congress or the States or some bureaucratic drafting committee. Institutions like those, the preamble made clear, exist to serve the people—not the other way around. In this way, the founders attempted a bold new experiment in government by and for the people.

In this way, too, the founders made clear that one of the great obligations of American citizens is to ensure that power continues to reside in the people. The promise of self-government is not self-executing or self-perpetuating. Keeping our republic, our experiment in self-government, is a shared responsibility—part of our duty as citizens. Each and every one of us has a role to play in passing along the blessings of liberty to our children and our children's children. I encourage you to participate in that task through speaking, voting, petitioning elected representatives, or performing public service. Our collective challenge is made easier and our efforts enriched by your presence, your voice, and your ideas. Today, you become part of the latest in a long line of patriots responsible for carrying the torch and ensuring that liberty will indeed prove secure for our posterity.

Then, too, there's the challenge posed by the opening passage of our Declaration of Independence. Although the Constitution is our basic law, it would be a lesser document had it not been preceded by the Declaration. In the Declaration, the founders sought to explain the reasons why they were seceding from Great Britain. And they began by explaining: "We hold these truths to be self-evident, that all men are created equal, that they are endowed by their Creator with certain unalienable Rights, [and] that among these are Life, Liberty and the pursuit of Happiness."

Today, you join a people still striving to make real the ideals of the Declaration's promise that all people are created equal and entitled to life, liberty, and the pursuit of happiness. Joining in that task is hard too. Among many other things, it comes with the duty of having to listen to and tolerate other points of view. That can be a challenge, especially in polarizing times. But democracy depends on our willingness, each one of us, to hear and respect even those with whom we disagree strongly. And polarizing times are nothing new. Alexander Hamilton wrote in the very first of *The Federalist Papers* that even "wise and good" people will disagree on questions of "the first magnitude." A fact, he said, that should "furnish a lesson of moderation" to us all. In a government by and for the people, we have to remember that those with whom we disagree, even vehemently, still have the best interests of the country at heart. We have to remember that democracy depends on our ability to reason and work with those who hold very different convictions and beliefs than our own. We have to learn not only to tolerate different points of view but to cherish the cacophony of democracy. As Benjamin Franklin reminded us, in a democracy we have the choice of either hanging together or hanging separately.

I join my colleagues here today in expressing our honor that you have chosen the path to citizenship in the United States. We welcome you to our ongoing experiment in self-government and are grateful for your help in our common struggle to make good this country's promise. I am delighted to call you my fellow Americans and I offer each and every one of you and your families my deepest congratulations.

2.

OUR
CONSTITUTION
AND ITS
SEPARATED POWERS

HOW DOES THIS CONSTITUTION SOUND? IN
lengthy and exacting detail it provides every
right you could possibly hope for. It promises the
"inviolability of the person" and the "privacy of cor-
respondence," the rights to vote and run for office,
and freedom of religion, "speech, the press, assembly
demonstration and association." It even guarantees
the right to an education, free medical care, and "re-
laxation." I'm not kidding. Sounds great, right?
Maybe even a big improvement over our own comparatively stingy Constitution?

Well, the Constitution I'm quoting from is North
Korea's. I could easily recite similar passages from
the Constitution of most any communist country:
They all sound about the same. But everyone knows

that the promises found in these documents aren't worth the paper they're written on. What would someone dragged from his bed in the middle of the night at the behest of the latest "Dear Leader" think about the right to "inviolability of the person"?

Our founders never knew the Kim family of North Korea, but they had plenty of experience with a tyrannical ruler. More than a few in the founding generation suffered at the hands of a capricious king, thrown in jail (or worse) without a fair trial. From their own experience and understanding of history, the framers knew that to prevent the rule of law from becoming the rule of men more is required than a Constitution full of nice promises. What's needed is a Constitution that counteracts the instinct to seek and misuse power, one that secures individual rights not so much by their enumeration as by real structural limits on the power of government and those who run it.

To this end, the framers divided the powers of the federal government into three branches. It was a radical innovation at the time, and it may be one of their most important contributions to human liberty. In Congress, the framers vested only certain enumerated "legislative Powers"—and to the framers that term had a distinct meaning. It meant the power to create new rules of general applicability with prospective application: a forward-looking function aimed at responding to new social and economic problems as they arise. To exercise that kind of power, the framers knew, required the collective wisdom of the people and their representatives. But the framers also understood that this awesome power could be used by majorities to invade the liberty of minority groups. So the framers divided the legislative power even further between a Senate and a House of Representatives. The result: Before Congress can impose new legal limits or obligations on the people, it must secure the concurrence of many different actors, answering to many different electorates, in many different elections. It is a process deliberately calculated to protect minority interests by effectively imposing a supermajority requirement for any new law.

Meanwhile, to the president the framers assigned the distinct authority to "execute[]" the law. The deliberative pace appropriate to the legislative branch, the framers believed, holds less purchase once a law survives the legislative process. If a law can pass both houses of Congress (and receive presidential approval or survive a veto override), the framers thought it should be executed with "energy." So the framers entrusted the executive power not to a committee, but to a single individual chosen by the nation as a whole. At the same time, the framers knew, separating the authority to *write* the law from the authority to *execute* it is essential to keep the executive branch from engaging in the sort of tyranny they experienced before the Revolution and that we see today in authoritarian regimes around the world.

Finally, the framers assigned the federal "judicial Power" to a Supreme Court and other lower courts. If the legislative power involves deciding what the law *should be* for everyone in the future, the framers conceived the judicial power as the task of applying that law as it *is* to specific disputes over past events. To exercise that particular kind of power, another and still different kind of decision-maker was needed: a neutral and impartial actor. To ensure what Hamilton called the "steady, upright, and impartial administration of the laws" to all persons regardless of their passing popularity, the founders guaranteed judges life tenure and salary protections. These protections make no sense, of course, for lawmakers in a republic where lawmaking is supposed to be responsive to the will of the people. But they are essential when the job description calls for the consistent application of the law even and especially for vulnerable and unpopular persons. And then, much as the framers divided Congress into two houses, they balanced the judiciary between independent and life-tenured judges responsible for deciding questions of law and juries drawn from the community responsible for deciding questions of fact; once more, power was checked and counterbalanced.

The separation of powers and its role in protecting individual liberty and the rule of law can sound pretty abstract. I confess it seemed that way to me in my high school civics class. I came to appreciate the genius of the founders' design more fully only years later, when as a judge I saw what happens to real people in real cases when the separation of powers goes unattended. Let me share with you a few of their stories, some of which you will see laid out more fully later. They're just a sampling of so many that came across my desk as a judge on the court of appeals, but they illustrate in practical terms the vital role of the separation of powers.

CARING HEARTS. Caring Hearts is a small business in Colorado that provides Medicare nursing services to the elderly. One year, the government performed an audit and concluded that Caring Hearts had improperly billed hundreds of thousands of dollars of services, so it slapped a fine of over $800,000 on the company. The trouble was, the government applied the wrong rules. Instead of applying the regulations in effect during the time Caring Hearts provided its services, it faulted the company for failing to abide more onerous rules that the agency adopted only years later. How did the government get its own rules so wrong? Every year, the *executive* agency administering Medicare has used the *legislative* authority delegated to it by Congress to issue a river of legally binding regulations and thousands more "subregulatory guidance documents" to explain those regulations. The agency had apparently written so many new legally binding rules that even it had lost track of all the changes.

MIGUEL GAMES-PEREZ. A federal prosecutor charged Mr. Games-Perez with "knowingly violat[ing]" a statute that makes it a crime to be (1) a felon and (2) in possession of a firearm. But the prosecutor failed to produce any evidence that Mr. Games-Perez *knew* he was a felon. In fact, at the time of his earlier conviction, the judge expressly (but erroneously) told Mr. Games-Perez that if he agreed to plead guilty (as he eventually did), he would leave the courtroom "*not* convicted of a felony." Still, rather than concede its inability to prove an essential element of the crime charged, the federal government invited judges to rewrite the law. The statute would be a better one, the government essentially told the Tenth Circuit, if it required the prosecution to prove only that Mr. Games-Perez knew he was in possession of a firearm. My court, relying on circuit precedent I thought mistaken, agreed. And so Mr. Games-Perez was sent to federal prison for violating a "statute" effectively written by judges rather than legislators, one neither Mr. Games-Perez nor anyone else could have found and taken notice of in the *United States Code* before the conduct leading to his "offense."

ALFONZO DE NIZ ROBLES. Mr. De Niz Robles is a Mexican citizen, married to a U.S. citizen, and the father of four U.S. citizens. Hoping to apply for lawful residency, he faced two competing federal statutory provisions that confused his path. The first seemed to suggest the government was free to adjust his status immediately and allow him to remain in this country. The second seemed to suggest he had to leave the country for at least a decade before applying for admission. In 2005, the Tenth Circuit held that the first statute trumped the second. Relying on that declaration of the law, Mr. De Niz Robles unsurprisingly decided to apply for an immediate adjustment of status. But then, years later, an administrative agency issued an edict purporting to "overrule" the Tenth Circuit's precedent on which Mr. De Niz Robles had relied. The agency said Mr. De Niz Robles and immigrants like him must always satisfy the ten-year waiting period outside the country. So, in essence, an *executive* agency claimed the power to overrule a *judicial* decision and tell Mr. De Niz Robles that he'd have to start the decade-long waiting clock now, after an eight-year wait for the agency's decision—even though if he'd known that was his only option at the beginning, his wait would've been nearly over.

At first, these stories might seem unrelated. They arise in different areas of law and implicate different questions of social policy. One is about Medicare and government contracts, the next about criminal law, the last about immigration. But despite their surface differences, over time I came to realize that cases like these reflect the same underlying problem: a mixing of what are supposed to be separated powers in ways that undermine the rule of law and diminish liberty. In the first case, the legislature delegated its lawmaking powers to the executive—and the result was that lawmaking had become so easy and came so quickly that no one could keep up with all the new restrictions. In the second case, the judiciary rewrote the legislature's statutes to make "better" policy, even though it meant sending a man to prison for breaking a law nowhere in the books or approved by the people's representatives. In the third case, the executive assumed the judicial power "to say what the law is" and left a family without fair notice of its demands on them. It's one thing to study the theory of the separation of powers. For me, it was another thing to witness how its disregard affects the lives of real people in real cases.

Just consider what happens when the judicial branch arrogates to itself the legislative function of deciding what the law *should be*. The people are excluded from the lawmaking process, replaced by a handful of unelected judges who are unresponsive to electoral will, unrepresentative of the country, and who come to the task armed only with four law clerks often barely out of law school. Their new "laws" apply not only prospectively to future conduct, but also retroactively to past actions that the affected parties can now do nothing to change. In this way, decisionmakers can see clearly the targets of their rulings and pick and punish them with impunity.

Consider, too, what happens when the executive assumes the power to make new laws restricting liberty. A slow process that's supposed to reflect and benefit from the views of the whole of the people is left to a single actor whose office is designed to be imbued with energy and vigor. Minority voices lose their impact, and lawmaking risks becoming so easy that no one can keep up. James Madison foresaw these problems when he warned that "[i]t will be of little avail to the people, that the laws are made by men of their own choice, if the laws be so voluminous that they cannot be read, or so incoherent that they cannot be understood; if they be repealed or revised before they are promulgated, or undergo such incessant changes that no man, who knows what the law is to-day, can guess what it will be to-morrow."

Consider, finally, what happens when the elected branches assume the judicial function. Instead of a neutral judge and a jury of their peers, the people are left with politicized decisionmakers who will be tempted to pick winners and losers based less on the merits than on their current electoral popularity. And in a world like that, what can we expect to happen to the constitutional and statutory rights of minorities, to the unpopular and marginalized?

However you mix what are supposed to be separated powers, the threats to the rule of law and liberty are much the same. At risk are the promise of knowable and stable law, fair notice, democratic self-rule, and equal protection under the law. Maybe a few will enjoy the riches needed to negotiate a world filled with endless lawmakers and endlessly changing law. These few might even be able to thrive in that environment, making the system work for themselves and against their rivals. Agencies, for example, can be captured by the powerful, and the regulated can become the regulators. But what about everyone else? In *Federalist No. 62*, James Madison warned that when the laws become too voluminous, incoherent, and malleable, they give "unreasonable advantage . . . to the sagacious, the enterprising, and the moneyed few over the industrious and uniformed mass of the people." The laws risk becoming a tool "made for the FEW, not for the MANY."

To be sure, even when powers that are supposed to be separated wind up fused, "law" might remain in some formal sense; after all, people are still obliged to obey what *someone* says the law commands. But is that really the *rule of law*? History (and our world today) contain too many examples of government enjoying so much discretion under the "law" that it can prosecute more or less anyone it wishes more or less anytime it wishes. The rule of law demands more. And I think Friedrich Hayek identified one of the most important demands of the rule of law when he said that, "[s]tripped of all technicalities," the rule of law "means that government in all its actions is bound by rules fixed and announced beforehand—rules which make it possible to foresee with fair certainty how the authority will use its coercive powers in given circumstances and to plan one's individual affairs on the basis of this knowledge."

The founding generation did not have the luxury of overlooking the importance of the separation of powers, but I sometimes wonder if we are at risk of forgetting or discounting it today. After all, the value of the separation of powers isn't always as obvious as the value of other sorts of constitutional protections. The Fourth Amendment's guarantee against unreasonable police searches of your iPhone is concrete; everyone readily understands the connection to individual liberty. The value of the First Amendment's right to speak your mind and its essential link to democratic self-government and individual freedom almost goes without saying. But it's easy to find distinguished people today who will argue that the separation of powers is undesirable or unnecessary. In a modern society, they will argue, it's not reasonable to expect the legislature to make the laws that govern us; legislation is too slow and cumbersome. Or, they say, juries and judges can't be trusted to get the right answer or do so efficiently, so we should allow executive agencies to decide the people's cases and controversies. And so on.

This chapter is about the separation of powers, its role in protecting individual liberty, and the dangers that follow when we forget. When the separation of powers goes ignored, those who suffer first may be the unpopular and least among us—immigrants like Mr. De Niz Robles, small businesses like Caring Hearts, and criminal defendants like Mr. Games-Perez. But they are not likely to be the last.

OF LIONS AND
BEARS, JUDGES AND
LEGISLATORS

In this speech, I focus on the differences between legislators and judges and what happens when we muddle those roles— the dangers that follow when judges assert the right to make new laws and when legislators claim the power to decide past disputes between the people. When I was first asked to give this talk as the Sumner Canary Memorial Lecture at Case Western Reserve University, I had a different topic in mind—I planned to talk about some of the access to justice challenges that concern me and are discussed later in the book. But then Justice Scalia died and, knowing how much he cared about this aspect of our separation of powers, I decided to dedicate this speech as a tribute to him and his legacy.

S OMETIMES PEOPLE ARE DESCRIBED AS LIONS OF THEIR PROFESsion and I have trouble understanding what exactly that means. Not so with Justice Scalia. He really was a lion of the law: docile in private life but a ferocious fighter when at work, with a roar that could echo for miles. Volumes will be rightly written about his contributions to American law, on the bench and off. Indeed, I have a hard time thinking of another justice who has written so many articles and books about the law even while serving on the Court. Writings like *A Matter of Interpretation* or *Reading Law* that are sure to influence generations of law students and lawyers.

But tonight I want to touch on a more thematic point and suggest that perhaps the great project of Justice Scalia's career was to remind us of the differences between judges and legislators. To remind us that legislators may appeal to their own moral convictions and to claims about social utility to reshape the law as they think it should be in the future. But that judges should do none of these things in a democratic society. That judges should instead strive (if humanly and so imperfectly) to apply the law as it is, focusing backward, not forward, and looking to text, structure, and history—not to their own moral convictions or the policy consequences they believe might serve society best. As Justice Scalia put it, "If you're going to be a good and faithful judge, you have to resign yourself to the fact that you're not always going to like the conclusions you reach. If you like them all the time, you're probably doing something wrong."

It seems to me that there can be little doubt about the success of this great project. We live in an age when the job of the federal judge is not so much to expound upon the common law as it is to interpret text—constitutional, statutory, regulatory, or contractual. And as Justice Kagan acknowledged in her Scalia Lecture at Harvard Law School in 2015, "we're all textualists now." Capturing the spirit of law school back when she and I attended, Justice Kagan went on to relate how professors and students often used to approach reading a statute with the question "[G]osh, what should this statute be[?]" rather than "[W]hat do the words in the statute say?" That much has changed and, as Justice Kagan said, "Justice Scalia had more to do with this [change] than anybody" because he "taught everyone to do statutory interpretation differently."

I don't think there is any better illustration of Justice Kagan's point than the very first opinion the Supreme Court issued after Justice Scalia's passing. That case—*Lockhart v. United States*—involved the question of how best to interpret a statute imposing heightened penalties for three types of offenses—"[1] aggravated sexual abuse, [2] sexual abuse," and "[3] abusive sexual conduct involving a minor or ward." The majority opinion by Justice Sotomayor relied on the rule of the last antecedent and argued that the phrase at the end of the sentence—"involving a minor or ward"—modifies only the last offense listed. So the statute's penalties apply whenever there is aggravated sexual abuse, or whenever there is sexual abuse, or whenever there is abusive sexual conduct involving a minor or ward. In dissent, Justice Kagan argued that the rule of the last antecedent sometimes gives way to "ordinary understanding[s] of how English works." And in Justice Kagan's estimation, an ordinary and average reader of the language here would think that the phrase "involving a minor or ward" modifies all three of its antecedents. So for the statutory penalties to apply, the government must always prove some kind of sexual abuse involving a minor. In support of her reading, Justice Kagan offered this gem: "Imagine a friend told you that she hoped to meet 'an actor, director, or producer involved with the new Star Wars movie.' You would know immediately that she wanted to meet an actor from the Star Wars cast—not an actor in, for example, the latest Zoolander."

As you can see, the two sides disagreed pretty avidly and colorfully. But notice, too, neither appealed to its views of optimal social policy. Their dispute focused instead on grammar, language, and statutory structure. In fact, I have no doubt several justices found themselves voting for an outcome they would have rejected as legislators. Now, one thing we know about Justice Scalia is that he loved a good fight—and it might be that he loved best of all a fight like this, over the grammatical effect of a participial phrase. If the Court were in the business of offering homages instead of judgments, it would be hard to imagine a more fitting one than this. Surely when the Court handed down its opinions that day, the justice sat smiling from some happy place.

But every worthwhile endeavor attracts its critics. And Justice Scalia's project is no exception. The critics come from different directions and with different agendas. Professor Ronald Dworkin, for example, once called the idea that judges should faithfully apply the law as written an "empty statement" because many legal documents like the Constitution cannot be applied "without making controversial judgments of political morality in the light of [the judge's] own political principles." My admirable colleague Judge Richard Posner has also proven a skeptic. He has said it's "naive" to think judges actually believe everything they say in their own opinions, for while they often deny the legislative dimension of their work, the truth is that judges must and should consult their own moral convictions or consequentialist assessments when resolving hard cases. Immediately after Justice Scalia's death, too, it seemed so many more added their voices to the choir. Professor Laurence Tribe, for example, wrote admiringly of the justice's contributions to the law. But he tempered his admiration by seemingly chastising the justice for having focused too much on the means of making judicial decisions and not enough on results, writing that "interpretive methods" don't "determine, much less eclipse, outcome[s]."

Well, I'm afraid you'll have to mark me down as naive, a believer that empty statements can bear content, and an adherent to the view that outcomes (ends) do not justify methods (means). Respectfully, it seems to me that an assiduous focus on text, structure, and history is essential to the judicial function. That, yes, judges should be in the business of declaring what the law *is,* using the traditional tools of interpretation, rather than pronouncing the law as they might wish it to be in light of their own political views, always with an eye on the outcome, and engaged perhaps in some Benthamite calculation of pleasures and pains along the way. Though the critics are loud and the temptations to join them may be many, mark me down, too, as a believer that the traditional account of the judicial role Justice Scalia defended will endure. Let me offer you three reasons for my faith on this score.

FIRST, CONSIDER THE CONSTITUTION. Judges must do more than merely consider it. They take an oath to uphold it. So any theory of judging in this country must at least be measured against that foundational duty. Yet it seems to me that those who would have judges behave like legislators, imposing their moral convictions and utility calculi on others, face an uphill battle when it comes to reconciling their judicial philosophy with our founding document.

After all, at the Constitutional Convention the framers debated a proposal very much like what the critics now suggest, one that would have incorporated the judiciary into a "council of revision"— one with sweeping powers to review and veto congressional legislation. But that proposal went down to defeat, overwhelmed by the contrary view that judges should expound upon the law only as it comes before them, free from the bias of having participated in its creation and from the burden of having to decide "the policy of public measures." In place of a system that mixed legislative and judicial powers, the framers chose one that carefully separated those powers. The Constitution reflects this design, devoting distinct articles to the "legislative Power[]" and the "judicial Power," creating separate institutions for each, and treating those powers in contradistinction.

Neither were these separate categories empty ones to the founding generation. Informed by a hard-earned intellectual inheritance—one perhaps equal parts English common law experience and Enlightenment philosophy—the founders understood the legislative power as the power to prescribe new rules of general applicability for the future. A power properly guided by the will of the people acting through their representatives, a task avowedly political in nature, and one unbound by the past except to the extent that any law must conform to the higher law of the Constitution itself.

Meanwhile, the founders understood the judicial power as a very different kind of power. Not a forward-looking but a backward-looking authority. Not a way for making new rules of general applicability but a means for resolving disputes about what existing law is and how it applies to discrete cases and controversies. Itself a necessary incident to civil society but a distinct one. One that calls for neutral arbiters, not elected representatives. One that is further bound to the past by its respect for precedent and analogy, its use of past cases as a tool for resolving current ones. And by its general rule limiting the court's focus to the arguments the parties have chosen to present for decision. To an adherent of this traditional view of judging, the task in any case is to interpret and apply the law as a reasonable and reasonably well-informed citizen might have understood when it engaged in the activity at issue in the case or controversy—not to amend or revise the law in some novel way.

So many specific features of the Constitution confirm what its larger structure suggests. For example, if the founders really thought legislators free to judge and judges free to legislate, why would they have gone to such trouble to limit the sweep of legislative authority—insisting that any new law must survive the arduous process of bicameralism and presentment (passage through two separate houses and presentment to the president for approval or veto)—if judges could perform the same essential function without similar safeguards? And why would they insist on legislators who are responsive to the people but then allow judges to act as legislators without accountability to the people? Why, too, would they have devised a system that allows equally unrepresentative litigants to define the scope of debate based on their narrow self-interest? And if judges were to legislate new rules of general applicability for the future, why would the founders have considered precedent as among the primary tools of the judicial trade rather than more forward-looking instruments like empirical data? And why would they have entrusted decisions to a single or few judges, aided only by the latest crop of evanescent law clerks, rather than on a larger body with more collective expertise?

In response to objections like these, Judge Posner has replied that "American appellate courts are councils of wise elders and it is not completely insane to entrust them with responsibility for deciding cases in a way that will produce the best results" for society. But, respectfully, even that's not exactly a ringing endorsement of judges as social utility optimizers, is it? I can think of a lot of things that aren't *completely* insane but still distinctly ill-advised (or so I try to convince my teenage daughters). And, respectfully too, wouldn't we have to be at least a little crazy to recognize the Constitution's separation of judicial and legislative powers and the duty of judges to uphold it, but then applaud when judges ignore all that to pursue what they have divined to be the best policy outcome? And crazy not to worry that if judges consider themselves free to disregard the Constitution's separation of powers, they might soon find other bothersome parts of the Constitution equally unworthy of their fidelity?

THIS OBSERVATION LEADS TO a second. It seems to me that the separation of legislative and judicial powers isn't just a formality dictated by the Constitution. To the founders, the legislative and judicial powers were distinct by nature and their separation was among the most important liberty-protecting devices of the constitutional design, an independent right of the people essential to the preservation of all other rights later enumerated in the Bill of Rights. Though much could be said on this subject, tonight permit me to suggest a few reasons why defending the legislative-judicial divide is critical to preserving our bedrock guarantees of due process and equal protection.

Consider if we allowed the legislator to judge. If legislatures were free to act as judges and create backward-looking rules, they would also be free to punish individuals for completed conduct they're unable to alter. And to do so without affording affected individuals any of the procedural protections that normally attend the judicial process, raising along the way serious due process questions. How can a citizen ever have fair notice of the law or order his or her affairs around it if the lawmaker can go back in time and outlaw what was reasonably thought lawful at the time? And how might the average citizen ever hope to intervene in that legislative process to prevent that very prospect? With due process concerns like these come equal protection problems too. If legislators could routinely act retroactively, what would happen to disfavored groups and individuals? With their past actions known and unalterable, they would be easy targets for discrimination. No doubt worries like these are exactly why the founders prohibited bills of attainder and ex post facto laws criminalizing completed conduct, and why baked into the "legislative Power[]" there's a presumption as old as the common law that all legislation bears only prospective effect.

Now consider the converse situation—if we allowed the judge to legislate. Unconstrained by the procedural hurdles of Article I, the judge would need only his or her own vote or those of just a few colleagues to change the law and the task of legislating would become a relatively simple thing. With the power to act retroactively, too, all the concerns just discussed about fair notice and equal protection would attend here with equal force. Could parties really hope to conform their conduct to the law's demands, or would they be left to the mercy of whatever retroactively applied rule whatever future judicial legislator they happen across might prefer? And what might the temptation be for the judge to use his or her newfound legislative authority to help favored parties and hurt disfavored ones? Notice as well how hard it would be to revise this so-easily-made judicial legislation to account for changes in the world or to fix mistakes. Unable to throw judges out of office in regular elections, you'd often have to wait for them to die before you'd have any chance of change. And even then you'd find it difficult to do so, for courts cannot so easily undo their errors given the weight they afford precedent. It seems to me that for reasons just like these Hamilton explained that "liberty can have nothing to fear from the judiciary alone," but "ha[s] everything to fear from [the] union" of the judicial and legislative powers. William Blackstone painted an even grimmer picture of a regime where judges are free to legislate, suggesting that there "men would then be[come] slaves to their magistrates."

AT THIS POINT I can imagine the critics replying this way. Sure, judges should look to the traditional tools of text, structure, history, and precedent. But in hard cases those materials will prove indeterminate. So *some* tiebreaker is needed and that's where the judge's political convictions, a consequentialist calculus, or something else comes into play. Respectfully, though, I'd suggest to you the critics' conclusion does not follow from their premise. If anything, replies along these lines seem to me to wind up supplying a third and independent reason for embracing the traditional view of judging—because it compares favorably against its alternatives.

Now, I do not mean to suggest that traditional legal tools will always yield a single definitive right answer in every case. Of course, Ronald Dworkin famously thought otherwise, contending that a Herculean judge could always land on the right answer. But at least in my experience most of us judges don't much resemble Hercules—there's a reason we wear loose-fitting robes—and I accept the possibility that some hard cases won't lend themselves to a clear right answer.

At the same time, though, I'd suggest to you that the amount of indeterminacy in the law is often exaggerated. Law students are fed a steady diet of hard cases in casebooks stuffed with the most vexing and difficult appellate opinions ever issued. Hard cases are, as well, the daily bread of the professoriate and a source of riches for the more perfumed advocates in our profession. But I wonder: How often do they share with you students these facts? Every year, more than 360,000 cases are filed in our federal courts and maybe 50 million more are filed in our state courts (not counting traffic cases). Yet in the federal system the vast majority of cases are resolved by our trial courts. Losing parties may not like the result, but they usually accept the outcome as reasonably just. In fact, only about 5.6 percent of federal lawsuits make it all the way to decision in an appellate court. And even among the small sliver of cases that make it so far, about 95 percent are resolved unanimously by the courts of appeals. That's no small thing, especially when you recall that on the courts of appeals we sit in panels of three and, as a Tenth Circuit judge, I sit with judges from six states appointed by presidents spanning from President Barack Obama all the way back to President Lyndon Johnson. Nor is that the end of it. Out of the millions of cases filed every year, only about seventy cases reach the Supreme Court. These are the very hardest cases, usually ones where lower courts have disagreed strongly. Yet even in these difficult matters, all nine justices (not just three judges) are able to agree unanimously about 40 percent of the time. That despite the fact the justices come from all across the country and were appointed by different presidents over a span of decades. And that figure has remained remarkably constant all the way back to World War II. Focusing on the hard cases may be fun, but doesn't it risk missing the forest for the trees?

And doesn't it also risk missing the *reason* why such a remarkable percentage of legal disputes are resolved this way? The truth is that the traditional tools of legal analysis do a remarkable job of eliminating or reducing indeterminacy. Yes, lawyers and judges may sometimes disagree about which canons of construction are most helpful in the art of ascertaining Congress's meaning in a complicated statute. We may sometimes disagree over the order of priority we should assign to competing canons of construction. And sometimes we may even disagree over the results they yield in particular cases. But when judges pull from the same toolbox and look to the same materials to answer the same narrow question—What might a reasonable person have thought the law was at the time?—we confine the range of possible outcomes and provide a remarkably stable and predictable set of rules people are able to follow. And even when a hard case does arise, once it's decided it takes on the force of precedent, becomes an easy case in the future, and contributes further to the determinacy of our law.

Besides, it seems to me that even accepting that some hard cases remain, it just doesn't follow that we must or should resort to our own political convictions, consequentialist calculi, or any other extralegal rule of decision. Just as Justices Sotomayor and Kagan did in *Lockhart,* we can make our choice based on a comparative assessment of the various legal clues: choosing whether the rule of the last antecedent or one of its exceptions best fits the case in light of the particular language at hand. At the end of the day, we may not be able to claim confidence that there's a certain and single right answer in every case, but there's no reason why we cannot make our best judgment depending on (and only on) conventional legal materials, relying on a sort of closed record, if you will, without peeking to outside evidence. No reason, too, why we cannot conclude for ourselves that one side has the better of it, even if by a nose, and even while admitting that a disagreeing colleague could see it the other way. As Justice Scalia once explained, "Every canon is simply *one indication* of meaning; and if there are more contrary indications (perhaps supported by other canons), it must yield. But that does not render the entire enterprise a fraud—not, at least, unless the judge wishes to make it so."

Neither do I see the critics as offering a better alternative. Consider a story Justice Scalia loved to tell. Imagine two men walking in the woods who happen upon an angry bear. They start running for their lives. But the bear is quickly gaining on them. One man yells to the other, "We'll never be able to outrun this bear!" The other replies, calmly, "I don't have to outrun the bear, I just have to outrun you." As Justice Scalia explained, just because the traditional view of judging may be imperfect for some small set of cases doesn't mean we should or must abandon it. The real question is whether the critics can offer anything better.

And about that, I have my doubts. Take the model of the judge as pragmatic social-welfare maximizer who seeks to weigh the various costs and benefits associated with the various possible outcomes of the case at hand and pick the one best calculated to maximize our collective social welfare. But in hard cases don't *both* sides usually have a pretty persuasive story about how deciding in their favor would advance the social good? In criminal cases, for example, we often hear arguments from the government that its view would promote public security or finality. Meanwhile, from the defense we often hear that its view would promote personal liberty and procedural fairness. How is a judge supposed to weigh or rank these radically different social goods? They all may seem like pretty good things and the pragmatic model of judging offers us no value or rule for determining which costs and benefits are to be preferred. At the end of the day, these critics risk inviting us only to trade one sort of indeterminacy problem for another. And the indeterminacy problem invited by the critics may well be a good deal more problematic given the challenges of trying to square their new models of judging with our constitutional design and its underlying values. So it seems to me that before we throw overboard our traditional views about the separation of judicial and legislative roles, we might do well to remember The Bear.

WITH THIS BRIEF SKETCH, I hope I've given you some sense of why I believe Justice Scalia's vision of the "good and faithful judge" is a worthy one. But so far I've discussed mostly principle, not experience. And I run the risk of an objection from those who might suggest that there's more in heaven and earth than is dreamt of in any philosophy. So as I close I want to make plain that the traditional view of law and judging not only makes the most sense to me as an intellectual matter but makes the most sense of my own lived and daily experiences in the trenches of the law. My life in the law has taught me that the law bears its own distinctive structure, language, coherence, and integrity. Lawyers seek to make judgments about the future based on a set of reasonably stable existing rules; they do so with a respect for and in light of the law as it is. That is not politics; that is the ancient and honorable practice of law. Now as a judge I see, too, that donning a black robe means something. It serves as a reminder of what's expected of us when we go about our business:

what Edmund Burke called the "cold neutrality of an impartial judge." In my decade on the bench, I have served with judges who strive daily and long and hard to do as Socrates said we should—to hear courteously, answer wisely, consider soberly, and decide impartially. Men and women who do not thrust themselves into the limelight but who tend patiently to the great promise of our legal system—that all litigants will receive equal protection under the law and due process for their grievances. Judges who assiduously seek to avoid the temptation to secure results they prefer. And who do, in fact, regularly issue judgments with which they disagree as a matter of policy, all because they think that's what the law fairly demands.

Justice Scalia's defense of this traditional view of our profession is a legacy every person in this room has inherited. And it is one you students will be asked to carry on soon enough. I remember as if it were yesterday sitting in a law school audience like this one. Listening to a newly minted Justice Scalia offer his Oliver Wendell Holmes lecture. He offered that particular salvo in his defense of the traditional view of judging and the law almost thirty years ago now. It all comes so quickly. But it was and remains, I think, a most worthy way to spend a life.

May he rest in peace.

"POWER WITHOUT LAW"?

———

*Where the last piece addressed the separation of powers be-
tween judges and legislators, this one, an amalgam of several
talks I've given, raises questions about the other two sides of
the separation of powers triangle: the executive-legislative
and executive-judicial divides.*

I MAGINE YOU'VE SPENT THE PAST FIVE YEARS WORKING ON A
new invention. You quit your job and even took out a second
mortgage. After many ups and downs, you finally hit on something
special. So now you endure the further cost and effort of applying for
a patent to protect your idea, devoting tens of thousands of dollars
and a few more years to that process alone. At the end of it all, the
Patent and Trademark Office agrees your invention is novel. It issues
a patent that affords you the exclusive right to make and sell your
invention for two decades, a reward for devising something that
stands to benefit everyone.

Or so you thought. Years down the road, someone emerges from
the woodwork and argues that your patent should be revoked because your invention merely replicated an existing patent. Until recently, only independent judges and juries could strip patent owners
of their vested property rights in duly issued patents. But lately
things have changed. Now, anyone who wants to take your patent
away can just file a petition with the director of the Patent and Trademark Office. And it turns out that the newly appointed director has
different views from those that prevailed when your patent was issued. You see, the new director's boss, the president, thinks other
people should be able to make products similar to yours without

having to pay you royalties; he and Congress these days are looking for "patent killers" to run the show. So the director sets out to ensure that your patent will be canceled. He starts by selecting the "administrative judges" who will hear the challenge to your patent, and he signals to them that invalidating the patent is a big priority for the new administration. It turns out, too, that these administrative judges can't easily brush off the director's pressure: They don't have life tenure, the director supervises them, and he even gets to select which of them will participate in your case. In fact, if (somehow) his hand-selected panel doesn't reach the outcome he prefers, he is free to add more administrative judges and order the case reheard. In the end, the outcome of your case comes as no surprise: The administrative judges unanimously vote to revoke your patent.

Sound like fiction—or maybe life in a regime where the rule of law isn't as jealously guarded as it is here? In fact, this scenario is (loosely) based on allegations involving a real statute in a real case: the America Invents Act and *Oil States v. Greene's Energy Group.* There, my Court upheld the act against a challenge alleging that it violated the separation of powers by allowing executive branch employees to exercise powers that previously belonged exclusively to the judiciary's independent judges and juries. (Needless to say by now, I dissented.) And it illustrates the topic I'd like to discuss with you: the dangers that follow when we fail to police the separation of powers.

I've spoken before about the importance of the separation of powers between judges and legislators, how that separation protects our liberties, and the dangers that can arise when the lines between those powers dissolve into a muddle. But that aspect of the separation of powers is, in some sense, the easy one. In the legal profession, we have spent a lot of time and effort in recent years focusing on the difference between legislators and judges—and seeking to refine our theories of interpretation to honor that divide. The return of textualism and originalism to the forefront of legal interpretation debates may be attributed in large part, I think, to a renewed appreciation that they are the only theories that respect the judge's proper role under the Constitution. But in all our debates over the boundaries between judges and legislators, I sometimes wonder if we have neglected attending with equal care to the boundaries between executive and judicial functions and between the executive and legislative roles.

Today, I would like to focus on those two sides of the separation of powers triangle. The framers firmly believed that the rule of law depends on keeping *all* three governmental powers in their proper spheres. They knew, too, that eliding these boundaries can prove powerfully tempting. Handing over judicial functions to the executive branch, for example, surely holds much allure, as my hypothetical illustrates: Agency employees may be more easily controlled than judges, their outcomes more easily assured, and their processes more efficient. But the founders also knew from hard experience with the Star Chamber and the Privy Council about the dangers of executive "courts." They knew that when the executive is free to withdraw your legal rights, those rights are no longer protected by neutral legal principles, the judgment of independent judges, and a jury of your peers. Instead, they may be taken with the efficient dispatch of a political agent with political designs. Now, I am not suggesting that we face dangers today remotely on the scale of those the framers confronted. But I do wonder if sometimes we are insufficiently attentive to the costs that accompany departures from the Constitution's design.

LATER, I WILL RETURN to some questions about the separation of powers between the executive and judiciary that cases like *Oil States* invite. But I'd like to start our discussion with the executive-legislative divide. The Constitution, of course, vested all federal legislative powers in Congress. And it deliberately made the legislative process a hard one, demanding the participation and assent of a large number of representatives in two separate houses before a new law can be enacted. Meanwhile, the framers did much the opposite when it came to designing a branch to enforce the laws. They vested executive authority in a single president on the conviction that, if a law can survive the arduous legislative process, it deserves faithful and vigorous execution of the sort you cannot expect from committees.

Today, these lines often appear blurrier to us than they did to the framers. More and more, Congress "delegates" its legislative authority to executive branch agencies and tasks them with solving the pressing problems of the day. And what happens when the power to legislate is effectively transferred from a branch the framers designed for deliberation to one they designed for prompt action? In the first place, you get exactly what you'd expect: a lot more law. For some time now, agency-made law has far outpaced congressional output. Consider the (admittedly crude) data from 2016. According to Clyde Wayne Crews, federal departments, agencies, and commissions issued 3,853 rules, while Congress passed and the president signed "just" 214 bills. That works out to about 18 agency-made rules for every congressional statute. Nor was 2016 an anomaly. The decade before that saw about 27 rules for every law. The comparison holds, too, not just when it comes to the number of laws but the number of pages they cover. At the end of 2012, the number of pages in the *Code of Federal Regulations* exceeded the number of pages in the *United States Code* by a factor of nearly four—topping out at over 160,000 pages. Nor does the *Code of Federal Regulations* include the many thousands of pages of other "sub-regulatory" proclamations, memoranda, guidance documents, bulletins, circulars, announcements, and the like that federal agencies issue every year. All of which are often practically as binding as any statute.

Naturally, some of this output is vitally important. It addresses the regulation of financial institutions, our national defense, and workplace safety, among many other things. But some of this energetic executive output also includes rules that regulate the very fine details of private conduct and back it up with the threat of serious criminal penalties. Consider this example unearthed by A Crime a Day: chapter 21, section 155.194 of the *Code of Federal Regulations,* a provision titled simply "Catsup." This regulation provides, among other things, that if you want to sell a food product called "ketchup" or "catsup," you must first test the consistency of the product in a contraption called a Bostwick Consistometer to ensure that it flows at a rate of no more than 14 centimeters per 30 seconds at a temperature of 20 degrees Celsius, give or take a degree. If your ketchup doesn't measure up, you may have to label it "Below Standard in Quality."

And if—heaven forbid—you sell ketchup that the federal government considers too runny without labeling it as such, you may have committed the federal crime of selling misbranded food, punishable by up to a year in prison for each violation. Madison warned that what we call "the rule of law" depends on the existence of laws that are reasonably clear, finite, and stable. Only then can people plan their lives and order their affairs. The rule of law comes under threat, he warned, when the laws become "so voluminous that they cannot be read, or so incoherent they cannot be understood." And you might reasonably wonder where we stand on those metrics today.

When lawmaking moves from the legislative to the executive branch, it's not just the *amount* of lawmaking that changes either. You may remember this story from your high school civics class. When Thomas Jefferson returned from France after the Constitution was written, he reportedly sat down for breakfast with George Washington. Jefferson criticized Washington for having agreed in his absence to a second chamber in the legislature, the Senate. Washington responded in this way: "Why," he asked, "did you pour that coffee into your saucer?" "To cool it," Jefferson answered. "Even so," replied Washington, "we pour legislation into the senatorial saucer to cool it."

As Washington saw it, the difficulties of the legislative process were essential to its design, purposefully placed there to ensure that laws would be more likely the product of deliberation than haste; more likely the product of compromise among the many than the will of the few; and more likely to respect minority interests than trample on their rights. As Hamilton explained, "The oftener the measure is brought under examination, the greater the diversity in the situations of those who are to examine it, the less must be the danger of those errors which flow from want of due deliberation, or of those missteps which proceed from the contagion of some common passion or interest." Because no bill in our legislative process can become law without the assent of a majority of both houses of Congress and the president—three entities elected at different times, by different constituencies—passing a statute almost always means compromising, and in particular compromising with those who represent minority interests. Meaning that minority groups have a strong bargaining chip to protect their interests, achieve concessions, or outright topple a bill. The whole point of the design is to involve a wide spectrum of viewpoints and distill the best each has to offer through deliberation and negotiation. Meanwhile, of course, only one party at a time controls the executive branch. So if the executive is allowed to make law, it has far less need to take account of minority interests; less incentive to deliberate than act; and less need to compromise. One can, as well, expect the law to flip-flop pretty much whenever one party takes the presidency from the other. The result: Our executive-made laws are more likely to be winner-take-all, less likely to reflect the virtues of compromise and deliberation, less likely to respect minority voices, and more likely to be the product of haste and partisan passion.

Here's still another question. What about the democratic accountability of those who make the laws? Under the Constitution, the answer is supposed to be pretty clear. Congress makes the laws and you are free to vote your representative in or out at regular intervals. But who do you blame for executive laws that you think ill-conceived, voluminous, or incoherent? Can you name the people who run the FCC, FTC, NLRB, or SEC? Even if you can, it's not like elections are held for those who lead these agencies. To be sure, many agencies report to the president, who is, in turn, democratically accountable to the people. But presidential elections tend to be about the big-picture questions—war and peace, not individual regulations. Nor can presidents always control these agencies. As Professor Jonathan Turley reminds us, only about 1 percent of executive agency positions are filled by presidential appointees, and entire sectors of our national life are regulated by "independent agencies" insulated from presidential control. Churchill once said that the world is divided into people who own their governments and governments who own their people, and it is vital we never cross that line.

Now, you might reply, at least our elected representatives in *Congress* maintain some level of control here, for Congress can always impose new restrictions on agencies, undo their work, or even eliminate them. Maybe. But maybe, too, it's sometimes rational for legislators to divest themselves of responsibility and hand off today's hot potato to an agency. After all, legislators can then tell constituents that they have "solved" the "problem" by adopting legislation directing the agency to fix it—and at the same time they can blame the agency later if their constituents don't like its chosen solution. Even more than that, maybe it's sometimes rational for legislators who cannot enact their full policy program consistent with the Constitution's demanding legislative process to pass what they can, delegate the rest to the agency to decide, and then try to cajole regulators to finish the job. So if we trust Congress to defend its legislative turf from the executive branch, we're likely to be disappointed. And, besides, why should we leave the enforcement of the separation of powers to trust? The Constitution didn't vest the legislative power in Congress to protect *Congress*. That assignment was just a means to an end, and the end is preserving the liberty of *the people*. When separated powers unite, it is *their* freedom that stands at risk.

NOW LET'S RETURN TO the executive-judicial side of the separation of powers triangle where I started with our inventor and the *Oil States* hypothetical. The Constitution assigns the executive the job of implementing our laws and the judiciary the responsibility for interpreting them. For these tasks, the framers created diametrically different institutions. Unlike the politically accountable and energetic executive, the judiciary was designed to be insulated from political pressures so that people could be confident that their cases and controversies over the meaning of existing laws and past facts would be resolved neutrally.

But here, too, the separation of powers has come under some strain, with power gravitating away from the more deliberative and neutral processes of the judiciary toward the more energetic and political ones of the executive. As *Oil States* illustrates, executive employees today often work under the nom de plume of "administrative judges" and claim the power to decide cases and controversies in proceedings that bear at least a passing resemblance to judicial trials and appeals. Nor do these administrative proceedings resolve only disputes over public rights. Often enough they claim the power to strip individuals even of their vested private rights. And often enough, as in *Oil States*, the administrative judges charged with deciding these cases are accountable to political bosses with agendas of their own; gone in these cases is the right to a neutral judge and a jury of your peers.

Even when it comes to the disputes that do remain within the judicial branch, executive agencies today enjoy considerable power. In relatively recent years, courts have decided to defer to agencies when it comes to the job of interpreting the law, effectively ceding to the executive a task previously thought a core judicial responsibility and competence. Perhaps the most well-known of these deference doctrines is the *Chevron* doctrine. *Chevron* says that if a statutory term is ambiguous, a judge must accept any reasonable gloss on the law the agency can supply—even if the judge is convinced it's not the *best* reading of the statute's terms. The related *Auer* doctrine requires judges to do much the same for an agency's interpretation of its own regulations. So now, not only do executive agencies get to write the regulations, not only may they enforce them too, but they are even allowed to resolve any ambiguities that later emerge in favor of their preferred policy outcomes.

In a short and recent span, as Justice Clarence Thomas has noted, courts have taken these doctrines and run with them. They've deferred to an agency's interpretation of a *different* agency's regulations. They've deferred to agency interpretations that were inconsistent with the agency's previous interpretations of the *same* statute or regulation. They've deferred to agency interpretations advanced for the first time in litigation. They've deferred to agency interpretations when it comes to criminal sentencing. Under the *Brand X* doctrine, the Supreme Court has even said that courts must sometimes overrule their preexisting judicial interpretations of the law when an executive agency wants a different result.

What's the upshot of affording the executive so great a role in judicial functions? In the first place, it can make it exceedingly difficult for ordinary people to know what the law is (and even where to look for it). Under our deference doctrines, it's not enough anymore to look to the statute books and the decisions of courts interpreting them. You *also* have to worry that a completely contrary and binding rule lies buried in the appendix to an agency's guidance manual— maybe the third manual issued in as many years. Even then, you *still* have to predict accurately *every* reasonable possibility of what the law *could be* in the future. For now an agency can disagree with a court's precedent as a matter of policy and demand its overruling. In a world like that, should we be concerned (as Hamilton was) about "subjecting . . . men to punishment for things which, when they were done, were breaches of no law," something that "ha[s] been, in all ages, [a] favorite and most formidable instrument[] of tyranny"?

Nor are these the only potential costs to consider. The founders insulated the judiciary from political pressures to ensure that judges would apply existing laws equally to everyone regardless of their present popularity. As Hamilton put it, this kind of independence was needed "to guard the Constitution and the rights of individuals from the effects of those ill humors, which the arts of designing men, or the influence of particular conjunctures, sometimes disseminate among the people themselves, and which, though they speedily give place to better information, and more deliberate reflection, have a tendency, in the meantime, to occasion dangerous innovations in the government, and serious oppressions of the minor party in the community." Remember, too, that when it comes to adjudicating cases and controversies, we're talking about assigning liability based on past actions that cannot be undone. It's not like the job of passing new legislation that usually applies only prospectively, with fair notice given to everyone about the need to conform their conduct to the new rule. In adjudicating cases and controversies, the decisionmaker knows exactly whose ox will be gored by his decisions and the victim has no chance to alter his conduct to conform to the judgment. So when independent judges and juries give way to political decisionmakers in deciding cases and controversies over past facts, should we worry about the consequences for unpopular persons and causes? And what happens when the *best* reading of the law a neutral judge can muster gives way under our deference doctrines to an *inferior* gloss produced by administrative judges who are handpicked for each case by a political boss?

Consider the case of *Yellowbear v. Lampert*. Andrew Yellowbear, in prison for murdering his daughter, is the kind of person who needs to be kept in special housing because his crime is so heinous other prisoners are likely to harm him. Given his unpopularity, it's perhaps unsurprising that, when he sought to access the prison's existing sweat lodge so he could exercise his Native American faith, executive officials refused. In response, my old court (the Tenth Circuit) had little difficulty applying a federal statute prohibiting religious discrimination to hold that Mr. Yellowbear was entitled to some access to the sweat lodge like other prisoners. Likewise, my court didn't hesitate to apply the same set of statutes to protect a Muslim prisoner who required halal food, or to shield a family-run business from federal mandates that would have forced family members to violate the dictates of their faith. None of these outcomes would have been possible if the original executive decision hadn't been reviewable by an independent judge. Can it be any surprise a *Wall Street Journal* study has found that, over a five-year period, the agency it studied won more than 90 percent of its cases before its own administrative judges but fewer than 70 percent of the cases it brought before federal judges?

Finally, consider the loss of civic involvement. The judiciary isn't just made up of life-appointed judges who have considerably more freedom to depart from majoritarian norms and political pressures than their counterparts in the other branches. It's also composed of juries. In this way, the judiciary might be said to be simultaneously the least *and* the most democratic of the branches. Yet like judges, juries are notoriously independent. They do not stand for election and they answer to no one. So while they are *of* the community, they do not have to answer *to* the community. It's the very independence and common sense of juries, their ability and willingness to cut through dogma and doctrine and technical legalese, that the founders and so many generations before and since have found so valuable. Of course, litigants in court may opt out of a jury trial, but they may also demand it, something they cannot do in administrative tribunals.

Nor is the loss only the litigants'. Participation in juries is the closest many people ever get to participating in their government. Studies suggest that serving on a jury may lead to increased electoral engagement, especially among those who have not previously participated in elections. Studies suggest, too, that participation in the jury system increases significantly participants' evaluation of our legal system. All of these civic goods disappear when cases are moved from judicial courtrooms to administrative conference rooms.

THE CONCERNS I'VE DISCUSSED here are nothing new. As long ago as 1933, the American Bar Association created a Special Committee on Administrative Law. Soon the committee voiced concerns that the cascade of new agencies was commingling executive, legislative, and judicial functions in ways that could prove problematic. Eventually, Congress adopted the Administrative Procedure Act as a step toward addressing these concerns. The APA created two ways for agencies to act—rulemaking and adjudication—and created two modes of proceeding for each—formal and informal. Unsurprisingly, formal proceedings offer considerably more procedural protections.

Generally speaking, in informal rulemakings an agency suggests a new rule, the public comments on that proposal, and then the agency makes adjustments accordingly before issuing a final rule—or deciding not to issue a final rule at all. When the agency does issue a final rule, that rule can and does often look different from the original proposal; to be permissible, a final rule only needs to be a "logical outgrowth" of the proposed one. Formal rulemaking, by contrast, requires an agency official to preside over a verbal or written proceeding featuring cross-examination and forbids that official from engaging in *ex parte* communications. The agency also bears the burden of proving that the rule is supported "on consideration of the whole record . . . and supported by . . . substantial evidence"—something the agency may not need to prove in an informal rulemaking.

The story is much the same when it comes to adjudication. In informal adjudication, the requirements are relatively few. Proceedings are presided over by officials who are often subject to oversight by others in the agency (just as in *Oil States*). These officials may even perform other duties within the agency in addition to their "judicial" responsibilities—including prosecuting and investigating other cases. By contrast, formal adjudications afford more protection for those involved. Parties may present their case by verbal or written evidence, conduct cross-examination, and submit rebuttal evidence. Parties are also entitled to a hearing where an administrative law judge (or the agency head) will preside. Administrative law judges do not enjoy the same independence as federal judges, but unlike some decisionmakers in more informal adjudications, these administrative law judges generally cannot have their pay cut without approval from a separate entity called the Merit Systems Protection Board.

When Congress adopted the APA, most everyone expected that formal proceedings would be quite common. That understanding held true for a while, as formal devices initially "dominated the administrative law landscape," in the words of the Administrative Conference of the United States. But today formal proceedings are a vanishing breed; formal rulemakings in particular, as Professor Aaron Nielson has explained, "ha[ve] been effectively exiled from administrative law." Nor can it come as a surprise either that agencies have pushed back against formal processes given the many advantages informal processes hold for them—or that courts have acquiesced in these agency efforts given our deference doctrines.

Agencies not only enjoy a great deal of leeway today when choosing whether to proceed informally or formally, they also have considerable discretion when choosing whether to proceed by rulemaking or adjudication. In a case called *Chenery II,* the Supreme Court held that an agency can sometimes even create a brand-new rule in an adjudication and apply that new rule retroactively to the parties before it (who, of course, lack any notice that might permit them to adjust their conduct to conform to the new regulatory demand). To be sure, this retroactive-rulemaking-by-adjudication has rested uneasily in our due process jurisprudence and has proven a frequent target of criticism. Justice Robert Jackson—President Franklin Roosevelt's attorney general and himself an architect of the administrative state—penned a forceful dissent in *Chenery II.* He argued that the Court was upholding an "assertion of power to govern the matter without law," something he thought would (in the words of Justice Benjamin Cardozo) reduce "[l]aw as a guide to conduct . . . to the level of mere futility."

In fairness to the *Chenery II* majority, it didn't think the retroactivity problem would prove significant in many cases because it didn't expect agencies to make a lot of new law through adjudication. Indeed, the majority wrote that agencies should use rulemaking procedures "as much as possible." But if that was the Court's expectation, reality has fallen far short. Agencies today routinely announce new rules while adjudicating individual cases. In fact, some agencies almost never engage in rulemaking and create virtually all of their new rules through adjudication. It's a result that may be at least a little ironic considering that Congress created some of these agencies precisely so that they could formulate clear *ex ante* rules for people to follow. But it's a result that cannot come as much of a surprise. For, again, what rational agency would choose to shoulder the burden of providing notice and allowing public comment from the whole of the people on a proposed rule when it could avoid that burden by simply announcing the same nationwide rule in the course of an informal adjudication of a discrete case against a single private party?

If you're beginning to wonder whether the APA's procedural protections designed to safeguard individual liberty on the front end may have fallen short of initial expectations, you might also wonder about the judicial review procedures the APA sought to provide on the back end. During the APA's drafting process, some suggested limiting judicial review of an agency's legal interpretations (at least sometimes) to the task of asking merely "whether the administrative construction is a permissible one." But in the end Congress chose a more robust formulation, directing that a "reviewing court shall decide all relevant questions of law, [and] interpret constitutional and statutory provisions." That language seems to suggest that courts must decide questions of law for themselves without deference to agency interpretations. Yet, as we have seen, modern courts may have nearly re-created for themselves this discarded standard of review through *Chevron* and related deference doctrines.

Nor is the problem limited to questions of law. Generally, the APA allows courts to strike down an agency's factual findings in adjudication only if they are unsupported by "substantial evidence." But in my time as a judge, I've seen at least some cases that might make you wonder if even that deferential standard has been watered down. Consider *Mathis v. Shulkin,* a case that came to the Supreme Court during my first term. There, lower courts seemingly created out of whole cloth a presumption that examiners at the Department of Veterans Affairs are competent to render expert medical opinions against veterans seeking compensation for service-related disabilities. So now substantial evidence can sometimes be effectively guaranteed by mere presumption. Or consider *Compass Environmental, Inc. v. Occupational Safety & Health Review Commission,* where the Tenth Circuit upheld an agency's sanction against a private company even though it presented no evidence that the company violated industry standards, as the law required; instead, the agency pointed only to alleged violations of the company's internal policies without seeking to show that they reflected (rather than exceeded) industry standards. Here, substantial evidence came from, really, no evidence at all.

But even putting all this aside and overlooking how the APA might have failed to realize its initial promise, you might wonder whether it was ever intended to be the final word. Those who enacted the APA in 1946 were well aware that, in the words of Justice Jackson, "[e]xperience may reveal defects." And both our world and our administrative state have changed massively since 1946. The federal civilian workforce outside the Department of Defense has grown by more than 70 percent, and the length of the *Code of Federal Regulations* has increased perhaps sevenfold. Not only are there far more agency rules, but they can bear far more significant impact. Today, a single federal rule can disrupt entire segments of our national life and change radically the way hundreds of millions of people work and live. Yet we still live under pretty much the same administrative law structure as we did in 1946, at least those portions of it that haven't been effectively brushed away in practice. If the men and women who helped draft the APA were acutely aware of the challenges agencies could pose in their time to the separation of powers and the liberties our constitutional design was meant to serve, you might wonder whether we may safely ignore these same concerns in our own time.

TO BE SURE, the practical benefits that flow from enforcing the separation of powers in an individual case can sometimes seem hard to see—maybe especially when compared (like apples vs. oranges) against the systemic efficiencies that fusing powers in executive agencies can provide. So what if a Caring Hearts, an Oil States, a De Niz Robles, or a Mathis suffers an injustice? That may be regrettable, but accommodating their individual concerns would be costly. What matters more, some might claim, is justice-in-gross; government must be allowed to work efficiently. But the founders saw virtue in the separation of powers and a government that is deliberately deliberate. Where others see inefficiency in the separation of powers, they saw fair notice; protection for the inherent value of every individual person, including especially dissenting voices; democratic accountability; and the rule of law as administered by independent judges and juries. By transferring more and more power from the legislature and judiciary to the executive, we alter piece by piece the framers' work and risk the underlying values it was designed to serve. Like a tower in the game of Jenga, pull out this block or that one and the tower may seem largely unaffected, especially if you do it with a bit of finesse—and the lawyers who come up with justifications for the blending of powers have plenty of that. But keep pulling out blocks, and eventually what started out as a strong and stable tower will begin to teeter.

Madison and the founders held the view that "[n]o political truth is" more important to "liberty" than the separation of powers because the "accumulation of" power "in the same hands" inevitably leads to "tyranny." We might ask ourselves today: Do we still agree? And if we do, how would we grade ourselves in bearing witness to that truth?

Alexis de Tocqueville was one of the keenest students of our new republic. He offered us this insight, which I leave with you tonight:

> After having thus successively taken each member of the community in its powerful grasp, and fashioned them at will, the

supreme power then extends its arm over the whole community. It covers the surface of society with a network of small complicated rules, minute and uniform, through which the most original minds and the most energetic characters cannot penetrate, to rise above the crowd. The will of man is not shattered, but softened, bent, and guided: men are seldom forced by it to act, but they are constantly restrained from acting: such a power does not destroy, but it prevents existence; it does not tyrannize, but it compresses, enervates, extinguishes, and stupefies a people, till each nation is reduced to be nothing better than a flock of timid and industrious animals, of which the government is the shepherd.

I have always thought that servitude of the regular, quiet, and gentle kind which I have just described, might be combined more easily than is commonly believed with some of the outward forms of freedom; and that it might even establish itself under the wing of the sovereignty of the people.

Gutierrez-Brizuela v. Lynch

With this piece we move from speeches about the separation of powers to cases showing its impact in the lives of real people. This first case, from my time on the Tenth Circuit, involved an immigrant who was seeking lawful admission to this country but who found himself caught up in complex regulatory red tape just like Mr. De Niz Robles. The government said he should lose even though existing judicial precedent supported him. In the government's view, the court had to defer to its view of the law's meaning—and even overrule the judicial precedent on which Mr. Gutierrez-Brizuela had relied. I addressed some of the underlying legal issues in a concurrence.

At issue were two Supreme Court decisions: Chevron and Brand X. Under the Chevron decision, handed down in the 1980s, if a court finds a statute's meaning ambiguous it may not resolve the ambiguity using the traditional tools of statutory interpretation that judges have employed for centuries. Instead, the court must defer to an executive agency's decision about the law's meaning. A court must do so even when the agency's decision is influenced by politics, and even if the agency later changes its position in response to a new election or other political pressure. Brand X built on Chevron and announced that a court is now also obliged to allow an agency to use its Chevron powers to overrule a preexisting judicial precedent. In this excerpt, I raise some questions about these doctrines and their consistency with the traditional judicial role, the rule of law, and fair notice to individuals like Mr. Gutierrez-Brizuela and Mr. De Niz Robles.

Some of the issues discussed here eventually found their way to the Supreme Court during my second full term, in Kisor v. Wilkie (2019).

THERE'S AN ELEPHANT IN THE ROOM WITH US TODAY. IN OTHER cases and opinions we have studiously attempted to work our way around it and even left it unremarked. But the fact is *Chevron* and *Brand X* permit executive bureaucracies to swallow huge amounts of core judicial and legislative power and concentrate federal power in a way that seems more than a little difficult to square with the Constitution of the framers' design. Maybe the time has come to face the behemoth.

In enlightenment theory and hard-won experience under a tyrannical king the founders found proof of the wisdom of a government of separated powers. In the avowedly political legislature, the framers endowed the people's representatives with the authority to prescribe new rules of general applicability prospectively. In the executive, they placed the task of ensuring the legislature's rules are faithfully executed in the hands of a single person also responsive to the people. And in the judiciary, they charged individuals insulated from political pressures with the job of interpreting the law and applying it retroactively to resolve past disputes. This allocation of different sorts of power to different sorts of decisionmakers was no accident. To adapt the law to changing circumstances, the founders thought, the collective wisdom of the people's representatives is needed. To faithfully execute the laws often demands the sort of vigor hard to find in management-by-committee. And to resolve cases and controversies over past events calls for neutral decisionmakers who will apply the law as it is, not as they wish it to be.

Even more importantly, the founders considered the separation of powers a vital guard against governmental encroachment on the people's liberties, including all those later enumerated in the Bill of Rights. What would happen, for example, if the political majorities who run the legislative and executive branches could decide cases and controversies over past facts? They might be tempted to bend existing laws, to reinterpret and apply them retroactively in novel ways and without advance notice. Effectively leaving parties who cannot alter their past conduct to the mercy of majoritarian politics and risking the possibility that unpopular groups might be singled out for this sort of mistreatment—and raising along the way, too, grave due process (fair notice) and equal protection problems. Conversely, what would happen if politically unresponsive and life-tenured judges were permitted to decide policy questions for the future or try to execute those policies? The very idea of self-government would soon be at risk of withering to the point of pointlessness. It was to avoid dangers like these, dangers the founders had studied and seen realized in their own time, that they pursued the separation of powers. A government of diffused powers, they knew, is a government less capable of invading the liberties of the people.

Founders meet *Brand X*. Precisely to avoid the possibility of allowing politicized decisionmakers to decide cases and controversies about the meaning of existing laws, the framers sought to ensure that judicial judgments "may not lawfully be revised, overturned or refused faith and credit by" the elected branches of government. Yet this deliberate design, this separation of functions aimed to ensure a neutral decisionmaker for the people's disputes, faces more than a little pressure from *Brand X*. Under *Brand X*'s terms, after all, courts are required to overrule their own declarations about the meaning of existing law in favor of interpretations dictated by executive agencies. By *Brand X*'s own telling, this means a judicial declaration of the law's meaning in a case or controversy before it is not "authoritative," but is instead subject to revision by a politically accountable branch of government.

Of course, *Brand X* asserts that its rule about judicial deference to executive revisions follows logically "from *Chevron* itself." And that assessment seems fair enough as far as it goes. If you accept *Chevron*'s claim that legislative ambiguity represents a license to executive agencies to render authoritative judgments about what a statute means, *Brand X*'s rule requiring courts to overturn their own contrary judgments does seem to follow pretty naturally.

But acknowledging this much only brings the colossus now fully into view. In the Administrative Procedure Act, Congress vested the courts with the power to "interpret . . . statutory provisions" and overturn agency action inconsistent with those interpretations. Congress assigned the courts much the same job in the immigration field where we happen to find ourselves today. And there's good reason to think that legislative assignments like these are often constitutionally compelled. After all, the question whether Congress has or hasn't vested a private legal right in an individual "is, in its nature, judicial, and must be tried by the judicial authority." Yet, rather than completing the task expressly assigned to us, rather than "interpret[ing] . . . statutory provisions," declaring what the law is, and overturning inconsistent agency action, *Chevron* tells us we must allow an executive agency to resolve the meaning of any ambiguous statutory provision. In this way, *Chevron* seems no less than a judge-made doctrine for the abdication of the judicial duty. Of course, some role remains for judges even under *Chevron*. Judges decide whether the statute is "ambiguous," and if it is, they decide whether the agency's view is "reasonable." But where in all this does a court interpret the law and say what it is? When does a court independently decide what the statute means and whether it has or has not vested a legal right in a person? Where *Chevron* applies that job seems to have gone extinct.

Transferring the job of saying what the law is from the judiciary to the executive unsurprisingly invites the very sort of due process (fair notice) and equal protection concerns the framers knew would arise if the political branches intruded on judicial functions. Under *Chevron* the people aren't just charged with awareness of and the duty to conform their conduct to the fairest reading of the law that a detached magistrate can muster. Instead, they are charged with an awareness of *Chevron*; required to guess whether the statute will be declared "ambiguous" (courts often disagree on what qualifies); and required to guess (again) whether an agency's interpretation will be deemed "reasonable." Who can even attempt all that, at least without an army of lawyers and lobbyists? And, of course, that's not the end of it.

Even if the people somehow manage to make it through this far unscathed, they must always remain alert to the possibility that the agency will reverse its current view 180 degrees anytime based merely on the shift of political winds and still prevail. Neither, too, will agencies always deign to announce their views in advance; often enough they seek to impose their "reasonable" new interpretations only retroactively in administrative adjudications. Perhaps allowing agencies rather than courts to declare the law's meaning bears some advantages, but it also bears its costs. And the founders were wary of those costs, knowing that, when unchecked by independent courts exercising the job of declaring the law's meaning, executives throughout history had sought to exploit ambiguous laws as license for their own prerogative.

Some claim to see a way out of our apparent predicament. They suggest that *Chevron* isn't so much about permitting agencies to assume the judicial function of interpreting the law as it is about permitting agencies to make the law, to effect their own preferences about optimal public policy when a statute is ambiguous. On this account, *Chevron*'s rule of deference isn't about trying to make judges out of agencies or letting them usurp the judicial function. Rather, it's about letting agencies fill legislative voids. When Congress passes ambiguous legislation, *Chevron* means we should read that as signaling a legislative "intention" to "delegate" to the executive the job of making any reasonable "legislative" policy choices it thinks wise. And, to be sure, *Chevron* itself espouses just this view.

But however that may be, none of it rescues us from our riddle. For whatever the agency may be doing under *Chevron*, the problem remains that courts are not fulfilling their duty to interpret the law and declare invalid agency actions inconsistent with those interpretations in the cases and controversies that come before them. A duty expressly assigned to them by the Administrative Procedure Act and one often likely compelled by the Constitution itself. That's a problem for the judiciary. And it is a problem for the people whose liberties may now be impaired not by an independent decisionmaker seeking to declare the law's meaning as fairly as possible—the decisionmaker promised to them by law—but by an avowedly politicized administrative agent seeking to pursue whatever policy whim may rule the day. Those problems remain uncured by this line of reply.

Maybe as troubling, this line of reply invites a nest of questions even taken on its own terms. *Chevron* says that we should infer from any statutory ambiguity Congress's "intent" to "delegate" its "legislative authority" to the executive to make "reasonable" policy choices. But where exactly has Congress expressed this intent? Trying to infer the intentions of an institution composed of 535 members is a notoriously doubtful business under the best of circumstances. And these are not exactly the best of circumstances. *Chevron* suggests we should infer an intent to delegate not because Congress has anywhere expressed any such wish, not because anyone anywhere in any legislative history even hinted at that possibility, but because the legislation in question is silent (ambiguous) on the subject. Usually we're told that "an agency literally has no power to act . . . unless and until Congress confers power upon it." Yet *Chevron* seems to stand this ancient and venerable principle nearly on its head.

Maybe worse still, *Chevron*'s inference about hidden congressional intentions seems belied by the intentions Congress has made textually manifest. After all and again, in the Administrative Procedure Act Congress expressly vested the courts with the responsibility to "interpret . . . statutory provisions" and overturn agency action inconsistent with those interpretations. Meanwhile not a word can be found here about delegating legislative authority to agencies. On this record, how can anyone fairly say that Congress "intended" for courts to abdicate their statutory duty under the Administrative Procedure Act and instead "intended" to delegate away its legislative power to executive agencies? The fact is, *Chevron*'s claim about legislative intentions is no more than a fiction—and one that requires a pretty hefty suspension of disbelief at that.

Even supposing, too, that we could overlook this problem—even supposing we somehow had something resembling an authentic congressional delegation of legislative authority—you still might wonder: can Congress really delegate its legislative authority—its power to write new rules of general applicability—to executive agencies? The Supreme Court has long recognized that under the Constitution "Congress cannot delegate legislative power to the president" and that this "principle [is] universally recognized as vital to the integrity and maintenance of the system of government ordained by the constitution." Yet on this account of *Chevron* we're examining, its whole point and purpose seems to be exactly that—to delegate legislative power to the executive branch.

Of course, in relatively recent times the Court has relaxed its approach to claims of unlawful legislative delegation. It has suggested (at least in the civil arena) that Congress may allow the executive to make new rules of general applicability that look a great deal like legislation, so long as the controlling legislation contains an "intelligible principle" that "clearly delineates the general policy" the agency is to apply and "the boundaries of [its] delegated authority." This means Congress must at least "provide substantial guidance on setting . . . standards that affect the entire national economy." Some thoughtful judges and scholars have questioned whether standards like these serve as much as a protection against the delegation of legislative authority as a license for it, undermining the separation between the legislative and executive powers that the founders thought essential.

But even taking the forgiving intelligible principle test as a given, it's no small question whether *Chevron* can clear it. For if an agency can enact a new rule of general applicability affecting huge swaths of the national economy one day and reverse itself the next (and that is exactly what *Chevron* permits), you might be forgiven for asking: where's the "substantial guidance" in that? And if an agency can interpret the scope of its statutory jurisdiction one way one day and reverse itself the next, you might well wonder: where are the promised "clearly delineated boundaries" of agency authority? The Supreme Court once unanimously declared that a statute affording the executive the power to write an industrial code of competition for the poultry industry violated the separation of powers. And if that's the case, you might ask how it is that *Chevron*—a rule that invests agencies with pretty unfettered power to regulate a lot more than chicken—can evade the chopping block.

Even under the most relaxed or functionalist view of our separated powers some concern has to arise, too, when so much power is concentrated in the hands of a single branch of government. After all, *Chevron* invests the power to decide the meaning of the law, and to do so with legislative policy goals in mind, in the very entity charged with enforcing the law. Under its terms, an administrative agency may set and revise policy (legislative), override adverse judicial determinations (judicial), and exercise enforcement discretion (executive). Add to this the fact that today many administrative agencies "wield[] vast power" and are overseen by political appointees (but often receive little effective oversight from the chief executive to whom they nominally report), and you have a pretty potent mix. Under any conception of our separation of powers, I would have thought powerful and centralized authorities like today's administrative agencies would have warranted less deference from other branches, not more. None of this is to suggest that *Chevron* is "the very definition of tyranny." But on any account it certainly seems to have added prodigious new powers to an already titanic administrative state—and spawned along the way more than a few due process and equal protection problems of the sort documented in the court's opinion today and in *De Niz Robles* [a case discussed on page 43]. It's an arrangement, too, that seems pretty hard to square with the Constitution of the founders' design and, as Justice Felix Frankfurter once observed, "[t]he accretion of dangerous power does not come in a day. It does come, however slowly, from the generative force of unchecked disregard of the restrictions" imposed by the Constitution.

What I suspect about *Chevron*'s compatibility with the separation of powers finds confirmation in what I know. The Supreme Court has expressly instructed us not to apply *Chevron* deference when an agency seeks to interpret a criminal statute. Why? Because, we are seemingly told, doing so would violate the Constitution by forcing the judiciary to abdicate the job of saying what the law is and preventing courts from exercising independent judgment in the interpretation of statutes. An admirable colleague, Judge Jeffrey Sutton, has noted that the same rationale would appear to preclude affording *Chevron* deference to agency interpretations of statutes that bear both civil and criminal applications. A category that covers a great many (most?) federal statutes today. And try as I might, I have a hard time identifying a principled reason why the same rationale doesn't also apply to statutes with purely civil application. After all, the Administrative Procedure Act doesn't distinguish between purely civil and other kinds of statutes when describing the interpretive duties of courts. Neither did the founders reserve their concerns about political decisionmakers deciding the meaning of existing law to criminal cases; Article III doesn't say judges should say what the law is or decide whether legal rights have or haven't vested and been violated only when a crime is alleged. And certainly *Marbury v. Madison* did not speak so meekly: it affirmed the judiciary's duty to say what the law is in a case that involved the interpretation of, yes, a civil statute affecting individual rights.

So what would happen in a world without *Chevron*? If this goliath of modern administrative law were to fall? Surely Congress could and would continue to pass statutes for executive agencies to enforce. And just as surely agencies could and would continue to offer guidance on how they intend to enforce those statutes. The only difference would be that courts would then fulfill their duty to exercise their independent judgment about what the law is. Of course, courts could and would consult agency views and apply the agency's interpretation when it accords with the best reading of a statute. But judicial review of the law's meaning would limit the ability of an agency to alter and amend existing law. It would avoid the due process and equal protection problems of the kind documented in our decisions. It would promote reliance interests by allowing citizens to organize their affairs with some assurance that the rug will not be pulled from under them tomorrow, the next day, or after the next election. And an agency's recourse for a judicial declaration of the law's meaning that it dislikes would be precisely the recourse the Constitution prescribes—an appeal to higher judicial authority or a new law enacted consistent with bicameralism and presentment. We managed to live with the administrative state before *Chevron*. We could do it again. Put simply, it seems to me that in a world without *Chevron* very little would change—except perhaps the most important things.

Caring Hearts v. Burwell

———

Where the last case addressed the mixing of executive and judicial powers, the next excerpt discusses what can happen when the executive assumes legislative powers. Freed from the constitutional constraints associated with the legislative process (bicameralism and presentment) and endowed with vigor and energy, the executive branch agency at issue here had little to stop it from churning out so many new regulations—thousands upon thousands of new documents every year—that eventually even it couldn't keep track of them all. A local company providing home health care to seniors found itself accused of violating rules that, as it turns out, weren't even in existence when it rendered its services.

EXECUTIVE AGENCIES TODAY ARE PERMITTED NOT ONLY TO enforce legislation but to revise and reshape it through the exercise of so-called "delegated" legislative authority. The number of formal rules these agencies have issued thanks to their delegated legislative authority has grown so exuberantly it's hard to keep up. The Code of Federal Regulations now clocks in at over 175,000 pages. And no one seems sure how many more hundreds of thousands (or maybe millions) of pages of less formal or "sub-regulatory" policy manuals, directives, and the like might be found floating around these days. For some, all this delegated legislative activity by the executive branch raises interesting questions about the separation of powers. For others, it raises troubling questions about due process and fair notice—questions like whether and how people can be fairly expected to keep pace with and conform their conduct to all this churning and changing "law." But what if the problem is even worse than that? What happens if we reach the point where even these legislating agencies don't know what their own "law" is?

That's the problem we confront in this case. And perhaps it comes as little surprise that it arises in the Medicare context. Medicare is, to say the least, a complicated program. The Centers for Medicare & Medicaid Services (CMS) estimates that it issues literally thousands of new or revised guidance documents (not pages) every single year, guidance providers must follow exactingly if they wish to provide health care services to the elderly and disabled under Medicare's umbrella. Currently, about 37,000 separate guidance documents can be found on CMS's website—and even that doesn't purport to be a complete inventory.

But how did CMS wind up confused about its own law? It began this way. Caring Hearts provides physical therapy and skilled nursing services to "homebound" Medicare patients. Of course, any Medicare provider may only charge the government for services that are "reasonable and necessary." But Congress hasn't exactly been clear about who qualifies as homebound or what services qualify as reasonable and necessary. So CMS has developed its own rules on both subjects—rules the agency has (repeatedly) revised and expanded over time. In a recent audit, CMS purported to find that Caring Hearts provided services to at least a handful of patients who didn't qualify as "homebound" or for whom the services rendered weren't "reasonable and necessary." As a result, CMS ordered Caring Hearts to repay the government over $800,000.

The trouble is, in reaching its conclusions CMS applied the wrong law. The agency didn't apply the regulations in force in 2008 when Caring Hearts provided the services in dispute. Instead, it applied considerably more onerous regulations the agency adopted only years later. Regulations that Caring Hearts couldn't have known about at the time it provided its services. Regulations that even CMS concedes bore only prospective effect. And Caring Hearts can make out a pretty good case that its services were entirely consistent with the law as it was at the time they were rendered. So this isn't (and never was) a case about willful Medicare fraud. Instead, it's a case about an agency struggling to keep up with the furious pace of its own rulemaking.

This case lays bare a strange world where the government itself— the very "expert" agency responsible for promulgating the "law" no less—seems unable to keep pace with its own frenetic lawmaking. A world Madison worried about long ago, a world in which the laws are "so voluminous that they cannot be read" and constitutional norms of due process, fair notice, and even the separation of powers seem very much at stake. But whatever else one might say about our visit to this place, one thing seems to us certain: an agency decision that loses track of its own controlling regulations and applies the wrong rules in order to penalize private citizens can never stand.

United States v. Nichols

———

As a group, criminal defendants have never been much liked—and the persons involved here may be the least popular of all. But what would you think of a government that allows its chief prosecutor to write the crimes he gets to prosecute? That's exactly what happened in this case, where Congress divested its legislative power and handed it to the attorney general, allowing him to write criminal laws for half a million people. In this Tenth Circuit dissent, I explore some of the consequences of this mixing of legislative and executive powers. After I joined the Supreme Court, these issues were to come before me again in Gundy v. United States *(2019).*

I F THE SEPARATION OF POWERS MEANS ANYTHING, IT MUST MEAN that the prosecutor isn't allowed to define the crimes he gets to enforce. Yet, that's precisely the arrangement the Sex Offender Registration and Notification Act purports to allow in this case and a great many more like it. In the Act, Congress left it to the Attorney General to decide whether and on what terms sex offenders convicted before the date of SORNA's enactment should be required to register their location or face another criminal conviction. So unusual is this delegation of legislative authority that to find an analogue you might have to look back to the time Congress asked the President to devise a code of "fair competition" for the poultry business—a delegation of legislative authority the Supreme Court unanimously rejected and Justice Cardozo called "unconfined and vagrant," a "delegation running riot." Even then you could be excused for thinking the delegation before us a good deal less cooped or caged than that one. After all, it doesn't just grant some alphabet soup agency the power to write rules about the chicken trade. It invests in the nation's chief prosecutor the authority to devise a criminal code governing a half-million people.

WHEN IT COMES TO sex offenders convicted after SORNA's enactment, the statute is exquisitely detailed. It divides those persons into three tiers based on the seriousness of their offense. It specifies which sex offenses place offenders in which tiers. It requires tier I offenders to register their location for 15 years; tier II offenders to do so for 25 years; and tier III offenders to carry on registering for life. It explains what conditions merit reducing the registration period. On and on it goes for 22 pages.

But none of this automatically applies to Mr. Lester Nichols and others convicted of sex offenses before the Act's passage. Instead, when it comes to past offenders, the Act says just this:

> The Attorney General shall have the authority to specify the applicability of the requirements of this subchapter to sex offenders convicted before the enactment of this chapter . . . and to prescribe rules for registration of any such sex offender.

Yes, that's it.

As the government acknowledges, this language leaves the Attorney General free to do nothing: the law "does not require the Attorney General to act within a certain time frame or by a date certain; it does not require him to act at all." Alternatively, "[u]nder his delegated authority in Subsection (d), the Attorney General could" require all past offenders to register or "require some but not all to register." Or, alternatively still, he could require those forced to register to "comply with some but not all of the registration requirements" applicable to future offenders in order to adapt the law as he thinks best for past offenders. After all, the statute grants the Attorney General authority to specify the applicability not of the Act as a whole, one way or another, but to specify the applicability of each of the various "requirements" contained within the Act. Even then, the

Attorney General remains free to "change his mind at any given time or over the course of different administrations." Given all this, it's perhaps unsurprising how many circuits and commentators have observed that the degree of discretion invested in the Attorney General here is vast. It is so vast, in fact, that some (including the government itself) once suggested a narrower interpretation of the relevant statutory language would make more sense of the Act.

A majority of the Supreme Court, however, carefully considered and rejected any alternative reading and made plain that, as a matter of statutory interpretation, SORNA's retroactive application hinges on the Attorney General. It went on to acknowledge that a statute investing so much authority in the Attorney General inevitably raises with it separation of powers questions. But, the Court said, it would leave those questions for another day. Justices Scalia and Ginsburg went further, expressing concern that the law "sail[s] close to the wind." The day to decide the constitutional question the Court left open is now upon us. And, as it turns out, the statute doesn't just sail close to the wind. It sails right into it.

ARTICLE I §1 PROVIDES that "[a]ll legislative powers herein granted shall be vested in a Congress of the United States." Many times over and in cases stretching back to the founding, the Supreme Court has held that this language limits the ability of Congress to delegate its legislative power to the Executive. There's ample evidence, too, that the framers of the Constitution thought the compartmentalization of legislative power not just a tool of good government or necessary to protect the authority of Congress from encroachment by the Executive but essential to the preservation of the people's liberty. As Madison put it, "[n]o political truth is . . . stamped with the authority of more enlightened patrons of liberty" than the separation of powers because "[t]he accumulation of all powers, legislative, executive, and judiciary in the same hands . . . may justly be pronounced the very definition of tyranny." By separating the lawmaking and law enforcement functions, the framers sought to thwart the ability of an individual or group to exercise arbitrary or absolute power. And by restricting lawmaking to one branch and forcing any legislation to endure bicameralism and presentment, the framers sought to make the task of lawmaking more arduous still. These structural impediments to lawmaking were no bugs in the system but the point of the design: a deliberate and jealous effort to preserve room for individual liberty.

Without a doubt, the framers' concerns about the delegation of legislative power had a great deal to do with the criminal law. The framers worried that placing the power to legislate, prosecute, and jail in the hands of the Executive would invite the sort of tyranny they experienced at the hands of a whimsical king. Their endorsement of the separation of powers was predicated on the view that "[t]he inefficiency associated with [it] serves a valuable" liberty-preserving "function, and, in the context of criminal law, no other mechanism provides a substitute."

Of course all this invites the question: how do you know an impermissible delegation of legislative authority when you see it? By its own telling, the Court has had a hard time devising a satisfying answer. But the difficulty of the inquiry doesn't mean it isn't worth the effort. After all, at stake here isn't just the balance of power between the political branches who might be assumed capable of fighting it out among themselves. At stake is the principle that the scope of individual liberty may be reduced only according to the deliberately difficult processes prescribed by the Constitution, a principle that may not be fully vindicated without the intervention of the courts. And "[a]bdication of responsibility is not part of the constitutional design."

Besides, putting the pieces together it turns out we do know a few things.

We know, for example, that Congress can leave "details" to the Executive. Congress can't punt to the President the job of devising a competition code for the chicken industry. Such widely applicable rules governing private conduct must be enacted by the Legislature. But once Congress enacts a detailed statutory scheme on its own— once it says, for example, that margarine manufacturers must pay a tax and place a stamp on their packages showing the tax has been paid—Congress may leave to the President "details" like designing an appropriate tax stamp.

Of course, defining what qualifies as a detail is itself no detail. But whether or not something fairly denominated a detail is involved, we also know Congress may pass legislation the operation of which is conditioned on a factual finding by the President. So, for example, Congress may direct the President to lift a statutorily imposed trade embargo against Great Britain if he determines as a factual matter that it is no longer violating the United States's neutrality. That's clearly no trivial question the President may answer. But answer it he may so long as a clear legislative consequence follows from his factual finding.

While these are the most traditional delegation tests—is it a detail? do we have a clear legislative consequence hinging on a factual finding?—in more recent times the Court has gone further, allowing legislation to stand so long as it contains an "intelligible principle" to guide the exercise of Executive discretion. How intelligible the "intelligible principle" must be to pass muster is much debated. But we know, by way of example, that Congress may ask the EPA to set national air quality standards which are "requisite to protect the public health" subject to "an adequate margin of safety" because, as used in the statute, the term "requisite" demands a standard neither higher nor lower than necessary to meet the legislatively directed objective of protecting the public health with an adequate margin of safety.

Still, the Court has never expressly held that an intelligible principle alone suffices to save a putative delegation when the criminal law is involved. To be sure, the Court has applied the intelligible principle test to regulations that may be enforceable through criminal penalties. But the Court hasn't endorsed the test in anything like the situation we face—legislation leaving it to the nation's top prosecutor to specify whether and how a federal criminal law should be applied to a class of a half-million individuals. In fact, the Court has repeatedly and long suggested that in the criminal context Congress must provide more "meaningful[]" guidance than an "intelligible principle."

Recently, the Supreme Court has suggested what a more "meaningful" standard might look like in the criminal context. Its discussion came in the course of a challenge to the Controlled Substances Act—legislation permitting the Attorney General to schedule various drugs as controlled substances, rendering their possession by unauthorized persons illegal. The Court allowed the law to stand, but instead of applying the intelligible principle test alone it proceeded to stress the presence and importance of certain specific statutory features.

At least three "meaningful" limitations emerged: (1) Congress must set forth a clear and generally applicable rule that (2) hinges on a factual determination by the Executive and (3) the statute provides criteria the Executive must employ when making its finding.

WITH THAT MUCH GUIDANCE about delegation doctrine in hand, a few things come clear when we return to the statute before us. For one, it's easy enough to see the similarities between our case and *Schechter Poultry* where the Court held Article I violated. Here as there Congress pointed to a problem that needed fixing and more or less told the Executive to go forth and figure it out. Meanwhile, it's hard to see how ours might be likened to any of the cases turning away delegation challenges.

True, some might try to pass off the question of SORNA's applicability to past offenders as a mere "detail." But the statute before us leaves the Attorney General with "unfettered discretion to determine both how and whether SORNA [is] to be retroactively applied" to a half-million individuals under threat of criminal prosecution from his own deputies. And however far you want to bend the boundaries of what qualifies as a "detail," it's hard to see how that might qualify. Our case just isn't anything like your grandfather's tax stamp challenge.

Fair enough, some might respond, but sex offenders are so unpopular that there's little chance an Attorney General would do anything other than apply SORNA retroactively to the fullest extent possible. Maybe there is no legislative mandate—conditional or otherwise—requiring him to follow this course, but there might as well be. A reply along these lines seems a likely enough answer to the question what a politically attuned Attorney General would do when the hot potato is passed his way. But it also seems an unlikely answer to the question whether Congress may constitutionally pass the potato in the first place. After all, in a delegation challenge the question isn't whether the Executive is likely to exercise the delegation in one way or another but whether Congress is empowered to delegate the decision at all. Indeed, the logic at play here would serve to ensconce even the most extreme and obviously unconstitutional delegations only because of a judicial intuition about contemporary political pressures. And not only do unelected judges make for notoriously poor political pundits: Ours is supposed to be an independent judiciary making decisions on the legal merits without respect to the vagaries of shifting political winds.

Some might claim an "intelligible principle" can be rummaged out of SORNA's preamble—a provision that expresses Congress's wish to "protect the public from sex offenders and offenders against children" by establishing "a comprehensive national system for the registration of those offenders." But Supreme Court cases rejecting delegation challenges on intelligible principle grounds don't usually rest on policy objectives voiced in a statute's preamble. To be sure, the Court has sometimes gone so far as to suggest that Congress need only "clearly delineate[] the general policy" to guide an agency's conduct. But this language usually seems to cover situations in which the legislative grant of discretion is tied to specific statutory provisions that expressly direct the exercise of that discretion. Meanwhile, no comparable guidance exists here.

Requiring a direct statutory link between discretion and direction makes sense too. After all, as the Court has acknowledged in recent years, it is most assuredly wrong to assume that "whatever" seems to further a "statute's primary objective must be the law." Legislation is the art of compromise and few (if any) statutes pursue a single pre-ambulatory purpose without condition, subtlety, or exception. For precisely these reasons, when it comes to the business of statutory interpretation it is usually the more specific and not the more general or aspirational direction that controls.

Our case illustrates the point. SORNA's prefatory provision expressing the desire to protect children and create a nationwide registration requirement hardly establishes that the statute meant to do so always and in every particular without exception or at any cost. In fact, SORNA is replete with examples of compromise even when it comes to future offenders. Congress indicated that some future offenders may be exempt from its registration requirements if they committed certain kinds of sex offenses but not others. Registration is required for life for some offenders but lesser periods for others. These periods can be reduced on good behavior. In these circumstances, it would seem strange to suppose that the statute's prefatory statement of purpose—or, for that matter, provisions of the law discussing the treatment of future offenders—provides intelligible guidance for the Attorney General's treatment of past offenders. Especially when Congress went on to address past offenders specifically, exempted them from the automatic application of any of the statute's registration requirements, and left their treatment to the Attorney General.

Separately but relatedly, the Supreme Court has instructed that under the intelligible principle test "the degree of agency discretion that is acceptable varies according to the scope of the power congressionally conferred." Faint echoes of detail doctrine can be found here: less direction may be required when Congress leaves it to the Executive to define what constitutes a "country elevator[]" and more may be required when Congress seeks to endow the Executive with the power to create regulations that affect the national economy. So even assuming that a preamble detached from the provision granting discretion to the Executive might suffice to supply an intelligible principle in some circumstances, it certainly won't always. And once again it's hard to see how the discretion conferred here is anything less than extraordinary—in its breadth (allowing the Attorney General to apply none, some, or all of SORNA's requirements to none, some, or all past offenders), in its subject matter (effectively defining a new crime), in its chosen delegate (the nation's top prosecutor), and in the number of people affected (half a million). All factors suggesting more, not less, guidance is required.

To be sure, Congress could have easily written a statute with such constraints, and to remedy the delegation problem here it might still. For example, Congress could have tasked the Attorney General with the job of determining what factors correlate with recidivism or present an unreasonable danger to the public and make his determinations based on those considerations. When deciding which past offenders should be required to register Congress could have required the Attorney General to examine, as well, factors like the recency of the violation; the nature of the sex offense; the number of past violations; the offender's age, family, residential, or occupational circumstances; or the offender's mental or physical health—or banned consideration of any of these factors. It's easy to imagine all sorts of ways Congress might have constrained—and might still constrain—the Attorney General's discretion. But, and by the government's own admission, we have nothing of the kind here.

Delegation doctrine may not be the easiest to tease out and it has been some time since the Court has held a statute to cross the line. But it has also been some time since the courts have encountered a statute like this one—one that, if allowed to stand, would require the Judiciary to endorse the notion that Congress may effectively pass off to the prosecutor the job of defining the very crime he is responsible for enforcing. By any plausible measure we might apply that is a delegation run riot, a result inimical to the people's liberty and our constitutional design.

Sessions v. Dimaya

———

This case shares some similarities with the one that precedes it. In the last case, a congressional statute expressly delegated to the executive branch the power to make the law. In this excerpt from a concurrence from my first full term on the Supreme Court, a vague statute effectively gave the power to make law to both prosecutors and judges.

VAGUE LAWS INVITE ARBITRARY POWER. BEFORE THE REVOLUTION, the crime of treason in English law was so capaciously construed that the mere expression of disfavored opinions could invite transportation to a penal colony or death. The founders cited the crown's abuse of "pretended" crimes like this as one of their reasons for revolution. Today's vague laws may not be as invidious, but they can invite the exercise of arbitrary power all the same—by leaving the people in the dark about what the law demands and allowing prosecutors and courts to make it up.

The law before us today is such a law. Before holding a lawful permanent resident alien like James Dimaya subject to removal for having committed a crime, the Immigration and Nationality Act requires a judge to determine that the ordinary case of the alien's crime of conviction involves a substantial risk that physical force may be used. But what does that mean? Just take the crime at issue in this case, California burglary, which applies to everyone from armed home intruders to door-to-door salesmen peddling shady products. How, on that vast spectrum, is anyone supposed to locate the ordinary case and say whether it includes a substantial risk of physical force? The truth is, no one knows. The law's silence leaves judges to their intuitions and the people to their fate. In my judgment, the Constitution demands more.

I BEGIN WITH A foundational question. Writing for the Court in *Johnson v. United States,* Justice Scalia held the residual clause of the Armed Career Criminal Act void for vagueness because it invited "more unpredictability and arbitrariness" than the Constitution allows. Because the residual clause in the statute now before us uses almost exactly the same language as the residual clause in *Johnson,* respect for precedent alone would seem to suggest that both clauses should suffer the same judgment.

But first in *Johnson* and now again today Justice Thomas has questioned whether our vagueness doctrine can fairly claim roots in the Constitution as originally understood. For its part, the Court has yet to offer a reply. I believe our colleague's challenge is a serious and thoughtful one that merits careful attention. At day's end, though, I am persuaded that void for vagueness doctrine, at least properly conceived, serves as a faithful expression of ancient due process and separation of powers principles the framers recognized as vital to ordered liberty under our Constitution.

Consider first the doctrine's due process underpinnings. The Fifth and Fourteenth Amendments guarantee that "life, liberty, or property" may not be taken "without due process of law." That means the government generally may not deprive a person of those rights without affording him the benefit of (at least) those "customary procedures to which freemen were entitled by the old law of England." Admittedly, some have suggested that the Due Process Clause does less work than this, allowing the government to deprive people of their liberty through whatever procedures (or lack of them) the government's current laws may tolerate. But in my view the weight of the historical evidence shows that the clause sought to ensure that the people's rights are never any less secure against governmental invasion than they were at common law. Lord Coke took this view of the English due process guarantee. John Rutledge, our second Chief Justice, explained that Coke's teachings were carefully studied and widely adopted by the framers, becoming " 'almost the foundations of our law.'" And many more students of the Constitution besides—from Justice Story to Justice Scalia—have agreed that this view best represents the original understanding of our own Due Process Clause.

Perhaps the most basic of due process's customary protections is the demand of fair notice. Criminal indictments at common law had to provide "precise and sufficient certainty" about the charges involved. Unless an "offence [was] set forth with clearness and certainty," the indictment risked being held void in court.

The same held true in civil cases affecting a person's life, liberty, or property. A civil suit began by obtaining a writ—a detailed and specific form of action asking for particular relief. Because the various civil writs were clearly defined, English subjects served with one would know with particularity what legal requirement they were alleged to have violated and, accordingly, what would be at issue in court. And a writ risked being held defective if it didn't provide fair notice.

The requirement of fair notice applied to statutes too. Blackstone illustrated the point with a case involving a statute that made "stealing sheep, or other cattle" a felony. Because the term "cattle" embraced a good deal more then than it does now (including wild animals, no less), the court held the statute failed to provide adequate notice about what it did and did not cover—and so the court treated the term "cattle" as a nullity. All of which, Blackstone added, had the salutary effect of inducing the legislature to reenter the field and make itself clear by passing a new law extending the statute to "bulls, cows, oxen," and more "by name."

This tradition of courts refusing to apply vague statutes finds parallels in early American practice as well. In *The Enterprise,* for example, Justice Henry Brockholst Livingston found that a statute setting the circumstances in which a ship may enter a port during an embargo was too vague to be applied, concluding that "the court had better pass" the statutory terms by "as unintelligible and useless" rather than "put on them, at great uncertainty, a very harsh signification, and one which the legislature may never have designed." In *United States v. Sharp,* Justice Bushrod Washington confronted a statute which prohibited seamen from making a "revolt." But he was unable to determine the meaning of this provision "by any authority . . . either in the common, admiralty, or civil law." As a result, he declined to "recommend to the jury, to find the prisoners guilty of making, or endeavouring to make a revolt, however strong the evidence may be."

Nor was the concern with vague laws confined to the most serious offenses like capital crimes. Courts refused to apply vague laws in criminal cases involving relatively modest penalties. They applied the doctrine in civil cases too. As one court put it, "all laws" "ought to be expressed in such a manner as that [their] meaning may be unambiguous, and in such language as may be readily understood by those upon whom it is to operate." " 'It is impossible . . . to dissent from the doctrine of Lord Coke, that acts of parliament ought to be plainly and clearly, and not cunningly and darkly penned, especially in penal matters.' "

These early cases, admittedly, often spoke in terms of construing vague laws strictly rather than declaring them void. But in substance void the law is often exactly what these courts did: rather than try to construe or interpret the statute before them, judges frequently held the law simply too vague to apply. Blackstone, for example, did not suggest the court in his illustration should have given a narrowing construction to the term "cattle," but argued against giving it any effect at all.

What history suggests, the structure of the Constitution confirms. Many of the Constitution's other provisions presuppose and depend on the existence of reasonably clear laws. Take the Fourth Amendment's requirement that arrest warrants must be supported by probable cause, and consider what would be left of that requirement if the alleged crime had no meaningful boundaries. Or take the Sixth Amendment's mandate that a defendant must be informed of the accusations against him and allowed to bring witnesses in his defense, and consider what use those rights would be if the charged crime was so vague the defendant couldn't tell what he's alleged to have done and what sort of witnesses he might need to rebut that charge. Without an assurance that the laws supply fair notice, so much else of the Constitution risks becoming only a "parchment barrie[r]" against arbitrary power.

Although today's vagueness doctrine owes much to the guarantee of fair notice embodied in the Due Process Clause, it would be a mistake to overlook the doctrine's equal debt to the separation of powers. The Constitution assigns "[a]ll legislative Powers" in our federal government to Congress. It is for the people, through their elected representatives, to choose the rules that will govern their future conduct. Meanwhile, the Constitution assigns to judges the "judicial Power" to decide "Cases" and "Controversies." That power does not license judges to craft new laws to govern future conduct, but only to "discer[n] the course prescribed by law" as it currently exists and to "follow it" in resolving disputes between the people over past events.

From this division of duties, it comes clear that legislators may not "abdicate their responsibilities for setting the standards of the criminal law," by leaving to judges the power to decide "the various crimes includable in [a] vague phrase." For "if the legislature could set a net large enough to catch all possible offenders, and leave it to the courts to step inside and say who could be rightfully detained, and who should be set at large[,] [t]his would, to some extent, substitute the judicial for the legislative department of government." Nor is the worry only that vague laws risk allowing judges to assume legislative power. Vague laws also threaten to transfer legislative power to police and prosecutors, leaving to them the job of shaping a vague statute's contours through their enforcement decisions.

These structural worries are more than just formal ones. Under the Constitution, the adoption of new laws restricting liberty is supposed to be a hard business, the product of an open and public debate among a large and diverse number of elected representatives. Allowing the legislature to hand off the job of lawmaking risks substituting this design for one where legislation is made easy, with a mere handful of unelected judges and prosecutors free to "condem[n] all that [they] personally disapprove and for no better reason than [they] disapprove it." Nor do judges and prosecutors act in the open and accountable forum of a legislature, but in the comparatively obscure confines of cases and controversies. For just these reasons, Hamilton warned, while "liberty can have nothing to fear from the judiciary alone," it has "every thing to fear from" the union of the judicial and legislative powers. No doubt, too, for reasons like these this Court has held "that the more important aspect of vagueness doctrine 'is not actual notice, but . . . the requirement that a legislature establish minimal guidelines to govern law enforcement'" and keep the separate branches within their proper spheres.

PERSUADED THAT VAGUENESS DOCTRINE enjoys a secure footing in the original understanding of the Constitution, the next question I confront concerns the standard of review. What degree of imprecision should this Court tolerate in a statute before declaring it unconstitutionally vague? For its part, the government argues that where (as here) a person faces only civil, not criminal, consequences from a statute's operation, we should declare the law unconstitutional only if it is "unintelligible." But in the criminal context this Court has generally insisted that the law must afford "ordinary people . . . fair notice of the conduct it punishes." And I cannot see how the Due Process Clause might often require any less than that in the civil context either. Fair notice of the law's demands, as we've seen, is "the first essential of due process." As we've seen, too, the Constitution sought to preserve a common law tradition that usually aimed to ensure fair notice before any deprivation of life, liberty, or property could take place, whether under the banner of the criminal or the civil law.

First principles aside, the government suggests that at least this Court's precedents support adopting a less-than-fair-notice standard for civil cases. But even that much I do not see. To be sure, the Court has sometimes "expressed greater tolerance of enactments with civil rather than criminal penalties because the consequences of imprecision are qualitatively less severe." But to acknowledge that truism does nothing to prove that civil laws must always be subject to the government's emaciated form of review. In fact, if the severity of the consequences counts when deciding the standard of review, shouldn't we take account of the fact that today's civil laws regularly impose penalties far more severe than those found in many criminal statutes? Ours is a world filled with more and more civil laws bearing more and more extravagant punishments. Today's "civil" penalties include confiscatory rather than compensatory fines, forfeiture provisions that allow homes to be taken, remedies that strip persons of their professional licenses and livelihoods, and the power to commit persons against their will indefinitely. Some of these penalties are routinely imposed and are routinely graver than those associated with misdemeanor crimes—and often harsher than the punishment for felonies. And not only are "punitive civil sanctions . . . rapidly expanding," they are "sometimes more severely punitive than the parallel criminal sanctions for the same conduct." Given all this, any suggestion that criminal cases warrant a heightened standard of review does more to persuade me that the criminal standard should be set above our precedent's current threshold than to suggest the civil standard should be buried below it.

WITH THE FAIR NOTICE standard now in hand, all that remains is to ask how it applies to the case before us. And here at least the answer comes readily for me: to the extent it requires an "ordinary case" analysis, the portion of the Immigration and Nationality Act before us fails the fair notice test for the reasons Justice Scalia identified in *Johnson* and the Court recounts today.

Just like the statute in *Johnson,* the statute here instructs courts to impose special penalties on individuals previously "convicted of" a "crime of violence." Just like the statute in *Johnson,* the statute here fails to specify which crimes qualify for that label. Instead, and again like the statute in *Johnson,* the statute here seems to require a judge to guess about the ordinary case of the crime of conviction and then guess whether a "substantial risk" of "physical force" attends its commission. *Johnson* held that a law that asks so much of courts while offering them so little by way of guidance is unconstitutionally vague. And I do not see how we might reach a different judgment here.

Any lingering doubt is resolved for me by taking account of just some of the questions judges trying to apply the statute using an ordinary case analysis would have to confront. Does a conviction for witness tampering ordinarily involve a threat to the kneecaps or just the promise of a bribe? Does a conviction for kidnapping ordinarily involve throwing someone into a car trunk or a noncustodial parent picking up a child from daycare? These questions do not suggest obvious answers. Is the court supposed to hold evidentiary hearings to sort them out, entertaining experts with competing narratives and statistics, before deciding what the ordinary case of a given crime looks like and how much risk of violence it poses? What is the judge to do if there aren't any reliable statistics available? Should (or must) the judge predict the effects of new technology on what qualifies as the ordinary case? After all, surely the risk of injury calculus for crimes like larceny can be expected to change as more thefts are committed by computer rather than by gunpoint. Or instead of requiring real evidence, does the statute mean to just leave it all to a judicial hunch? And on top of all that may be the most difficult question yet: at what level of generality is the inquiry supposed to take place? Is a court supposed to pass on the ordinary case of burglary in the relevant neighborhood or county, or should it focus on statewide or even national experience? How is a judge to know? How are the people to know?

The implacable fact is that this isn't your everyday ambiguous statute. It leaves the people to guess about what the law demands— and leaves judges to make it up. You cannot discern answers to any of the questions this law begets by resorting to the traditional canons of statutory interpretation. No amount of staring at the statute's text, structure, or history will yield a clue. Nor does the statute call for the application of some preexisting body of law familiar to the judicial power. The statute doesn't even ask for application of common experience. Choice, pure and raw, is required. Will, not judgment, dictates the result.

NO ONE SHOULD BE surprised that the Constitution looks unkindly on any law so vague that reasonable people cannot understand its terms and judges do not know where to begin in applying it. A government of laws and not of men can never tolerate that arbitrary power. And, in my judgment, that foundational principle dictates today's result.

3.

THE
JUDGE'S TOOLS

WHEN I WAS IN LAW SCHOOL, MANY PROFESsors and students seemed to assume that in disputes over a statute's meaning a judge should turn to its legislative history, seek to discern the law's purpose, and then do whatever is necessary to promote that perceived purpose in the case at hand. I might be exaggerating a bit—but not by much. We were fed a healthy diet of cases in which judges themselves worried that paying too much attention to a statute's terms might risk producing results "at variance with the policy of the legislation." When it came to constitutional law, things were not much different. We were told that the Constitution is a "living" document. Most everyone seemed to agree with Justice Felix Frankfurter's view that "the words of the Constitution . . . are so unrestricted by their intrinsic meaning or by their history or by tradition or by prior decisions that they leave the individual justice free, if indeed they do not compel him, to gather meaning not from reading the Constitution but from reading life."

I remember the first time I heard anyone seriously challenge this kind of thinking. It came when Justice Scalia, still new to the Supreme Court, visited my law school to deliver a lecture entitled "The Rule of Law as a Law of Rules." Although nominally about the importance of avoiding balancing tests in the law, the lecture was suffused with the conviction that when charged with interpreting congressional statutes and constitutional texts, judges should follow the law as written and originally understood, and that judges who seek to do anything else act inconsistently with the judicial function in our system of separated powers. It was a breath of fresh air, inspiring, like little I had heard in my classes.

Still, I don't think I fully appreciated that moment at the time. It wasn't until after I graduated and was lucky enough to serve as a law clerk for Judge David Sentelle on the D.C. Circuit that I began to see the importance of interpreting written laws as originally understood. I began to see what happens to ordinary people in real cases, to the rule of law, and to the role of the judge when courts abandon that task in favor of "evolving" the law in ways they think preferable. My concerns only grew as I became a lawyer and, later, a judge. I saw people sent to jail or fined for conduct the written law did not proscribe. I saw contracts rewritten based on little more than a judicial policy preference. I saw the scope of regulatory statutes and obligations rewritten entirely based on comments buried in congressional debates. I came to realize that when judges abandon the original meaning of a law to pursue some other goal they find worthy, they risk exercising political will rather than legal judgment. And, in the process, they threaten the legitimacy of the judicial enterprise and the right of the people to fair notice of the law's demands.

I became persuaded that a judge must learn the lessons of originalism and textualism. Really, the two terms may be little more than different ways to say the same thing. A judge faithful to textualism seeks to enforce a statute's ordinary meaning at the time of its enactment. And what textualism seeks to accomplish for statutes, originalism seeks to accomplish for the Constitution. An originalist judge seeks to enforce the original meaning of our nation's supreme statute.

Over time I learned, too, that there's nothing revolutionary about any of this. Originalism and textualism sounded new and exciting to me when I first heard Justice Scalia speak. But I later learned that was only because I was taught in something of a bubble where fads largely ruled the day—fads like the Judge as Greek Hero or the Judge as Pragmatic Social Engineer. The notion that judges should more modestly interpret written laws according to their original meaning wasn't in vogue then but it is anything but new. It turns out to be the view the Supreme Court has expressed in scores of cases through most of its history. It is, as well, how many of the founders conceived of the judge's job when they wrote the Constitution. Textualism and originalism are our history, the mainstream and traditional accounts of the judge's job in our republic. What follows are two speeches and a few cases that illustrate my journey to this realization.

ORIGINALISM AND
THE CONSTITUTION

———

*Being an originalist sometimes seems like being stuck in a
game of whack-a-mole. Whenever you talk about the theory,
the same old objections keep popping up. We need a "living"
Constitution in a modern society; the Constitution's too old
and cryptic to be able to know its original meaning; originalism leads to awful results that society can't abide. Whack
down one of these challenges and the next is sure to appear.
In this piece, I seek to address the usual objections and explain why I believe originalism is the theory of interpretation
that fits best with our Constitution.*

IMAGINE YOU'RE HAULED INTO COURT, FALSELY ACCUSED OF MUR-
der in a classic case of mistaken identity. The prosecution's case
hinges on an eyewitness's written statement given to the police only
minutes after the crime. But the witness's story has holes in it. For
starters, the statement says he was present at the time of the crime.
But you find out he only stumbled onto the scene after the fact. You
also discover that the officer who took the statement seemed to
threaten the witness—telling him "it would be good for him to talk"
about your alleged involvement in the crime because the police
"would be taking a hard look at everyone at the scene."

At trial, the prosecution seeks to introduce the witness's written
statement and your lawyer immediately objects. Now, your lawyer is
no slouch. She quickly directs the court's attention to the Sixth
Amendment's Confrontation Clause, which guarantees a criminal
defendant the right to "confront[] . . . the witnesses against him."
That clause, your lawyer argues, requires live testimony from the

witness, not just a piece of paper. After all, she says, there's no sub-stitute for cross-examination to uncover the flaws in a witness's story and to assess a witness's credibility. In reply, the prosecutor argues that testimony isn't necessary. He says the written statement bears plenty of hallmarks of reliability. He adds, too, that it would be bur-densome and inefficient to require the witness to testify on the stand. Ultimately, the judge sides with the prosecution and, without an op-portunity to undermine the key piece of evidence, you're out of luck; the jury quickly convicts.

Something like this unfortunate saga unfurled regularly in court-rooms in America during *Ohio v. Roberts*'s twenty-four-year reign. In *Roberts,* the Court disregarded the Sixth Amendment's plain and firm language that guarantees defendants the right to confront their accusers. In its place, the Court invented a wobbly new balancing test. Under its terms, the so-called "competing interests" of "effec-tive law enforcement" could justify "dispensing with" the defen-dant's right to confront a witness at trial so long as a witness's prior written statement bore "adequate 'indicia of reliability.'" Now, if you're puzzled by what the term "adequate indicia of reliability" means or how a standard like that might be applied in a principled manner, you are not alone. Under *Roberts*'s rule, identical cases were often treated very differently. Some judges found indicia of reliability only in detailed statements; others found even brief ones just fine too. Some judges found indicia of reliability because the witness was in custody; others because the witness was out of custody. Some judges found indicia of reliability where a statement was given im-mediately after the events; others because years had intervened.

Happily, this particular story took a turn for the better when the Supreme Court finally overruled *Roberts* in *Crawford v. Washington.* After carefully reviewing historical sources, the Court in *Crawford* concluded that, as originally understood, the Confrontation Clause prohibited the "admission of testimonial statements of a witness who did not appear at trial unless he was unavailable to testify, and the defendant had had a prior opportunity for cross-examination." *Crawford* also reminded us that judges are not supposed to substi-tute a conditional guarantee they prefer for an absolute one found in the Constitution's text.

The story of *Roberts* and *Crawford* is instructive. It shows just how profoundly a judge's approach to the job of interpreting the Constitution can affect the lives of ordinary Americans. It reveals, too, the central divide in constitutional theory today. On one side, *Roberts* exemplifies what is often called "living constitutionalism." Now, living Constitution theories come in more varieties than ice cream flavors at Baskin-Robbins. Every day, more and more aspiring constitutional law professors churn out more and more "paradigm-shifting" theories of constitutional law. Often they bear sonorous-sounding names like Pragmatic Constitutionalism, Progressive Constitutionalism, even Postmodern Constitutionalism. I'm not making this up. While differing in their particulars, many of these theories share the conviction that the Constitution's meaning *changes* over time and that *judges* should determine what changes should be made based on external policy considerations. Just like the Court did in *Roberts*.

On the other side of the debate lies originalism. Originalists believe that the Constitution should be read in our time the same way it was read when adopted. Like the *Crawford* Court, originalists believe that a defendant's right to confrontation today can mean no less than it did at the founding. In an originalist's view, it is not for judges to decide how to balance the competing interests of efficient law enforcement on the one hand and accurate criminal convictions on the other. The people themselves decided the appropriate balance when they adopted the Sixth Amendment and agreed on an unequivocal right to confrontation. That right, an originalist believes, must be honored always and never rewritten by judges who happen to see things differently. Naturally, originalists sometimes disagree on methods and results. But just like living constitutionalism has a core, so does originalism: that the Constitution's meaning was fixed at its ratification and the judge's job is to discern and apply that meaning to the people's cases and controversies.

Tonight, I want to explain how I came to conclude that originalism is the method of interpretation most consonant with the Constitution—why *Crawford* is right and *Roberts* and all those living Constitution theories are wrong. I confess I hope I will manage to persuade you too. But I do not come before you without a backup plan. If I cannot convince you that originalism is the *proper* interpretive theory for our Constitution, I hope to convince you (to borrow from Churchill) that originalism is the worst form of constitutional interpretation, except for all the others.

BEFORE I GET TO the real case for originalism, though, let's clear out some underbrush. No discussion of originalism gets very far these days before someone interjects "We *need* a living Constitution to govern a modern society." Originalism, they say, is a terrible thing because it will haul us back to the horse-and-buggy days and is hopelessly impractical for our shiny modern world. But when someone tells you this, hold on to your wallet; you're about to be swindled. Originalism teaches only that the Constitution's original *meaning* is fixed; meanwhile, of course, new *applications* of that meaning will arise with new developments and new technologies. Consider a few examples. As originally understood, the term "cruel" in the Eighth Amendment's Cruel and Unusual Punishments Clause referred (at least) to methods of execution deliberately designed to inflict pain. That never changes. But that *meaning* doesn't just encompass those particular forms of torture known at the founding. It also applies to deliberate efforts to inflict a slow and painful death by laser. Take another example. As originally understood, the First Amendment protected speech. That guarantee doesn't just apply to speech on street corners or in newspapers; it applies equally to speech on the Internet. Or consider the Fourth Amendment. As originally understood, it usually required the government to get a warrant to search a home. And that meaning applies equally whether the government seeks to conduct a search the old-fashioned way by rummaging through the place or in a more modern way by using a thermal imaging device to see inside. Whether it's the Constitution's prohibition on torture, its protection of speech, or its restrictions on searches, the meaning remains constant even as new applications arise.

Well, if that canard doesn't work, living constitutionalists often reply with another quick objection. They complain we can't know the original understanding because the document's too old and cryptic. Hardly. We figure out the original meaning of old and difficult texts all the time. Just ask any English professor who teaches Shakespeare or Beowulf. Does anyone seriously suggest that it's useless to discuss the original meaning of "to be, or not to be"; "to thine own self be true"; or "[a]ll that glisters is not gold"? The fact is, we have even deciphered the Rosetta Stone. Note, too, the sleight of hand here. If the Constitution is too old to understand, what about old precedents? Surely (*hopefully*) living constitutionalists don't mean to suggest we should throw out *Marbury v. Madison* just because it's almost as old and cryptic as the Constitution itself.

Backing away slightly at this point, living constitutionalists often pursue their indeterminacy argument this way. They point to cases where originalist justices on the Supreme Court have disagreed about the Constitution's original meaning. They say, "Aha! See, the promise of being able to figure out the original meaning of the Constitution is such a sham even they can't agree." But what does the occasional disagreement between originalists really prove? We all know that the cases that land in the Supreme Court are the hardest ones in our legal system. So why should it surprise anyone that faithful originalists on the Court sometimes disagree on the original meaning of some of its provisions? And why should that be an indictment against the methodology?

After all, if there's one piece of terrain that living constitutionalists do not want to pitch their battle upon, it's determinacy. Originalism makes many of the living constitutionalists' hard cases quite easy. Is the death penalty constitutional? Yes, the Constitution expressly mentions it multiple times. Does the Sixth Amendment require confrontation or are there a bunch of balancing tests and unenumerated exceptions we must devise? We know the answer because the text tells us. And while originalists may sometimes disagree on outcomes, they are at least constrained by the same value-neutral methodology and the same closed record of historical evidence. Come to us with arguments from text, structure, and history and we are bound to listen with care and do our best to reason through them. Allow me to reign over the country as a living constitutionalist and you have no idea how I will exercise that fickle power.

Fine, the living constitutionalist usually says. Maybe we could make originalism work reasonably well, but why should we be ruled by the dead hand of the past? But beware: This argument proves too much. This isn't an attack against *originalism* so much as it is an attack on *written law*. After all, as soon as the people ratify a constitutional provision or the legislature passes a new statute, it becomes a law written by a past rather than a present majority. And at exactly what point does continued adherence to that law become the dreaded rule of the dead hand? When a majority of those who voted to ratify it have died? When everyone who voted to ratify it has died? Lives in being plus twenty-one years? If laws enacted by the dead hand are presumptively problematic, then what about the Civil Rights Act of 1964 and the Voting Rights Act of 1965? Or the Equal Protection, the Due Process, and the Cruel and Unusual Punishments Clauses?

If living constitutionalists can't *really* believe the dead hand critique, what are they trying to get at here? I suspect their real complaint isn't with old laws generally so much as it is with the particular *terms* of this old law. The Constitution is short—only about 7,500 words, including all its amendments. It doesn't dictate much about the burning social and political questions they care about. Instead, it leaves the resolution of those matters to elections and votes and the amendment process. And it seems this is the real problem for the critics. For when it comes to the social and political questions of the day they care most about, many living constitutionalists would prefer to have philosopher-king judges swoop down from their marble palace to ordain answers rather than allow the people and their representatives to discuss, debate, and resolve them. You could even say the real complaint here is with our democracy.

Others argue that originalism fails to afford sufficient respect to precedent. They suggest, for example, that originalism is incompatible with important judicial decisions like *Brown v. Board of Education*. Note here, again, that on this view (some) dead hands are just fine. But even more important, note that this critique contains at least two errors. First, it assumes that the precedents in question cannot be squared with the original understanding. But that's not always so. Take a look, for example, at Michael McConnell's, Steven Calabresi's, and Michael Perl's originalist defenses of *Brown* itself and count me convinced. Second, this argument overlooks the fact that adopting a theory of *interpretation* for unsettled questions and adopting a theory of *precedent* for settled questions are two different things. A living constitutionalist, no less than an originalist, must decide when to abide and when to discard judicial precedents with which he may disagree. And, of course, getting your theory of precedent right is important (and I deal with that question elsewhere, including in a very long book with several judicial colleagues). But it also runs orthogonal to our current discussion.

A final, frequent, and related objection to originalism goes something like this. Originalism should be rejected because it leads to bad results. I can't help but notice, though, that many of the supposedly "bad" results critics cite often just reflect their own erroneous and sometimes even farcical understandings of originalism. Take one example I hear often these days: Some critics assert that originalism should be rejected because it means a woman cannot be president. After all, they note, the Constitution refers to the chief executive as "he." But this is nonsense. When the Constitution was ratified, "he" served as a standard pronoun of indefinite gender—it covered women too. (As it often does today.) Plainly, a woman can be elected president under the written terms of the Constitution.

Beyond that, let me pose this question. Suppose originalism *does* lead to a result you happen to dislike in this or that case. *So what?* The "judicial Power" of Article III of the Constitution isn't a promise of all good things. Letting dangerous and obviously guilty criminals who have gravely injured their victims go free just because an officer forgot to secure a warrant or because the prosecutor neglected to bring a witness to trial for confrontation seems like a bad idea to plenty of people. But do you really want judges to revise the Constitution to avoid those "bad" results? Or do you believe that judges should enforce the law's protections equally for everyone, regardless of how inefficient or unpopular or old the law might be? Regardless of who benefits today—the criminal or the police; the business or the employee; immigrants or ICE?

Of course, some suggest that originalism leads to bad results because the results inevitably happen to be politically conservative results. Rubbish. Originalism is a theory focused on *process,* not on *substance*. It is not "Conservative" with a big *C* focused on politics. It is conservative in the small *c* sense that it seeks to conserve the meaning of the Constitution as it was written. The fact is, a good originalist judge will not hesitate to preserve, protect, and defend the Constitution's original meaning, regardless of contemporary political consequences. Whether that means allowing protesters to burn the American flag (the First Amendment); prohibiting the government from slapping a GPS tracking device on the underside of your car without a warrant (the Fourth Amendment); or insisting that juries—not judges—should decide the facts that increase the penalty you face in a criminal case (the Sixth Amendment). In my own judicial career, I've written many originalist rulings with so-called "liberal" results. Like *United States v. Carloss,* where I ruled that the police violated a criminal defendant's Fourth Amendment rights by entering the curtilage of his home without a warrant despite four conspicuously posted no trespassing signs. Or *Sessions v. Dimaya,* where I ruled that an immigrant couldn't constitutionally be punished according to a law so vague that judges were forced to give it content by fiat. Or *Carpenter v. United States,* where I explained that simply giving your property to another doesn't necessarily mean you lose all your Fourth Amendment rights in it. I could go on and on. So could any originalist judge.

Besides, if we're going to measure an interpretive theory by its results, consider this. Virtually the entire anticanon of constitutional law we look back upon today with regret came about when judges chose to follow their own impulses rather than follow the Constitution's original meaning. Look, for example, at *Dred Scott* and *Korematsu*. Neither can be defended as correct in light of the Constitution's original meaning; each depended on serious judicial invention by judges who misguidedly thought they were providing a "good" answer to a pressing social problem of the day. A majority in *Korematsu,* unmoored from originalist principles, upheld the executive internment without trial of American citizens of Japanese descent despite our Constitution's express guarantees of due process and equal protection of the laws. A majority in *Dred Scott,* also disregarding originalist principles, held that Congress had no power to outlaw slavery in the Territories, even though the Constitution clearly gave Congress the power to make laws governing the Territories. In both cases, judges sought to pursue policy ends they thought vital. Theirs was a living and evolving Constitution. And often enough it may be tempting for a judge to do what he thinks best for society in the moment, to bend the law a little to an end he desires, to trade just a bit of judicial integrity for political expediency. After all, passing majorities will applaud judicial efforts to follow their wishes. But as *Korematsu* and *Dred Scott* illustrate, the pursuit of political ends through judicial means will often and ironically bring about a far worse result than anticipated—a sort of constitutional karma.

Even when it comes to more prosaic cases, leaving things to the moral imagination of judges invites trouble. Just consider the "reasonable expectation of privacy" test the Court invented in the 1960s to redefine what qualifies as a search for Fourth Amendment purposes. Oh, it sounded nice enough. But under that judge-made doctrine, the Court has held—and I'm not making this up—that a police helicopter hovering 400 feet above your home doesn't offend a "reasonable expectation of privacy." The Court has even held that the government can snoop through materials you've entrusted to the care of third parties because, in its judgment, that, too, doesn't invade a "reasonable expectation of privacy." But who really believes that? The car you let the valet park; the medical records your doctor promised to keep confidential; the emails you sent to your closest friend. You don't have a reasonable expectation of privacy against the government in any of those things? Really?

WITH SOME OF THE sillier objections against originalism cleared out of the way, let's turn to the real business. Any serious discussion of constitutional interpretation must begin with the Constitution itself. After all, a judge's oath and most important job is to preserve that document and its guarantees. And while the Constitution doesn't speak directly to the proper mode of its interpretation, a careful inspection of its terms and structure shows that originalism is anticipated and fairly commanded by its terms.

Start with what the Constitution says about itself: "This Constitution . . . [is] the supreme Law of the Land." Underscoring its status as "supreme Law," the Constitution requires "all . . . judicial Officers . . . [to] be bound by Oath or Affirmation, to support" it. In England, of course, the constitution was largely a set of unwritten customs. Our founders deliberately rejected that model when they decided to adopt a written Constitution. And the Constitution's self-conscious language emphasizing its written-ness, its status as a law, and the judge's duty to abide its terms tell us some important things about the judge's job. It tells us that the Constitution's express limitations on the scope of governmental action are not merely aspirational or customary or advisory. Or at least that they are not supposed to be. It tells us that the Constitution is itself a law, the supreme law. It tells us, too, that only the terms of this written document and nothing else, not any unreferenced norm or custom, constitutes that supreme law. And it tells us that judges are bound to enforce this law before any other. As Chief Justice John Marshall explained, "The powers of the [government] are defined, and limited; and [so] that those limits may not be mistaken, or forgotten, the constitution is written." In Marshall's view, it would be "immoral" for a judge to take an oath to support the Constitution only then to serve later as "the knowing instrument[], for violating what [he has sworn] to support!"

For a judge bound to respect and not violate the terms of a written law he has sworn to support, the natural starting point for resolving any dispute over its meaning must be the ordinary meaning of that term at the time of its enactment. After all, that's how we interpret most *every* text. When Hamlet threatens to "make a ghost of him that *lets* me," the reference may seem unclear to a modern reader. But when you look at a contemporaneous dictionary you quickly discover that "let" meant "hinder" (as the term is still used in tennis today, when the ball is hindered by the net). So, most everyone today would agree that Hamlet was not threatening to kill someone who *wanted* to be killed; it's clear that Hamlet was threatening to kill anyone who *got in his way*. Confusion solved by the original public meaning.

To be sure, the law sometimes assigns specialized meanings to words and terms and we must ask what the ordinary reader familiar with the law's specialized meanings would have understood of the word or term's usage at the time of the law's adoption. After all, to know what "let" meant in Shakespeare's time we must ask what a person familiar with the word and its usages would make of it, and exactly the same holds here. Some of the Constitution's terms had long-established and very particular meanings in the common law familiar to lawyers and judges.

But the notion that the same rules of interpretation that apply to other written laws should apply to the written law of our Constitution is an ancient one and exactly what the framers expected. As Hamilton put it, the Constitution should be interpreted "according to the usual and established rules of construction." It's an idea, too, that the Supreme Court and many other courts have reaffirmed repeatedly over the course of our history. In 1790, for example, the General Court of Maryland explained that "[i]n expounding the Federal Constitution, the same rules will be observed which are attended to in the exposition of a statute." After all, a group full of *lawyers* wrote a *legal* document. Should it be any surprise that they expected the document to be interpreted in accord with long-accepted principles of legal interpretation?

In fact, while the founders and early justices disagreed on much else, many agreed on this. Chief Justice Marshall explained that the Constitution's "words are to be understood in that sense in which they are generally used." James Madison "entirely concur[red] in the propriety of resorting to the sense in which the Constitution was accepted and ratified by the nation. In that sense alone it is the legitimate Constitution." Justice Joseph Story said that "the Constitution must be expounded . . . as it stands" and should not "be subject to . . . fluctuations" but should mean the same thing "forever." Thomas Jefferson argued that the Constitution should not be interpreted by "what meaning may be squeezed out of the text, or invented against it" but instead by "the probable one in which it was passed." Even George Washington, no lawyer himself, explained that "the Constitution, which at any time exists, 'till changed by an explicit and authentic act of the whole People, is sacredly obligatory upon all. . . . [L]et there be no change by usurpation; for though this, in one instance, may be the instrument of good, it is the customary weapon by which free governments are destroyed." Living constitutionalists reject this by asking us, admittedly and frankly, to allow judges to bend the Constitution in new and evolving ways. After all, living constitutionalism only has purchase and purpose when it *departs* from the original understanding.

Notice, too, this inconsistency in the living constitutionalist's argument. *Sometimes* even they will admit the original public meaning should control. For example, when the Constitution speaks of allowing the government to raise the militia in cases of "domestic Violence," no one thinks the government can call forth the troops in response to an instance of spousal abuse; everyone accepts that the phrase "domestic Violence" should be understood according to its original meaning as referring to an insurrection. Take another example. The Constitution says that the president must be thirty-five. That provision was written in a time when the average life expectancy was thirty-six. But you'd be committed if you argued that we should adjust for inflation, and only those (say) seventy-five or older could be president. So the truth is that *everyone*—even the living constitutionalists—agrees that we must interpret the Constitution according to its original meaning at least *sometimes*. But what persuasive explanation is there for the living constitutionalists' suggestion that we should *only sometimes* adhere to the original public meaning of the Constitution's written text? For my part, I can think of none.

LET'S TURN NEXT TO the Constitution's ratification and amendment procedures. The Constitution leaves to democratic processes, Hamilton explained, the job of "prescrib[ing] the rules by which the duties and rights of every citizen are to be regulated." So before the Constitution could take effect, the founders called on the states to convene special conventions of the people's representatives. And they insisted on a supermajority of those conventions to ratify the original Constitution. Later, to amend the Constitution's terms, the founders required a supermajority of states agree. None of this was an accident. All of it was part of a self-conscious design, as Madison said, aimed at "secur[ing] the public good and private rights against the danger of such a [majority] faction, and at the same time . . . preserv[ing] the spirit and the form of popular government."

Originalism honors this design by respecting both *whom* the Constitution entrusts with its adoption and amendment and *how* those things are supposed to be accomplished. Originalism seeks to enforce the Constitution and its amendments consistent with the understandings of the people who were alone legally authorized to adopt them. And it seeks to prevent any alterations to the meaning of those terms through other legally unauthorized means. When we interpret a legal text, we usually follow the ancient principle of *expressio unius*—recognizing that when the law prescribes a particular way of accomplishing something, it means to exclude other possible and unmentioned alternatives. So when the Constitution tells us how to ratify and amend its terms through carefully calibrated democratic processes calculated to respect minority interests, an originalist knows that it necessarily means to exclude other potential methods of altering its content—whether by means of a bare majority of states, by Congress alone, or (worse yet) by a handful of willful judges.

Living constitutionalism seems far harder to square with the Constitution's design on these scores. Ask yourself: What is the point of the promise that the people and their representatives alone may make and amend the Constitution's written terms if judges feel free to "evolve" the meaning of those terms to include whatever content they think appropriate? In the living constitutionalist's world, it seems that the promise of self-rule risks becoming little more than a ruse and the amendment process a remnant. The Constitution's ratification and amendment procedures assure that before any change to our foundational law can be made everyone will have the chance to be heard. It is a process that deliberately engages the collective wisdom and judgment of the nation. It is also one that commands deliberation and caution, guarding against overeasy changes by passing political factions in response to the latest fads. All these promises of self-government and safeguards for minority interests go out the window when the job is assumed by a committee of nine lawyers who feel free to do as they wish. And if constitutional amendment can be accomplished so easily now through judges, why bother with the real amendment process? Is it any wonder that, as living constitutionalism has risen, the more democratic amendment process has atrophied? From 1789 to 1971 the people amended the Constitution twenty-six times, an average of one amendment every seven years. Even if you discount this number for the Bill of Rights, which adopted ten amendments at once, from 1792 to 1971 the average is still one amendment about every eleven years. Meanwhile, in the past forty-seven years, a period more or less coinciding with the reign of living constitutionalism, the Constitution has been amended just once.

Notice, too, another incongruity in the living constitutionalists' position. Once again, they will concede that *sometimes* the only proper mode for lawmaking is through the processes prescribed by the original understanding of the Constitution. Article I, for example, provides that a bill cannot become law until it passes both houses of Congress and is signed by the president (or passed over his veto). No one seriously argues that the legislature can make a new law except through bicameralism and presentment. So why argue that the judiciary should be able to effectively rewrite the ordinary and original public meaning of the Constitution and its amendments outside the prescribed amendment processes? What justification is there for abiding only *some* constitutionally prescribed formalities for new lawmaking? Again, I struggle to imagine a persuasive reply.

BEYOND ALL THIS LIES another set of clues our Constitution offers about its proper interpretation. The Constitution vests only the "judicial Power" to resolve "cases" and "controversies" in the federal judiciary. It then goes on to insulate the judicial branch from political control through life tenure and salary protection. These terms and protections, it seems to me, also point firmly in originalism's direction.

Start with the term the "judicial Power." In our Constitution, the framers took pains to divide the legislative from the judicial powers—to divide the power to *make* law and the power to *interpret* it. Our Constitution reserves all lawmaking power (statutory and constitutional) to the people and their representatives. The framers understood the lawmaking power as the authority to make rules of conduct governing our society. Often enough, that power involves little more than choosing between competing and incommensurable goods. Should we prioritize improving our Internet or transportation infrastructure? There is no right decision here, just choice, and it is a choice properly left to a self-governing people and their representatives to make. Because of the immense power of legislation to affect the people's lives, liberty, and property, the framers not only created a deliberately difficult process for adopting new laws but also usually required new laws to apply only prospectively and generally to all persons, the better to safeguard fair notice of the law's demands and equality in its application.

Meanwhile, when the framers spoke of the judicial power, they understood it to be entirely distinct and involve none of these things. To them the judicial power wasn't to be used for making new rules of general applicability for society that often require raw choices between competing goods, but a neutral authority for resolving disputes over the application of existing laws to completed events. While the business of making new laws calls for value judgments and self-governance, the business of ensuring that existing laws are fairly applied to everyone calls for a dispassionate arbiter who is not responsive to majoritarian pressures.

That the legislative and judicial powers are distinct in these ways finds confirmation in the Constitutional Convention, where the framers considered four proposals to mix the two sorts of powers. Yet time and time again, these proposals went down to defeat. Elbridge Gerry said that it "was quite foreign from the nature of [the judicial] office to make them judges of the policy of public measures." Rufus King added that judges should "expound the law as it should come before them, free from the bias of having participated in its formation." And Caleb Strong said that "the power of making ought to be kept distinct from that of expounding, the laws. No maxim [is] better established." In fact, I am aware of no evidence that anyone at the framing or during the ratification debates thought that the Constitution permitted judges to update its meaning over time. To the contrary, when the Anti-Federalists raised fears that judges might *improperly* treat the Constitution as a living document, the Federalists defending the Constitution responded not by arguing that judicial updating was *proper* but by asserting that impeachment would be an available and adequate remedy.

Insulating judges from democratic accountability also reveals the founders' assumption that judges would resolve ambiguity using neutral and well-known rules of interpretation, not their own "living" and "evolving" values. Life tenure makes little sense if judges are supposed to be nothing more than politicians wearing robes. Insulating the federal judiciary from the political process—and exempting judges from the procedural safeguards placed on the exercise of legislative power—cannot be easily explained if you expect them to make value judgments on policy grounds. Only because he understood judging to be a distinct discipline guided by neutral interpretive principles could Hamilton credibly argue that the judiciary would be the "least dangerous" branch and would exercise merely "judgment" and not "will."

Originalism fits with the framers' design. It respects the line between making new law and the far more modest judicial power of interpreting law according to neutral principles. Consider first the goal of originalism: to ascertain the ordinary and public meaning of the Constitution's text at the time of ratification. Notice that originalism can describe a judge's goal in interpretation without reference to any value judgments or subjective preferences. The goal is not to "do justice" as the judge personally may see it, but to enforce the Constitution as written. Consider, too, the originalist's tools, each one value-neutral. Originalists often begin their inquiry by examining dictionary definitions and other contemporaneous written sources to determine the ordinary public meaning of a word at the time the constitutional provision at issue was enacted. Because the Constitution is a law and invokes legal terms of art, originalists will also consult how those terms were understood and used at the time of the founding. Even seemingly broad phrases take on more concrete meaning this way. So, for example, "due process" doesn't mean free-floating notions of "fairness"; it isn't a license for judges to inject their own value judgments. Rather, this phrase was long used in the common law and was understood to refer to specific, ancient, and traditional procedures afforded to free persons in England before the government could take their lives, liberty, or property. Considering an interpretation in light of the Constitution's structure also helps to confirm or disprove a possible understanding of a term. So, for example, the relationship between the various vesting clauses (which grant different powers to legislative, executive, and judicial actors) helps us to understand what each of those clauses was understood to include and exclude. Finally, originalists will compare their interpretation against early practice. So, for example, if the First Congress unanimously hired a chaplain to say a prayer before conducting legislative business and no member of the public complained, that might be some evidence the practice didn't violate the original meaning of the Establishment Clause. With a yardstick and tools of interpretation that are reasonably objective, you can criticize a judge's handiwork in an objective manner.

By contrast, living constitutionalism cannot easily claim such consonance with the separation of powers and the limited nature of the judicial power. Why would the Constitution bother to distinguish so carefully between the legislative and judicial powers if judges were really just supposed to be superlegislators free to alter not just statutes but the Constitution according to their own evolving sensibilities? And on what account does it make sense to insulate judges from democratic processes if they do not seek to apply neutral principles to discern what the law is but feel free to enforce the law as they think it *should be*? Jefferson warned that "[t]o take a single step beyond the boundaries" established in the Constitution "is to take possession of a boundless field of power." Exactly so.

HAVING SAID SO MUCH about particular constitutional clues, I should be careful not to overlook the forest for the trees. Each of the constitutional clues I've discussed so far was adopted as part of a broader project: to ensure the rule of law. At a minimum, the rule of law demands fair notice of the law and equality in its application. The government must be bound by fixed rules announced in advance; the people must be able to conform their conduct to these rules; and the government must be prevented from using retroactive or malleable rules to single out unpopular groups for disfavored treatment. "Freedom of men under government," John Locke wrote, "is, to have a standing rule to live by, common to every one of that society . . . and not to be subject to the inconstant, uncertain, unknown, arbitrary will of another man." At the end of the day, that's what our Constitution sought to achieve.

Originalism reinforces these rule-of-law values of notice and equality. Most obviously, by interpreting the text according to its ordinary public meaning, and accepting that it cannot be changed outside the amendment process, originalism ensures that citizens know with some predictability the content of their constitutional rights. And that, in turn, means the people know when their rights are violated, the better to hold the government to account. Originalism, too, helps to ensure equality in the law's application. *Everyone* gets the benefit of the written law's terms. The least powerful among us get the same treatment as the most powerful, and cannot have their rights balanced away by judges. It does not matter, say, whether the judge prefers law enforcement interests to criminal defendants.

Meanwhile, what happens to the rule-of-law values of notice and equality before the law if we abandon originalism for living constitutionalism? Judges are endowed with the extraordinary power to rule retroactively with a full view of each party's completed and unchangeable actions. That's fine when judges are limited to applying value-neutral rules to enforce the original understanding of the Constitution's written terms. But what happens when judges can "evolve" constitutional commands in light of their own values? Who can guess how they will rule? And who stands to benefit? Maybe the few will be able to speculate successfully about (and perhaps even influence) what judges will do in this unbounded world. The many, and certainly the least among us, cannot be expected to fare so well.

IN CASE YOU THINK I overstate the inconsistency of living constitutionalism with our written Constitution and the rule of law, consider the theory's first serious manifestation in the Supreme Court's case law: *Dred Scott v. Sandford*, a case I discussed earlier. There, the Court found a substantive due process right to own slaves in Territories of the United States that even Congress could not extirpate. Perhaps no decision before or since has sent such a lightning bolt through society. And for good reason. Where exactly in the Due Process Clause or anywhere else in the Constitution can you find such a right? The truth is, *Dred Scott* conjured it out of thin air and the only good thing to come of the decision was that it spurred an inspiring originalist dissent from Justice Benjamin Robbins Curtis, who, in my judgment, put the originalists' case about as well as it has ever been put. He said that "when a strict interpretation of the Constitution, according to the fixed rules which govern the interpretation of laws, is abandoned, and the theoretical opinions of individuals are allowed to control its meaning, we have no longer a Constitution; we are under the government of individual men, who for the time being have power to declare what the Constitution is, according to their own views of what it ought to mean." Just so.

Nor is there any guessing where this boundless power the living constitutionalists claim will lead. If the Constitution isn't to be interpreted by the same traditional rules that govern the interpretation of other written laws, by what rule is it to be interpreted? Living constitutionalists say we should depart from the original and ordinary meaning of the text in service of extraneous substantive values. But which values should guide us? Maybe it should come as little surprise that, as Professor Raoul Berger put it, as soon as we depart from the original meaning we wind up with "as many theories as writers." Today, some living constitutionalists say judges should recalibrate the political processes to promote more democracy; others wish us to promote economic efficiency; and on and on the proposals parade. But the divergence of all these theories betrays a common truth: If we do not seek to enforce the law's original public meaning, we must introduce some extraneous value to guide our work.

Don't take my word for it; take it from some of the more prominent living constitutionalists. Professor Mark Tushnet has said: "I am invariably asked, 'Well, yes, but how would *you* decide the X case?' . . . My answer, in brief, is to make an explicitly political judgment: which result is, in the circumstances now existing, likely to advance the cause of socialism? Having decided that, I would write an opinion in some currently favored version of Grand Theory."

Dean Erwin Chemerinsky has suggested that justices "inevitably" need to "make value judgments that come down to their own ideology and life experience." And Judge Richard Posner has explained that he "tr[ies] to improve things within certain bounds"—"to figure out, what is a sensible solution to this problem" without worrying "about doctrine, precedent, and all that stuff" and then he adopts it, unless Supreme Court precedent blocks his path. Maybe originalism isn't perfectly determinate or doesn't always lead where you would like to go. But in a world of imperfect choices, which vision of the judge's role do you think fits best with our written Constitution? And which vision of a judge's role fits best with a republic premised on self-rule?

IN CLOSING, I'D LIKE to share one final thought with you. When these constitutional interpretation debates arise, often the first place my mind takes me is not to the Constitution or *The Federalist Papers*. Instead, I recall a scene from Robert Bolt's play about Sir Thomas More, *A Man for All Seasons*. There, More's family urged him to arrest a man they thought evil even though no law clearly forbade his conduct. More objected, asking: "What would you do? Cut a great road through the law to get after the Devil?" Without hesitation, his son-in-law replied, "I'd cut down every law in England to do that!" To which More answered, "Oh? And when the last law was down, and the Devil turned round on you—where would you hide . . . the laws all being flat? . . . [I]f you cut them down . . . d'you really think you could stand upright in the winds that would blow then? Yes, I'd give the Devil benefit of law, for my own safety's sake."

Sometimes, debates between living constitutionalists and originalists become mired in minutiae. But in the end constitutional theory is about who decides the most important questions in our society. Will it be unaccountable judges? Or will it be the people themselves? For my part, you can count me with those who would conserve the law's forests, and with Jefferson, who reminds us that "[o]ur . . . security [lies in] the possession of a written constitution. Let us not make it a blank paper by construction."

A CASE FOR
TEXTUALISM

———

Statutory interpretation may be the accounting of the legal field. Nothing else quite puts people to sleep in the same way, but few things are as important. The statutes that Congress and state legislatures pass govern everything from the air we breathe, to the food we eat, to whether someone must spend the rest of his life in prison. Selecting (and refining) a sound theory for interpreting those laws, then, is a critical task for a judge. As I seek to explain here, I believe that many of the same clues that suggest judges should use originalism in the interpretation of the Constitution also suggest we should use textualism in the interpretation of statutes.

IMAGINE YOU'RE HAULED INTO COURT, FACING UP TO A DECADE in federal prison. The prosecutor tells you that you've violated a federal criminal statute prohibiting a previously convicted felon from possessing a firearm. But wait, you say, you didn't know you were a felon. In fact, when you faced trouble with the law before, the judge expressly said that you were not convicted of a felony; that it was only a misdemeanor. So you decide to look up the statute the prosecutor has now charged you with violating—surely you can't be guilty. And, aha! The statute prohibits individuals from "knowingly" being both (1) a felon and (2) in possession of a firearm.

That doesn't matter, the prosecutor replies. She asks the judge to look to the statute's legislative history—the flotsam Congress leaves in its wake when it pushes through a new law. The legislative history here, she says, shows that when it adopted the felon-in-possession law, Congress was seeking to recodify an older statute. And that older statute only required the government to prove that the defendant knew he possessed a firearm—not that he knew he was a felon. The prosecutor says something called a "House Report" makes all this clear. And that's not all, she says. Proving that you knew you were a felon would be too burdensome on the government as a matter of policy, in light of the growing problem of gun violence. For these reasons, the prosecutor urges, it just wouldn't make sense to read the statute as written. In the end, the court agrees and you're headed to federal prison.

Sound far-fetched? This scenario comes pretty close to what happened in *United States v. Games-Perez,* a case I considered on the Tenth Circuit. A majority of my court relied on legislative history to determine the purpose of the statute and then read that purpose into the statute to rule against the defendant, Mr. Games-Perez. Lawyers often call this interpretive approach "purposivism."

I dissented. Everyone agreed that the word "knowingly" modified the second element, so the government had to prove the defendant knowingly possessed the gun. And if that's so, I asked, how could the statute's knowledge requirement leapfrog over the first element and only touch down at the second? Any ordinary reader, I argued, would understand that the statute as written requires the government to prove the defendant's knowledge of not just the second statutory element but the first as well. With all this focus on text, it's no surprise that this approach to statutory interpretation is often called "textualism."

At my confirmation hearing for the Supreme Court, one senator took a different view still. Commenting on Mr. Games-Perez's case, she said simply: "[H]e was a felon with a gun and his probation [officer] instructed him that he was not to carry that weapon. So I have very strong feelings about that." In reply, I tried to explain that "I am just trying to follow the plain words of the law—'knowingly be a felon in possession.'" The senator's response? "I do accept that that is your view. . . . It is not my view. . . . He was a felon." Never mind the text or even unexpressed potential legislative purposes. On this account, whatever ruling leads to the best social consequences should and must be the law. By this point, you can probably guess what this approach to statutory interpretation is sometimes called: "consequentialism."

As *Games-Perez* illustrates, how judges go about interpreting statutes matters a great deal. While my Court's constitutional law docket gets the most play in the media, the truth is that we spend the bulk of our time trying to make sense of Congress's handiwork in cases that rarely capture press attention but still have major impacts on the lives of our fellow citizens. And which approach a judge adopts in interpreting a statute often makes all the difference.

Of course, there are variations within the competing schools of thought I've outlined and others besides them. As Professor William Eskridge has put it, "[T]heories of statutory interpretation have [bloomed] like dandelions in spring." So anyone seeking to enter this field has to proceed with some trepidation. Still, I think we've now endured enough springs—and enough debate—to be able to distinguish the blossom from the weeds. Even many who once subscribed to other theories are happy these days to call themselves textualists. Tonight, I'd like to argue, they do so for good reasons.

IT SEEMS TO ME that the place to start is with the Constitution. After all, the judge's highest obligation is to preserve and protect its promises. And while the Constitution doesn't speak directly to the question of statutory interpretation, I think its structure tells us quite a lot.

Take these three clues.

First, Article I of the Constitution endows Congress (and only Congress) with "[a]ll legislative Powers" granted to the federal government. The legislative power, the framers understood, is the power to create prospective new rules of general applicability to govern private conduct. This is, as Hamilton put it, the power to "prescribe[] the rules by which the duties and rights of every citizen are to be regulated"—the power to make value judgments concerning morals, on how to weigh competing goods, and which to preference.

Second, the Constitution describes a demanding process for the creation of new laws. Before the people's liberties may be restricted by law, a statute must survive the gauntlet of two popularly accountable houses of Congress. Even then, it must still receive the assent of an electorally accountable president (or win a legislative override).

Pretty plainly, lawmaking is supposed to be a very public and very hard business, not something that can be accomplished in the privacy of chambers or by the flick of a pen.

Third, when new laws do emerge they must be honored. All people deserve their benefit, not just the popular or powerful. For that reason, Article III assigns the resolution of "cases" and "controversies," including those involving the application of federal statutes, not to popularly accountable politicians but to independent judges with life tenure. Nor may judges play any part in the legislative process. When it comes to statutes, Article III authorizes judges only to ensure that the laws Congress adopts are applied neutrally—"without respect to persons," as our federal judicial oath says.

Collectively, this separation of powers seeks to foster the rule of law. The vesting clause of Article I ensures that the legislature alone may make law and that it usually must do so only with prospective application and only in terms applicable to all persons. The demand that all legislation must survive two separate houses and presidential review guarantees that these laws will be debated in public and by electorally accountable representatives so the people will know and have a chance to shape the rules they must live by. And an insulated judiciary exists so these new rules will be neutrally applied to all persons without regard to their present popularity. In a society governed by the rule of law, the people can expect to come upon the law in the books; the law does not come upon the people out of nowhere.

Given all this, it seems to me that any theory of interpretation seeking to comply with the Constitution and the values it seeks to serve must respect the divide between making legislation and interpreting it; honor the grueling legislative process, not seek to invent new shortcuts; and protect the people from political pressures when it comes to the application of the laws in their cases and controversies.

Textualism does all this. When interpreting statutes, it tasks judges with discerning (only) what an ordinary English speaker familiar with the law's usages would have understood the statutory text to mean at the time of its enactment. Rather than beginning with legislative history or making economic hypotheses about social consequences, a textualist starts with dictionary definitions, rules of grammar, and the historical context in which a law was adopted to see what its language meant to those who adopted the law. In this way, textualism offers a known and knowable methodology for judges to determine impartially and fix what the law is, not simply declare what it ought to be—a method to discern the written law's content without extraneous value judgments about persons or policies.

Maybe the most prominent interpretive tools used by textualists are the so-called "canons of construction." But don't let the arcane name fool you. The canons are little more than commonplace rules of English usage and grammar—like the rule that the verb "includes" followed by a list introduces examples and not an exhaustive list. So when I say that my colleagues include Justice Sotomayor and Justice Thomas, everyone knows that I didn't mean to exclude Justice Breyer.

Using preexisting, neutral, and objective interpretive tools like these ensures that the people can discern with some certainty what the law demands of them. It prevents, too, any agent of the government from twisting statutory terms to help those with deep pockets or harm the least among us. Celebrities and traitors alike are subject to the rule of the last antecedent or the rule that inclusion of one thing implies the exclusion of others. Rules of grammar play no favorites.

Textualism, too, holds the legislature to the constitutionally prescribed processes for making new law. Textualism honors only what's survived bicameralism and presentment—and not what hasn't. The text of the statute and only the text becomes law. Not a legislator's unexpressed intentions, not nuggets buried in the legislative history, and certainly not a judge's policy preferences. Textualism appreciates this. As Justice Jackson explained, "[I]t is only the words of the bill that have presidential approval, where that approval is given. It is not to be supposed that, in signing a bill, the President endorses the whole Congressional Record. For us to undertake to reconstruct an enactment from legislative history"—or, you might add, from its underlying policy goals—is, as Jackson put it, "merely to involve the Court in political controversies which are quite proper in the enactment of a bill but should have no place in its interpretation."

There's more here. Bicameralism and presentment effectively impose a supermajority requirement on new laws. Often, even small minority groups can stop the majority from acting or insist on concessions in exchange for needed votes. So when judges do anything other than interpret statutes according to the ordinary meaning of their terms, they risk undoing carefully wrought compromises and robbing political minorities of their constitutionally afforded bargaining chip, handing a victory to a faction that couldn't convince others to go as far as they'd like in the legislative arena.

And there's still another important point nested in here. Much of the value of bicameralism and presentment lies in the seemingly paradoxical fact that it allows for results less coherent, principled, or maximal than those produced by judicial power. A statute may not always look rational to the outsider; its premises may not always proceed to a neat logical conclusion. But that's not a problem crying out for a judicial solution; that's part of the genius of the legislative process. A statute represents the work of a wide swath of the people's representatives and reflects compromises both complex and crude so that a large nation might live together in peace. Meanwhile, judicial decisions aren't about compromise: Someone must win and someone must lose. Judges aren't supposed to compromise principle but reach their decisions through the consistent application of logical premises to a natural end. The judicial process, moreover, doesn't invite participation by the whole of the people but only those few parties who have standing and can afford to litigate. So allowing judges to enforce something other than what can be found in, yes, often messy statutory texts risks denying society an important tool for releasing social pressures in a large republic, replacing delicate legislative trade-offs with maybe more rational but often rigid judicial syllogisms that lack the democratic provenance the Constitution demands.

It's easy enough to see, too, how textualism fits with an insulated judiciary. The founders afforded the judiciary the extraordinary protections they did because (and only because) they expected judges to decide cases using neutral interpretive techniques. And, in fact, many of the techniques embodied in the canons of construction that textualists use today were pretty ancient even by the time of the founding and familiar to the framers. The colonial and English law books were crammed with cases using them. Nothing about textualism is new; it is what was expected.

Meanwhile, if judges were free to disregard these traditional rules of statutory construction in order to further some hidden purposes or to promote their own views of the social good, what would make them worthy of life tenure and salary protections? I cannot think of a good reply—and neither could William Blackstone. If the law is left only to what can be found "in the breast of the judge," he wrote, it would only serve to "make every judge a legislator." Who, after all, would hire nine people to write laws for a continental nation and then insulate them from any electoral accountability? Let alone pick for the job nine lawyers from fancy law schools, with a majority from East Coast urban centers? That sounds more like the monarchy the Constitution rejected than the republic it ordained.

Textualism fits with an insulated judiciary in another way as well. Judges are more likely to fulfill their assigned mission of protecting disfavored persons from intemperate majorities when they can point to a neutral interpretive method to support their decisions. They can say, "I didn't rule against you because I disagree with your values and goals, but because the law required me to." Unfortunately, history has proven time and time again that when judges abandon neutral interpretive rules and allow outside considerations to infect their work—take *Dred Scott* and *Korematsu,* to name just a couple of examples—it becomes all the harder for them to stand firm against the weight of majoritarian pressures.

OF COURSE, CHALLENGES CAN be leveled at textualism. But, to my mind at least, a careful inspection of the leading charges only serves to confirm its case.

Some say that statutes should be treated by judges more or less like the common law. Perhaps no one has pressed the point more thoughtfully than Judge Guido Calabresi in his book *A Common Law for the Age of Statutes.* As I understand it, the essence of this position is that judges should update statutes when they grow out of touch with the legal topography. In his view, the "judicial Power" preserved by the Constitution includes the power to interpret statutes in a common law manner; tweaking a statute just a little when

needed so that it might work more efficiently. Perhaps even sometimes nullifying an otherwise constitutional statute if it has become
too much of an outlier in the legal fabric.

Now, I confess that I agree to an extent with this argument's premise. Surely the "judicial Power" bestowed upon federal courts in the
Constitution includes the power of common law adjudication in some
circumstances. But, respectfully, I do not see how Judge Calabresi's
conclusion follows. A federal judge's power to expound the common
law exists only in a relatively few arenas—admiralty law, for example.
And the judge's common law power does *not* extend to those arenas
where Congress has prescribed rules of decision by statute.

Neither is this simply a problem of labels. As Professor Samuel
Estreicher points out, equating common and statutory law ignores
critical differences between them. The common law derives its legitimacy in no small part from ensuring "consisten[t] and principled" rulings by judges. Statutes, by contrast, derive their legitimacy
from following the Constitution's process for creating new legislation. They are valid even if their rationales seem unpersuasive to
judges or stick out like a sore thumb from surrounding doctrine;
indeed, as we have seen, the compromise nature of statutes is one of
their key virtues. And those compromises reached in the political
sphere are supposed to be revisable only in that same sphere. At bottom, I think that Professor Estreicher is exactly right: Judge Calabresi's "vision of the courts' role in the legal process—as guarantors
of an overarching coherence in the legal fabric, irrespective of
whether the rules are judge-made or forged in legislative chambers—
contemplates a common law superseding legislative will and threatens a profound displacement of legislative initiative and, ultimately,
accountability."

Others level a different objection to textualism. They complain
that textualism does not yield determinate answers. Some versions
of this critique, most notably ones developed by critical legal theorists, posit that all texts are radically indeterminate, and that meaning is always and ultimately controlled by the interpreter, not the text
itself.

While this argument perhaps contains a nugget of truth, I'd like to suggest that it's mostly fool's gold. Words have meaning, and texts are not all or usually indeterminate. Ask most any federal judge and I bet they will tell you what Judge Ray Kethledge has said so well: "[S]tatutory ambiguities are less like dandelions on an unmowed lawn than they are like manufacturing defects in a modern automobile: they happen, but they are pretty rare, given the number of parts involved."

Obviously, there will be some close cases. And in those close cases we can expect that lawyers and judges of good faith will debate vigorously what the traditional tools of statutory interpretation suggest about a particular text's meaning. But at least when we use the value-neutral tools of textualism the dispute remains a distinctly legal one carried out in legal terms. Textualism allows us to assess and critique the work of others on objective terms too. Rather than arguing that an opposing party's position yields bad social policy and praying the judge sees social policy the same way we do, we can say an opposing party misapplies the canon that words are known by the company they keep, or seeks to interpret a statute in a way that causes a term to be unnecessarily superfluous, or violates some other traditional rule of sound interpretation.

Admittedly, there will be those rare occasions when the statutory manufacturing defect is so grave that everyone will agree that stubborn ambiguity remains even after their careful application. But even then textualists aren't left impoverished. The law has long encountered this sort of problem and it has long since adapted answers. Ancient canons of construction and traditional rules of procedure tell judges how to handle these situations too. By way of illustration, consider a few examples. Start with the rule of lenity. Lenity teaches us that, when an ambiguity remains in a penal statute after the traditional interpretive tools are exhausted, the tie goes to liberty and the defendant—not to the prosecutor and prison. In even more extreme circumstances—when a statute is so ambiguous that a judge simply cannot divine its meaning consistent with the judicial role—textualists have long employed the void for vagueness doctrine as a backstop. In that case, the judge must stop enforcing the statute altogether rather than seek to continue by making it up. And if a judge cannot know whether or not a statute applies to certain conduct, then the party bearing the burden of persuasion must lose.

IF AT THIS POINT you still harbor doubts about textualism, I'd ask you to consider the old truism that you can't beat something with nothing. For if you're inclined to abandon textualism, it falls to you to offer the judge something else in return. And when you try, I wonder if you might just find yourself wishing you hadn't started down that road in the first place. Take two of the leading contenders we've already encountered: "purposivism" and "consequentialism." While views diverge within these schools of thought, I think we can safely summarize their basics this way.

Purposivists seek to give primacy to the perceived spirit of a statute—to further its primary purpose—even at the expense of the letter of the law. What evil was this statute aimed at? The proper interpretation of the statute, purposivists say, should seek to eradicate that evil. In construing a statute, purposivists sometimes hypothesize a reasonable legislator and ask what he would have wanted it to mean if he had faced the facts at hand. Perhaps an especially defining characteristic of purposivist theories is their reliance on legislative history—the committee reports, floor statements, and other papers Congress produces as it considers a bill—all in an effort to discover the hidden intention lurking behind the law. Sometimes, too, purposivists seek guidance about a statute's purpose from administrative agencies charged with superintending the law at issue.

Similarly but distinctly, consequentialists believe that judges should interpret legal texts to produce the best outcome for society. Some seek to maximize overall social welfare; others to protect favored persons or interests; still others to produce the equitable result in the case at hand. But whatever their particular stripe, consequentialists differ from purposivists in that they seek to select the outcome calculated to produce optimal policy results along some metric regardless what those in Congress might have intended.

As I see it, though, purposivism and consequentialism quickly begin to run into problems when measured against our constitutional benchmarks. They take us dangerously far from interpreting the text and toward legislating a new one, encouraging the judge to adopt a meaning that furthers some purpose or social policy outside the statute's metes and bounds. After all, it's only when these theories invite us to depart from the statutory text that they do any real work. In issuing this invitation, these theories also begin to tear at the fabric of the separation of powers. On their account, judges don't just honor what's survived the constitutionally compelled legislative process. They seek to implement some other values that haven't survived (and often probably couldn't survive) that process. Legislating limits on liberty no longer remains a deliberately difficult business—or an open and public one. You no longer have to persuade 535 members of Congress and the president. You no longer have to engage all of society in a compromise. You only need to engage with one opponent (or a relative handful) in a sterile brief writing exercise directed to a few judges. And often lost in the process of judicial efforts to rationalize the law more perfectly are the compromise bargains that are the hallmark virtues of the legislative process.

These theories also sit uneasily with the idea of an insulated federal judiciary. If judges are allowed to revise the terms of otherwise entirely constitutional legislation based on extratextual policy considerations, why are they unelected and endowed with life tenure? In Britain, members of the House of Lords served as appellate judges and could participate in the lawmaking process too. Our Constitution did not adopt this familiar structure but expressly rejected it by reserving all federal lawmaking powers to Congress and establishing an independent judiciary. That difference in design implies a difference in function: a judiciary that must "be bound down by strict rules" and neutral interpretive principles and one that must leave the business of making social policy judgments to Congress.

Purposivism and consequentialism seem to me equally at odds with the rule of law values the Constitution's structure seeks to serve. How are the people to know in advance what atextual purpose a purposivist judge might ascribe to a statute? Or which portions of the hidden legislative history behind the law's text a judge might find probative? Let alone know what rule a consequentialist judge might think best for society? And what's the point of writing down laws anyway if they are but jumping-off points for the judicial imagination? Purposivist and consequentialist theories, too, mean that judges may constantly update statutes in light of a changing world in order to fulfill an unexpressed congressional purpose or to ensure a rule best for society. So not only is meaning not limited to the text, it's never fixed either, always shifting shape. What's left of fair notice then?

I worry, too, what these theories do to our commitment to equality. If a statute's meaning isn't determined by value-neutral rules seeking to enforce its written terms, who stands to benefit? Despite some popular belief, judges are only human. The more leeway a judge is given, the more likely the judge will engage, consciously or not, in motivated reasoning or bias in reaching a result. And it should come as little surprise if this bias will often harm minorities and disfavored groups, given that judges are, by and large, drawn from the majority or more powerful groups in society. The increase in flexibility gained by these theories comes with increased risks to equality. So if you think you might want judges to enact into law hidden legislative intentions or social policy, I ask you this. What happens when they come for you? Yes, if you are popular or powerful, maybe you will have them on your side. But what if you are neither of those things?

After years of facing strong challenges along just these lines, purposivism and consequentialism have recently seen some scholarly efforts to stem their retreat. For example, Judge Robert Katzmann and my friend Chris Mammen have thoughtfully sought to rehabilitate purposivism in their books *Judging Statutes* and *Using Legislative History in American Statutory Interpretation*. They contend that limited uses of legislative history can help in interpreting a statute, and they point to committee reports as particularly reliable sources of information about Congress's intended meaning. Committee reports generally accompany bills presented to Congress and, as Judge Katzmann puts it, provide members of Congress with information about "a bill's context, purposes, policy implications, and details."

But, respectfully, I do not think that these arguments answer the most fundamental objections we've already encountered. Like the fact that only a bill's text survives the process our supreme law prescribes for making laws; that judges are vested with the authority to enforce that which is written in the law, not that which isn't; and that doing anything else but discerning the fair meaning of the text cannot be easily squared with our insulated federal judiciary. And even taking the argument on its own terms, I can't help but wonder whether it paints a rather rosy picture of committee reports. Consider again Judge Kethledge, who has described his experience as a Senate staffer drafting legislative history. To him, the job was sort of "like being a teenager at home while your parents are away for the weekend: there was no supervision. I was able to write more or less what I pleased. . . . [M]ost members of Congress . . . have no idea at all about what is in the legislative history for a particular bill." A famous colloquy involving my old boss and home state senator, Bill Armstrong of Colorado (I interned for him as a young man), and Senator Bob Dole illustrates the point even when it comes to the supposedly reliable committee report:

> MR. ARMSTRONG: Mr. President, will the Senator tell me whether or not he wrote the committee report?

> MR. DOLE: Did I write the committee report?

> MR. ARMSTRONG: Yes.

> MR. DOLE: No; the Senator from Kansas did not write the committee report.

> MR. ARMSTRONG: Did any Senator write the committee report?

> MR. DOLE: I have to check.

> MR. ARMSTRONG: Does the Senator know of any Senator who wrote the committee report?

> MR. DOLE: I might be able to identify one, but I would have to search. I was here all during the time it was written, I might say, and worked carefully with the staff as they worked. . . .

MR. ARMSTRONG: Mr. President, has the Senator from Kansas, the chairman of the Finance Committee, read the committee report in its entirety?

MR. DOLE: I am working on it. It is not a bestseller, but I am working on it.

MR. ARMSTRONG: Mr. President, did members of the Finance Committee vote on the committee report?

MR. DOLE: No.

MR. ARMSTRONG: . . . The report itself is not considered by the Committee on Finance. It was not subject to amendment by the Committee on Finance. It is not subject to amendment now by the Senate. . . . If there were matter within this report which was disagreed to by the Senator from Colorado or even by a majority of all Senators, there would be no way for us to change the report. I could not offer an amendment tonight to amend the committee report. . . . [L]et me just make the point that this is not the law, it was not voted on, it is not subject to amendment, and we should discipline ourselves to the task of expressing congressional intent in the statute.

I think my old boss had it right. He might have added that legislative history can also suffer from two more paradoxical problems. The more it's used, the more unreliable it's likely to become and the less incentive legislators will have to legislate. After all, canny politicians will have every reason to try to achieve their lawmaking dreams through ever more enterprising uses of legislative history and have even less incentive to attend to the much harder job of pushing their ideas through the full legislative process.

My concerns with purposivism and consequentialism parallel those expressed by two men who preceded me in the seat on the Court I now occupy. In their pre-judicial political lives, they couldn't have been more different. Before their appointments to the Court, one served as Franklin Delano Roosevelt's attorney general; the other worked in Richard Nixon's Justice Department. But when it came to the judge's job of interpreting statutes, they were of one mind. Justice Jackson explained that "[w]hen we decide . . . what Congress probably had in mind, we must put ourselves in the place of a majority of Congressmen and act according to the impression we think this history should have made on them. Never having been a Congressman, I am handicapped in that weird endeavor. That process seems to me not interpretation of a statute but creation of a statute." Decades later, Justice Scalia echoed the point when he said that "[w]hen you are told to decide, not on the basis of what the legislature said, but on the basis of what it *meant* . . . your best shot at figuring out what the legislature meant is to ask yourself what a wise and intelligent person *should* have meant; and that will surely bring you to the conclusion that the law means what you think it *ought* to mean."

AT THIS POINT, it might help to make the comparison between our competing theories more concrete. We've already seen how they played out in the Tenth Circuit in *Games-Perez*. Now let's consider two cases recently decided by the Supreme Court. During my first full term on the Court, we heard *Digital Realty Trust v. Somers,* a case about the scope of the Dodd-Frank Act's whistleblower protections. In the Dodd-Frank Act, Congress protected "whistleblower[s]" from retaliation by their employers. But in that particular statute Congress defined the term "whistleblower[s]" to mean those who report lawbreaking to the Securities and Exchange Commission. The plaintiff in the case before us didn't report his complaint to the SEC, only to his boss. Later, the boss allegedly retaliated against him. The plaintiff sought whistleblower protections under the Act, arguing the law's purpose is (or should be) to maximize whistleblower reports and protect those who report questionable activity. The Ninth Circuit agreed with him.

My Court unanimously reversed. We did so for the very sort of reasons I've outlined. Extending the scope of protected whistleblowers beyond those Congress chose to protect might be a great policy idea and no doubt it would seem to take a purpose latent in the statute to its logical end. But it also would have required the Court to upset a congressional compromise. With the passage of time and tumult of the legislative process, it might be hard to know why Congress chose to go as far as it did but no further. But we do know that the legislative process isn't about pursuing an idea to the nth degree and the compromise represented in the statute was the only one that managed to run the legislative gauntlet and become law.

A similar story unfolded in *Wisconsin Central v. United States.* There, we confronted the Railroad Retirement Tax Act of 1937. The statute allows the government to tax railroad employees' "money" income. The government argued that this provision permitted it to tax the stock options an employee receives from his employer. As a matter of ordinary usage, of course, the term "money" meant then (as it does now) "a medium of exchange." And pretty obviously, "stock" isn't a medium of exchange; after all, no one buys groceries or pays rent in stock. Of course, stock can be *converted* into money. But then again, so can baseball cards. The truth is, most *anything* can be converted into money. Yet no one would seriously suggest that everything *is* money.

Maybe so, the government responded. But, it argued, there are strong purposivist and consequentialist reasons for eliding the difference between money and things convertible into money. If the statute's purpose was to tax money income, it said, then we should follow that thought to its logical end and allow other things easily convertible into money to be taxable too. Distinguishing between monetary and nonmonetary income might, as well, yield a suboptimal tax policy by encouraging companies to award more remuneration in stock and less in money, leaving the federal fisc to suffer.

The Court rejected the government's arguments. It explained that the judicial power doesn't include a power to steer tax policy or pursue every good idea found in legislation to its logical conclusion or update statutes we think outdated. Nor is it a power to flatten out legislative compromises found in one area of the law but not another. That Congress chose to tax nonmonetary income elsewhere in the tax code showed that it knew very well how to do so if it wished. So we invoked the familiar textualist canon of interpretation that the expression of an idea in one place means its absence in another must be given effect. The fact that Congress made different choices in different statutes, we said, deserved respect, not a rewrite.

Notice the strong temptation judges face in both cases to revise the statute. To bend the statutory terms to reach a short-term policy victory for a popular whistleblower or against an unpopular tax-avoiding corporate shareholder. To feel like they've "made a difference." Because textualism is value-neutral, it hands out victories based on the strength of consistency with a statutory text, not passing popularity. So, yes, one day textualism means the criminal defendant should win and the next day a corporate railroad shareholder must. Judges may not like every policy outcome they reach. But if they did, we should think less of them.

IN THE END, TEXTUALISM is about ensuring that our written law is our actual law. There's no doubt that inventing a new law instead of applying the written one can be tempting. Often enough, a good judge will look at a statute and immediately know three things: One, the law is telling me to do something really stupid; two, the law is perfectly constitutional; and, three, if I follow the stupid-but-constitutional law, everyone who's not a lawyer is going to think I am stupid too. But despite temptations like these, textualism has come to dominate the interpretation of statutes today because so many inside and outside the legal profession have come to appreciate that something more important is at stake. People have come to respect that lawmaking belongs to legislators; that judges should seek to act by neutral principle; that people deserve to know in advance the laws that govern them. And that everyone—whether it's today's hero or tomorrow's villain—deserves the protections of the written law.

United States v. Carloss

———

The next four cases illustrate originalism and textualism in action. I've picked two from each category. The first case, United States v. Carloss, belies the old objection that originalism will leave rights underprotected. It's a case about a type of government search called the "knock and talk." Officers approach a home and knock on the front door, hoping for a receptive welcome so they might enter by consent and without the need for a warrant. But the homeowners in this case had several No Trespassing signs lining the path to their front door. Should that have barred the officers' approach, at least without a warrant, under the Fourth Amendment? My colleagues on the Tenth Circuit took the view that government officials were free to ignore the warnings and walk up the homeowner's path and knock on the front door without a warrant. I dissented. To me, this case is what originalism is all about: ensuring that the liberties the people enjoyed at the founding remain no less secure today.

THE "KNOCK AND TALK" HAS WON A PROMINENT PLACE IN TODAY'S legal lexicon. The term is used to describe situations in which police officers approach a home, knock at the front door, and seek to engage the homeowner in conversation and win permission to search inside. Because everything happens with the homeowner's consent, the theory goes, a warrant isn't needed. After all, the Fourth Amendment prohibits "unreasonable" searches, and consensual searches are rarely that. No doubt for just this reason law enforcement has found the knock and talk an increasingly attractive investigative tool and published cases approving knock and talks have grown legion. But in the constant competition between constable and quarry, officers sometimes use knock and talks in ways that test the boundaries of the consent on which they depend. So, for example, courts have found that a homeowner's consent isn't freely given when officers appear with a display of force designed to overbear. Courts have found consent lacking and a constitutional violation, too, when officers mislead homeowners into thinking they have no choice but to cooperate.

Today's case comes at us along similar lines but from a different vector. A home's curtilage—that area "immediately surrounding and associated with the home"—is protected by the Fourth Amendment much like the home itself. So not only do officers need a warrant, exigent circumstances, or consent to enter a home, they also generally need one of those things to reach the home's front door in the first place. Typically, of course, officers contend that their intrusion into the curtilage for a knock and talk is justified by the homeowner's implied consent. And usually there's no question about it, for the Supreme Court has recognized that the "knocker on the front door" normally supplies an implied "invitation or license" for visitors of all kinds to enter the home's curtilage and knock at the front door. By placing a knocker on the front door (or, I'm sure, a doorbell next to it), the homeowner is traditionally said to invite even "solicitors" and "hawkers" to "approach the home by the front path, knock promptly, wait briefly to be received, and then (absent invitation to linger longer) leave." For this same reason and to the same extent, the Court has explained, law enforcement agents, no less than anyone else, may approach the front door and seek entry.

But what happens when the homeowner manifests an obvious intention to revoke the implied license to enter the curtilage and knock at the front door? When the owner literally substitutes the knocker with a No Trespassing sign, one smack in the middle of the front door? When she adds two more No Trespassing signs at the driveway's mouth to the street, one on either side of the only clear access route from the street to the front door—and along the very route any visitor would use to approach the home? And when, for good measure, she posts still another No Trespassing sign between the driveway and the house? So that to enter the home's front porch, its constitutionally protected curtilage, visitors would have to disregard four separate and plainly visible warnings that their presence is wholly unwelcome? May officers still—under these circumstances— enter the curtilage to conduct an investigation without a warrant and absent an emergency?

That's the question we're asked to address today. Most ambitiously, the government suggests that its officers enjoy an irrevocable right to enter a home's curtilage to conduct a knock and talk. On this view, a homeowner may post as many No Trespassing signs as she wishes. She might add a wall or a medieval-style moat, too. Maybe razor wire and battlements and mantraps besides. Even that isn't enough to revoke the state's right to enter.

This argument seems to me difficult to reconcile with the Constitution of the founders' design. We know that the Fourth Amendment, at a minimum, protects the people against searches of their persons, houses, papers, and effects to the same degree the common law protected the people against such things at the time of the founding, for in prohibiting "unreasonable" searches the Amendment incorporated existing common law restrictions on the state's investigative authority. We know, too, that at the time of the founding the common law permitted government agents to enter a home or its curtilage only with the owner's permission or to execute legal process. No trace of some sort of permanent easement belonging to the state (and state alone) can be found in the common law of the founders' time. In fact, state officials no less than private visitors could be liable for trespass when entering without the homeowner's consent.

The government disputes none of this apparently dispositive authority. In fact, it doesn't even address it. Instead, the government replies by pointing to the Supreme Court's observation that officers usually enjoy the homeowner's implied consent to enter the curtilage to knock at the front door. But nothing in that prosaic observation purported to upend the original meaning of the Fourth Amendment or centuries of common law recognizing that homeowners may revoke by word or deed the licenses they themselves extend. In fact, the Court took pains to emphasize that the implied license that might have permitted the officers to enter the curtilage in that case was the same common law license generally enjoyed by private visitors—one entitling the officers to do "no more than any private citizen might."

If we decline to adopt its main theory on appeal, the government asks us to entertain another alternative ground for affirmance. Accepting now for argument's sake that the implied license to enter the curtilage extends no more to law enforcement agents than it does to other visitors, the government contends that No Trespassing signs aren't the proper way to revoke it. According to the government, a homeowner may avoid a knock and talk only by hiding in the home and refusing to answer the door. Or maybe by opening the door and commanding officers to leave.

This argument is no more persuasive than the last. Actually, it's no different from the last. A homeowner who refuses to answer the door, or who opens it to say "go away," does so after the officers have already entered the home's front porch and knocked on the door—everything the implied license permits the officers to do. In the government's two scenarios, then, a homeowner hasn't revoked the license to enter the curtilage and knock at the front door so much as the officers have exhausted the terms of that license.

Unsurprisingly, this variation on the theme finds no more of a place in the Constitution than the theme itself. The government points to the Supreme Court's observation that a homeowner in response to a knock and talk may choose to refuse to answer the door or the questions put to him. But in endorsing that principle the Court hardly suggested that it was denying another—that it meant to deny the homeowner the power to revoke the implied license before visitors reach the front door.

RATHER THAN REJECT THE government's two arguments and call it a day, my colleagues choose to pursue two (more) alternative arguments for affirmance all their own. For its part, the concurrence appears to take the view that No Trespassing signs cannot revoke the implied license in the "residential context" unless they are coupled with a "fence or other physical obstacle." But the concurrence supplies no authority to support its judgment, and indeed there seems to be ample authority running the other way, suggesting that the common law at the time of the founding did not require a property owner to express his intent to revoke a license to enter in any particular way. Indeed, all that was traditionally required were "express words . . . or . . . an act . . . indicating an intention to revoke." Nothing in this common law rule of decision required both notice by word (a sign) and notice by deed (a fence). In fact, despite the relatively low literacy rates in mid-18th century England and early America, there appears to be considerable authority suggesting that posted signs or other types of published notice could suffice as a matter of law to ward off unwanted visitors.

In place of authority, the concurrence rests predominantly on certain intuitions about what "reasonable people" think. The concurrence suggests that "reasonable person[s]" do not consider No Trespassing signs, absent a fence or other obstacle, as speaking to the implied license to enter in the "residential context." In the concurrence's judgment, most people know that it's illegal to "trespass" on private property, and they also know that it generally isn't "trespassing" to walk up to the front door of a house and knock. So, the reasoning appears to go, "reasonable persons" visiting a residential neighborhood understand the particular words "no trespassing" to refer to conduct other than the exercise of the implied license.

This intuitive appeal, though, seems to invite further problems of its own. First, the Fourth Amendment is, after all, supposed to protect the people at least as much now as it did when adopted, its ancient protections still in force whatever our current intuitions or preferences might be. Second, as a matter of fact, you can't help but wonder if millions of homeowners (and solicitors) might be surprised to learn that even a long line of clearly posted No Trespassing signs are insufficient to revoke the implied license to enter a home's curtilage—that No Trespassing signs have become little more than lawn art. Certainly the concurrence offers no evidence to support its intuition about social customs and the opposite intuition seems no less and maybe a good deal more defensible, especially in light of our common law heritage. Third, as a matter of logic, even on its own terms the concurrence's argument fails to sustain the conclusion that fences or other obstacles are necessary to revoke the implied license in the residential setting. Consider. If a single No Trespassing sign communicates only the already obvious fact that trespassing isn't permitted and says nothing that might be reasonably interpreted as revoking the implied license, how does the addition of a fence transform the message so drastically, as the concurrence supposes? And if adding a fence does transform the meaning of a single No Trespassing sign, then why can't a large number of signs, collectively and strategically placed, have the same effect? The concurrence simply doesn't say. Along similar lines, if, as the concurrence suggests, No Trespassing signs cannot revoke the implied license because they use the word "trespassing" and that term has become encrusted with a very particular meaning that just doesn't speak to the implied license, what about signs that avoid the term and say instead Keep Out? Keep Off? Do Not Enter? Or how about this?

THE IMPLIED LICENSE DISCUSSED
BY THE UNITED STATES SUPREME COURT
IN *BREARD V. ALEXANDRIA,* 341 U.S. 622 (1951)
AND *FLORIDA V. JARDINES,* 133 S. CT. 1409 (2013)
IS HEREBY REVOKED

Respectfully, the concurrence's argument doesn't seem to suggest a rule requiring fences or other obstacles so much as a reason for differentiating between the precise text found on signs—in a way no statute or case I've found has seen fit to do—and simply avoiding the word "trespass" and its variants. And if that's the case, you have to wonder if following the concurrence's lead would do no more than invite a new cottage industry, one spitting out lawn signs with long and lawyerly (and no doubt less intuitive and commonsensical) messages instead of the tried and true "No Trespassing."

The majority opinion offers yet another alternative theory for affirmance. Addressing the three signs leading to the front porch, the majority begins by noting that they were posted on ground leading to the curtilage rather than on the curtilage itself. And this fact, it suggests, means a reasonable visitor wouldn't have understood them to forbid entry into the curtilage. But it's unclear why that conclusion follows from these facts. All three signs lined the path any visitor would follow (and the path the officers did follow) to reach the curtilage and front door. The signs came one upon the other, hard and in short order, and near the bounds of the curtilage itself. All were clearly visible and clearly unwelcoming. And from this it's difficult to see how a reasonable visitor could have felt at liberty to venture into the curtilage.

What's more, at least one sign was undeniably on curtilage and clearly visible to those preparing to enter it. To be sure, the majority opinion finds this last sign insufficient, too, if for a different reason. The majority suggests that the terms of this particular sign were too ambiguous. But in large bold letters the sign said this:

POSTED

PRIVATE PROPERTY

HUNTING, FISHING, TRAPPING, OR TRESPASSING

FOR ANY PURPOSE IS STRICTLY FORBIDDEN

VIOLATORS WILL BE PROSECUTED

The majority opinion emphasizes the sign's discussion of hunting, fishing, and trapping, and notes that those activities don't usually take place on a front porch. From this, the majority opinion reasons, the sign could have been reasonably interpreted by a visitor as forbidding him only from engaging in these recreational activities elsewhere on the property and not as speaking to his entry into the curtilage where the sign was posted. But I would have thought it equally (or maybe even a good deal more) likely that a reasonable person—considering whether to enter a stranger's front porch and staring at a large "PRIVATE PROPERTY" sign forbidding "TRESPASSING FOR ANY PURPOSE"—would take it as directed at him and his activities rather than as directed only at someone interested in hunting or fishing somewhere else on the property. Especially when there's no evidence in the record that any hunting, fishing, or trapping took place in the yard of this home in the middle of town along a paved street.

WHETHER IN ARGUING THAT the state enjoys an irrevocable license to enter or in suggesting that No Trespassing signs are categorically insufficient to bar its agents, the government appears to be moved by the same worry: that if clearly posted No Trespassing signs can revoke the right of officers to enter a home's curtilage their job of ferreting out crime will become marginally more difficult. But obedience to the Fourth Amendment always bears that cost and surely brings with it other benefits. Neither, of course, is it our job to weigh those costs and benefits but to apply the Amendment according to its terms and in light of its historical meaning.

Besides, it is hardly the case that following the Fourth Amendment's teachings would leave the government as bereft of lawful alternatives as it seems to suppose. The Amendment and the common law from which it was constructed leave ample room for law enforcement to do its job. A warrant will always do. So will emergency circumstances. After-the-fact consent may suffice if freely given. And, of course, there's no need for consent when officers search only open fields rather than curtilage. Neither is there need for consent when officers enter curtilage for a non-investigative purpose. Our duty of fidelity to the law requires us to respect all these law enforcement tools. But it also requires us to respect the ancient rights of the people when law enforcement exceed their limits. In this case the two arguments the government offers to justify its conduct can claim no basis in our constitutional tradition. And, respectfully, I just do not see the case for struggling so mightily to save the government's cause with arguments of our own devise—especially when what arguments we are able to muster suffer so many problems of their own and the benefits of exposing them to at least a modest encounter with the adversarial process seem so obvious.

Carpenter v. United States

———

This case deals with a new technology, your cell phone loca-
tion data, and the government's attempt to collect and search
it without a warrant. Supreme Court decisions from the
1970s suggested that, once you give an item to a third party,
you lose all Fourth Amendment protections in that item and
the government can search it without a warrant. Because
your cell phone location data is shared with your phone car-
rier, the government in this case argued that it should be able
to search that data without a warrant under this so-called
"third-party doctrine." In this dissent from my first full term
on the Supreme Court, I suggested that the original meaning
of the Fourth Amendment demands more protection for the
people and their "persons, houses, papers, and effects" than
"third-party doctrine" affords. I then sought to sketch out
what it might look like to return to the Fourth Amendment's
original meaning and what that meaning might hold for the
question of cell phone location data.

IN THE LATE 1960S THIS COURT SUGGESTED FOR THE FIRST TIME IN
a case called *Katz* that a search triggering the Fourth Amendment
occurs when the government violates an "expectation of privacy"
that "society is prepared to recognize as 'reasonable.'" Then, in a
pair of decisions in the 1970s applying the *Katz* test, *Smith v. Mary-*
land and *United States v. Miller,* the Court held that a "reasonable
expectation of privacy" doesn't attach to information shared with
"third parties." By these steps, the Court came to conclude, the Constitution does nothing to limit investigators from searching records

you've entrusted to your bank, accountant, and maybe even your doctor.

What's left of the Fourth Amendment? Today we use the Internet to do most everything. Smartphones make it easy to keep a calendar, correspond with friends, make calls, conduct banking, and even watch the game. Countless Internet companies maintain records about us and, increasingly, *for* us. Even our most private documents—those that, in other eras, we would have locked safely in a desk drawer or destroyed—now reside on third party servers. *Smith* and *Miller* teach that the police can review all of this material, on the theory that no one reasonably expects any of it will be kept private. But no one believes that, if they ever did.

What to do? It seems to me we could respond in at least three ways. The first is to ignore the problem, maintain *Smith* and *Miller,* and live with the consequences. If the confluence of these decisions and modern technology means our Fourth Amendment rights are reduced to nearly nothing, so be it. The second choice is to set *Smith* and *Miller* aside and try again using the *Katz* "reasonable expectation of privacy" jurisprudence that produced them. The third is to look for answers elsewhere.

START WITH THE FIRST option. *Smith* held that the government's use of a pen register to record the numbers people dial on their phones doesn't infringe a reasonable expectation of privacy because that information is freely disclosed to the third party phone company. *Miller* held that a bank account holder enjoys no reasonable expectation of privacy in the bank's records of his account activity. That's true, the Court reasoned, "even if the information is revealed on the assumption that it will be used only for a limited purpose and the confidence placed in the third party will not be betrayed." Together, those cases announced this categorical rule: Once you disclose information to third parties, you forfeit any reasonable expectation of privacy you might have had in it.

So can the government demand a copy of all your e-mails from Google or Microsoft without implicating your Fourth Amendment rights? Can it secure your DNA from 23andMe without a warrant or probable cause? *Smith* and *Miller* say yes it can—at least without running afoul of *Katz*. But that result strikes most lawyers and judges today—me included—as pretty unlikely. In the years since its adoption, countless scholars, too, have come to conclude that the "third-party doctrine is not only wrong, but horribly wrong." The reasons are obvious. "As an empirical statement about subjective expectations of privacy," the doctrine is "quite dubious." People often *do* reasonably expect that information they entrust to third parties, especially information subject to confidentiality agreements, will be kept private. Meanwhile, if the third party doctrine is supposed to represent a normative assessment of when a person should expect privacy, the notion that the answer might be "never" seems a pretty unattractive societal prescription.

What, then, is the explanation for our third party doctrine? The truth is, the Court has never offered a persuasive justification. The Court has said that by conveying information to a third party you " 'assum[e] the risk' " it will be revealed to the police and therefore lack a reasonable expectation of privacy in it. But assumption of risk doctrine developed in tort law. It generally applies when "by contract or otherwise [one] expressly agrees to accept a risk of harm" or impliedly does so by "manifest[ing] his willingness to accept" that risk and thereby "take[s] his chances as to harm which may result from it." That rationale has little play in this context. Suppose I entrust a friend with a letter and he promises to keep it secret until he delivers it to an intended recipient. In what sense have I agreed to bear the risk that he will turn around, break his promise, and spill its contents to someone else? More confusing still, what have I done to "manifest my willingness to accept" the risk that the government will pry the document from my friend and read it *without* his consent?

One possible answer concerns knowledge. I know that my friend *might* break his promise, or that the government *might* have some reason to search the papers in his possession. But knowing about a risk doesn't mean you assume responsibility for it. Whenever you walk down the sidewalk you know a car may negligently or recklessly veer off and hit you, but that hardly means you accept the consequences and absolve the driver of any damage he may do to you.

Some have suggested the third party doctrine is better understood to rest on consent than assumption of risk. "So long as a person knows that they are disclosing information to a third party," the argument goes, "their choice to do so is voluntary and the consent valid." I confess I still don't see it. Consenting to give a third party access to private papers that remain my property is not the same thing as consenting to a *search of those papers by the government*. Perhaps there are exceptions, like when the third party is an undercover government agent. But otherwise this conception of consent appears to be just assumption of risk relabeled—you've "consented" to whatever risks are foreseeable.

Another justification sometimes offered for third party doctrine is clarity. You (and the police) know exactly how much protection you have in information confided to others: none. As rules go, "the king always wins" is admirably clear. But the opposite rule would be clear too: Third party disclosures *never* diminish Fourth Amendment protection (call it "the king always loses"). So clarity alone cannot justify the third party doctrine. In the end, what do *Smith* and *Miller* add up to? A doubtful application of *Katz* that lets the government search almost whatever it wants whenever it wants. The court of appeals had to follow that rule and faithfully did just that, but it's not clear why we should.

THERE'S A SECOND OPTION. What if we dropped *Smith* and *Miller*'s third party doctrine and retreated to the root *Katz* question whether there is a "reasonable expectation of privacy" in data held by third parties? Rather than solve the problem with the third party doctrine, I worry this option only risks returning us to its source: After all, it was *Katz* that produced *Smith* and *Miller* in the first place.

Katz's problems start with the text and original understanding of the Fourth Amendment. The Amendment's protections do not depend on the breach of some abstract "expectation of privacy" whose contours are left to the judicial imagination. Much more concretely, it protects your "person," and your "houses, papers, and effects." Nor does your right to bring a Fourth Amendment claim depend on whether a judge happens to agree that your subjective expectation to privacy is a "reasonable" one. Under its plain terms, the Amendment grants you the right to invoke its guarantees whenever one of your protected things (your person, your house, your papers, or your effects) is unreasonably searched or seized. Period.

History too holds problems for *Katz*. Little like it can be found in the law that led to the adoption of the Fourth Amendment or in this Court's jurisprudence until the late 1960s. The Fourth Amendment came about in response to a trio of 18th century cases "well known to the men who wrote and ratified the Bill of Rights, [and] famous throughout the colonial population." The first two were English cases invalidating the Crown's use of general warrants to enter homes and search papers. The third was American: the Boston Writs of Assistance Case, which sparked colonial outrage at the use of writs permitting government agents to enter houses and business, breaking open doors and chests along the way, to conduct searches and seizures—and to force third parties to help them. No doubt the colonial outrage engendered by these cases rested in part on the government's intrusion upon privacy. But the framers chose not to protect privacy in some ethereal way dependent on judicial intuitions. They chose instead to protect privacy in particular places and things—"persons, houses, papers, and effects"—and against particular threats—"unreasonable" governmental "searches and seizures."

Even taken on its own terms, *Katz* has never been sufficiently justified. In fact, we still don't even know what its "reasonable expectation of privacy" test *is*. Is it supposed to pose an empirical question (what privacy expectations do people *actually* have) or a normative one (what expectations *should* they have)? Either way brings problems. If the test is supposed to be an empirical one, it's unclear why judges rather than legislators should conduct it. Legislators are responsive to their constituents and have institutional resources designed to help them discern and enact majoritarian preferences. Politically insulated judges come armed with only the attorneys' briefs, a few law clerks, and their own idiosyncratic experiences. They are hardly the representative group you'd expect (or want) to be making empirical judgments for hundreds of millions of people. Unsurprisingly, too, judicial judgments often fail to reflect public views. Consider just one example. Our cases insist that the seriousness of the offense being investigated does *not* reduce Fourth Amendment protection. Yet scholars suggest that most people *are* more tolerant of police intrusions when they investigate more serious crimes. And I very much doubt that this Court would be willing to adjust its *Katz* cases to reflect these findings even if it believed them.

Maybe, then, the *Katz* test should be conceived as a normative question. But if that's the case, why (again) do judges, rather than legislators, get to determine whether society *should be* prepared to recognize an expectation of privacy as legitimate? Deciding what privacy interests *should be* recognized often calls for a pure policy choice, many times between incommensurable goods—between the value of privacy in a particular setting and society's interest in combating crime. Answering questions like that calls for the exercise of raw political will belonging to legislatures, not the legal judgment proper to courts. When judges abandon legal judgment for political will we not only risk decisions where "reasonable expectations of privacy" come to bear "an uncanny resemblance to those expectations of privacy" shared by Members of this Court. We also risk undermining public confidence in the courts themselves.

My concerns about *Katz* come with a caveat. *Sometimes*, I accept, judges may be able to discern and describe existing societal norms. That is particularly true when the judge looks to positive law rather than intuition for guidance on social norms. So there may be *some* occasions where *Katz* is capable of principled application—though it may simply wind up approximating the more traditional option I will discuss in a moment. Sometimes it may also be possible to apply *Katz* by analogizing from precedent when the line between an existing case and a new fact pattern is short and direct. But so far this Court has declined to tie itself to any significant restraints like these.

As a result, *Katz* has yielded an often unpredictable—and sometimes unbelievable—jurisprudence. *Smith* and *Miller* are only two examples; there are many others. Take *Florida v. Riley*, which says that a police helicopter hovering 400 feet above a person's property invades no reasonable expectation of privacy. Try that one out on your neighbors. Or *California v. Greenwood*, which holds that a person has no reasonable expectation of privacy in the garbage he puts out for collection. In that case, the Court said that the homeowners forfeited their privacy interests because "[i]t is common knowledge that plastic garbage bags left on or at the side of a public street are readily accessible to animals, children, scavengers, snoops, and other members of the public." But the habits of raccoons don't prove much about the habits of the country. I doubt, too, that most people spotting a neighbor rummaging through their garbage would think they lacked reasonable grounds to confront the rummager. Making the decision all the stranger, California state law expressly *protected* a homeowner's property rights in discarded trash. Yet rather than defer to that as evidence of the people's habits and reasonable expectations of privacy, the Court substituted its own curious judgment.

Resorting to *Katz* in data privacy cases threatens more of the same. Just consider. The Court today says that judges should use *Katz*'s reasonable expectation of privacy test to decide what Fourth Amendment rights people have in cell-site location information, explaining that "no single rubric definitively resolves which expectations of privacy are entitled to protection." But then it offers a twist. Lower courts should be sure to add two special principles to their *Katz* calculus: the need to avoid "arbitrary power" and the importance of "plac[ing] obstacles in the way of a too permeating police surveillance." While surely laudable, these principles don't offer lower courts much guidance. The Court does not tell us, for example, how far to carry either principle or how to weigh them against the legitimate needs of law enforcement. At what point does access to electronic data amount to "arbitrary" authority? When does police surveillance become "too permeating"? And what sort of "obstacles" should judges "place" in law enforcement's path when it does? We simply do not know.

The Court's application of these principles supplies little more direction. The Court declines to say whether there is any sufficiently limited period of time "for which the Government may obtain an individual's historical [location information] free from Fourth Amendment scrutiny." But then it tells us that access to seven days' worth of information *does* trigger Fourth Amendment scrutiny—even though here the carrier "produced only two days of records." Why is the relevant fact the seven days of information the government *asked for* instead of the two days of information the government *actually saw*?

Why seven days instead of ten or three or one? And in what possible sense did the government "search" five days' worth of location information it was never even sent? We do not know.

Later still, the Court adds that it can't say whether the Fourth Amendment is triggered when the government collects "real-time cell-site location data or 'tower dumps' (a download of information on all the devices that connected to a particular cell site during a particular interval)." But what distinguishes historical data from real-time data, or seven days of a single person's data from a download of *everyone's* data over some indefinite period of time? Why isn't a tower dump the *paradigmatic* example of "too permeating police surveillance" and a dangerous tool of "arbitrary" authority—the touchstones of the majority's modified *Katz* analysis? On what possible basis could such mass data collection survive the Court's test while collecting a single person's data does not? Here again we are left to guess. At the same time, though, the Court offers some firm assurances. It tells us its decision does *not* "call into question conventional surveillance techniques and tools, such as security cameras." That, however, just raises more questions for lower courts to sort out about what techniques qualify as "conventional" and why those techniques would be okay *even if* they lead to "permeating police surveillance" or "arbitrary police power."

Nor is this the end of it. After finding a reasonable expectation of privacy, the Court says there's still more work to do. Courts must determine whether to "extend" *Smith* and *Miller* to the circumstances before them. So apparently *Smith* and *Miller* aren't quite left for dead; they just no longer have the clear reach they once did. How do we measure their new reach? The Court says courts now must conduct a *second Katz*-like balancing inquiry, asking whether the fact of disclosure to a third party outweighs privacy interests in the "category of information" so disclosed. But how are lower courts supposed to weigh these radically different interests? Or assign values to different categories of information? All we know is that historical cell-site location information (for seven days, anyway) escapes *Smith* and *Miller*'s shorn grasp, while a lifetime of bank or phone records does not. As to any other kind of information, lower courts will have to stay tuned.

In the end, our lower court colleagues are left with two amorphous balancing tests, a series of weighty and incommensurable principles to consider in them, and a few illustrative examples that seem little more than the product of judicial intuition. In the Court's defense, though, we have arrived at this strange place not because the Court has misunderstood *Katz*. Far from it. We have arrived here because this is where *Katz* inevitably leads.

THERE IS ANOTHER WAY. From the founding until the 1960s, the right to assert a Fourth Amendment claim didn't depend on your ability to appeal to a judge's personal sensibilities about the "reasonableness" of your expectations of privacy. It was tied to the law. The Fourth Amendment protects "the right of the people to be secure in their persons, houses, papers, and effects, against unreasonable searches and seizures." True to those words and their original understanding, the traditional approach asked if a house, paper or effect was *yours* under law. No more was needed to trigger the Fourth Amendment. Though now often lost in *Katz*'s shadow, this traditional understanding persists. *Katz* only "supplements, rather than displaces the traditional property-based understanding of the Fourth Amendment."

Beyond its provenance in the text and original understanding of the Amendment, this traditional approach comes with other advantages. Judges are supposed to decide cases based on "democratically legitimate sources of law"—like positive law or analogies to items protected by the enacted Constitution. A Fourth Amendment model based on positive legal rights "carves out significant room for legislative participation in the Fourth Amendment context," too, by asking judges to consult what the people's representatives have to say about their rights. Nor is this approach hobbled by *Smith* and *Miller,* for those cases are just *limitations* on *Katz,* addressing only the question whether individuals have a reasonable expectation of privacy in materials they share with third parties. Under this more traditional approach, Fourth Amendment protections for your papers and effects do not automatically disappear just because you share them with third parties.

Given the prominence *Katz* has claimed in our doctrine, American courts are pretty rusty at applying the traditional approach to the Fourth Amendment. We know that if a house, paper, or effect is yours, you have a Fourth Amendment interest in its protection. But what kind of legal interest is sufficient to make something *yours*? And what source of law determines that? Current positive law? The common law at 1791, extended by analogy to modern times? Both? Much work is needed to revitalize this area and answer these questions. I do not begin to claim all the answers today, but (unlike with *Katz*) at least I have a pretty good idea what the questions *are*. And it seems to me a few things can be said.

First, the fact that a third party has access to or possession of your papers and effects does not necessarily eliminate your interest in them. Ever hand a private document to a friend to be returned? Toss your keys to a valet at a restaurant? Ask your neighbor to look after your dog while you travel? You would not expect the friend to share the document with others; the valet to lend your car to his buddy; or the neighbor to put Fido up for adoption. Entrusting your stuff to others is a *bailment*. A bailment is the "delivery of personal property by one person (the *bailor*) to another (the *bailee*) who holds the property for a certain purpose." A bailee normally owes a legal duty to keep the item safe, according to the terms of the parties' contract if they have one, and according to the "implication[s] from their conduct" if they don't. A bailee who uses the item in a different way than he's supposed to, or against the bailor's instructions, is liable for conversion. This approach is quite different from *Smith* and *Miller*'s (counter)-intuitive approach to reasonable expectations of privacy; where those cases extinguish Fourth Amendment interests once records are given to a third party, property law may preserve them.

Our Fourth Amendment jurisprudence already reflects this truth. In *Ex parte Jackson*, this Court held that sealed letters placed in the mail are "as fully guarded from examination and inspection, except as to their outward form and weight, as if they were retained by the parties forwarding them in their own domiciles." The reason, drawn from the Fourth Amendment's text, was that "[t]he constitutional guaranty of the right of the people to be secure in their papers against unreasonable searches and seizures extends to *their papers,* thus closed against inspection, *wherever they may be.*" It did not matter that letters were bailed to a third party (the government, no less). The sender enjoyed the same Fourth Amendment protection as he does "when papers are subjected to search in one's own household."

These ancient principles may help us address modern data cases too. Just because you entrust your data—in some cases, your modern-day papers and effects—to a third party may not mean you lose any Fourth Amendment interest in its contents. Whatever may be left of *Smith* and *Miller,* few doubt that e-mail should be treated much like the traditional mail it has largely supplanted—as a bailment in which the owner retains a vital and protected legal interest.

Second, I doubt that complete ownership or exclusive control of property is always a necessary condition to the assertion of a Fourth Amendment right. Where houses are concerned, for example, individuals can enjoy Fourth Amendment protection without fee simple title. Both the text of the Amendment and the common law rule support that conclusion. "People call a house 'their' home when legal title is in the bank, when they rent it, and even when they merely occupy it rent free." That rule derives from the common law. That is why tenants and resident family members—though they have no legal title—have standing to complain about searches of the houses in which they live.

Another point seems equally true: just because you *have* to entrust a third party with your data doesn't necessarily mean you should lose all Fourth Amendment protections in it. Not infrequently one person comes into possession of someone else's property without the owner's consent. Think of the finder of lost goods or the policeman who impounds a car. The law recognizes that the goods and the car still belong to their true owners, for "where a person comes into lawful possession of the personal property of another, even though there is no formal agreement between the property's owner and its possessor, the possessor will become a constructive bailee when justice so requires." At least some of this Court's decisions have already suggested that use of technology is functionally compelled by the demands of modern life, and in that way the fact that we store data with third parties may amount to a sort of involuntary bailment too.

Third, positive law may help provide detailed guidance on

evolving technologies without resort to judicial intuition. State (or sometimes federal) law often creates rights in both tangible and intangible things. In the context of the Takings Clause we often ask whether those state-created rights are sufficient to make something someone's property for constitutional purposes. A similar inquiry may be appropriate for the Fourth Amendment. Both the States and federal government are actively legislating in the area of third party data storage and the rights users enjoy.

State courts are busy expounding common law property principles in this area as well. If state legislators or state courts say that a digital record has the attributes that normally make something property, that may supply a sounder basis for judicial decisionmaking than judicial guesswork about societal expectations.

Fourth, while positive law may help establish a person's Fourth Amendment interest there may be some circumstances where positive law cannot be used to defeat it. *Ex parte Jackson* reflects that understanding. There this Court said that "[n]o law of Congress" could authorize letter carriers "to invade the secrecy of letters." So the post office couldn't impose a regulation dictating that those mailing letters surrender all legal interests in them once they're deposited in a mailbox. If that is right, *Jackson* suggests the existence of a constitutional floor below which Fourth Amendment rights may not descend. Legislatures cannot pass laws declaring your house or papers to be your property except to the extent the police wish to search them without cause. As the Court has previously explained, "we must 'assur[e] preservation of that degree of privacy against government that existed when the Fourth Amendment was adopted.'" Nor does this mean protecting only the specific rights known at the founding; it means protecting their modern analogues too. So, for example, while thermal imaging was unknown in 1791, this Court has recognized that using that technology to look inside a home constitutes a Fourth Amendment "search" of that "home" no less than a physical inspection might.

WHAT DOES ALL THIS mean for the case before us? To start, I cannot fault the court of appeals for holding that *Smith* and *Miller* extinguish any *Katz*-based Fourth Amendment interest in third party cell-site data. That is the plain effect of their categorical holdings. Nor can I fault the Court today for its implicit but unmistakable conclusion that the rationale of *Smith* and *Miller* is wrong; indeed, I agree with that. The court of appeals was powerless to say so, but this Court can and should. At the same time, I do not agree with the Court's decision today to keep *Smith* and *Miller* on life support and supplement them with a new and multilayered inquiry that seems to be only *Katz*-squared. Returning there, I worry, promises more trouble than help. Instead, I would look to a more traditional Fourth Amendment approach. Even if *Katz* may still supply one way to prove a Fourth Amendment interest, it has never been the only way. Neglecting more traditional approaches may mean failing to vindicate the full protections of the Fourth Amendment.

Our case offers a cautionary example. It seems to me entirely possible a person's cell-site data could qualify as *his* papers or effects under existing law. Yes, the telephone carrier holds the information. But 47 U.S.C. §222 designates a customer's cell-site location information as "customer proprietary network information" (CPNI), §222(h)(1)(A), and gives customers certain rights to control use of and access to CPNI about themselves. The statute generally forbids a carrier to "use, disclose, or permit access to individually identifiable" CPNI without the customer's consent, except as needed to provide the customer's telecommunications services. It also requires the carrier to disclose CPNI "upon affirmative written request by the customer, to any person designated by the customer." Congress even afforded customers a private cause of action for damages against carriers who violate the Act's terms. Plainly, customers have substantial legal interests in this information, including at least some right to include, exclude, and control its use. Those interests might even rise to the level of a property right.

The problem is that we do not know anything more. Before the district court and court of appeals, Mr. Carpenter pursued only a *Katz* "reasonable expectations" argument. He did not invoke the law of property or any analogies to the common law, either there or in his petition for certiorari. Even in his merits brief before this Court, Mr. Carpenter's discussion of his positive law rights in cell-site data was cursory. He offered no analysis, for example, of what rights state law might provide him in addition to those supplied by §222. In these circumstances, I cannot help but conclude—reluctantly—that Mr. Carpenter forfeited perhaps his most promising line of argument.

Unfortunately, too, this case marks the second time this Term that individuals have forfeited Fourth Amendment arguments based on positive law by failing to preserve them. Litigants have had fair notice since at least *United States v. Jones* (2012) and *Florida v. Jardines* (2013) that arguments like these may vindicate Fourth Amendment interests even where *Katz* arguments do not. Yet the arguments have gone unmade, leaving courts to the usual *Katz* hand-waving. These omissions do not serve the development of a sound or fully protective Fourth Amendment jurisprudence.

United States v. Games-Perez

———

Now, a pair of cases showing textualism at work. This first one I've alluded to already: The government prosecuted Miguel Games-Perez for "knowingly violat[ing]" a statute that prohibits (1) a convicted felon from (2) possessing a firearm in interstate commerce. In response, Mr. Games-Perez argued that he didn't know about his felony status. After all, the court that convicted him told him the crime wasn't a felony. But Mr. Games-Perez's argument was a losing one under Tenth Circuit precedent, which did not require the government to prove the defendant's knowledge of his felony status. So Mr. Games-Perez asked the whole circuit to rehear his case and revisit its precedent. A majority declined, and what follows is an excerpt from my dissent in which I argued that the text's terms favored Mr. Games-Perez. Tellingly, the government didn't much dispute this and instead rested its case largely on legislative history. The result? On its view, people were left to sit imprisoned—for close to five years in the case of Mr. Games-Perez—on the basis of something other than the written law. (After I joined the Supreme Court, we took up a similar case in Rehaif v. United States *[2019], and came to a very different judgment.)*

PEOPLE SIT IN PRISON BECAUSE OUR CIRCUIT'S CASE LAW ALLOWS the government to put them there without proving a statutorily specified element of the charged crime. Today, this court votes narrowly, 6 to 4, against revisiting this state of affairs. So Mr. Games-Perez will remain behind bars, without the opportunity to present to a jury his argument that he committed no crime at all under the law of the land. Of course, rehearing *en banc* is reserved only for questions of exceptional importance. And I fully appreciate the considered judgment of my colleagues who vote against reconsidering our circuit precedent: after all, it is both longstanding and consistent with the rulings of several other courts. Even so, I respectfully submit this extraordinary situation warrants reconsideration.

Mr. Games-Perez was prosecuted for "knowingly violat[ing]" a statute that prohibits (1) a convicted felon (2) from possessing a firearm (3) in interstate commerce. But to win a conviction under our governing panel precedent, the government had to prove *only* that Mr. Games-Perez knew he possessed a firearm, *not* that he also knew he was a convicted felon. And, as I have explained before, it is difficult to see how someone might "knowingly violate[]" this statute without knowing he satisfies all the substantive elements that make his conduct criminal—especially the *first* substantive element Congress expressly identified. Just stating our precedent's holding makes the problem clear enough: its interpretation—reading Congress's *mens rea* (mental state) requirement as leapfrogging over the first statutorily specified element and touching down only at the second listed element—defies grammatical gravity and linguistic logic. Ordinarily, after all, when a criminal statute introduces the elements of a crime with the word "knowingly," that *mens rea* requirement must be applied "to *all* the subsequently listed [substantive] elements of the crime." Nor is this a situation where "knowingly" begins a long statutory phrase containing several elements and a reasonable question arises how far into the thicket the "knowingly" adverbial modifier extends. If the statute before us had said "whoever knowingly possesses a firearm after being convicted of a crime," it might be possible to argue that "knowingly" modifies only "possesses a firearm" and not the later prepositional phrase, "after being convicted of a crime." But that's just not the grammar we face here. Here, Congress gave us three elements in a particular order. And it makes no sense to read the word "knowingly" as so modest that it might blush in the face of the very first element only to regain its composure and reappear at the second.

This court's failure to hold the government to its congressionally specified burden of proof means Mr. Games-Perez might very well be wrongfully imprisoned. After all, a state court judge repeatedly (if mistakenly) represented to him that the state court deferred judgment on which his current conviction hinges did not constitute a felony conviction. Given these repeated misstatements from the court itself, Mr. Games-Perez surely has a triable claim he didn't know his state court deferred judgment amounted to a felony conviction. Yet the government never had to face a trial on this question; it never had to prove its case that Mr. Games-Perez knew of his felon status. It was allowed instead to imprison him without the question even being asked.

There can be fewer graver injustices in a society governed by the rule of law than imprisoning a man without requiring proof of his guilt under the written laws of the land. Yet that is what our precedent permits, excusing the government from proving an essential element of the crime Congress recognized. I believe that mistaken decision should be overruled.

What's particularly noteworthy is that the government offers no colorable defense of our precedent on the basis of the statutory language at issue. While not dispositive of the statute's meaning, this glaring omission surely says something, and something not at all good, about the plausibility of our precedent and the appropriateness of Mr. Games-Perez's conviction.

What's more, the extra-textual argument the government does press in response to the petition for rehearing hardly fills the void. The government rests its case entirely on the basis of a legislative history exegesis found in a divided decision of the Fourth Circuit. According to the government, that opinion shows that, although our statute's predecessors did not contain an explicit *mens rea*, courts interpreting them required the government to prove that the defendant knew the object he possessed was a firearm—but not that the defendant knew of his felon status. From this, the government surmises, when Congress added the word "knowingly" to our statute, it must have meant only to adopt this judicial gloss and no more.

The problem with all this is that hidden intentions never trump expressed ones. Whatever weight courts may give to judicial interpretations of predecessor statutes when the current statute is ambiguous, those prior interpretations of now defunct statutes carry no weight when the language of the current statute is clear. When the current statute's language is clear, it must be enforced just as

Congress wrote it. And whatever the legislative history may or may not suggest about Congress's collective "intent" (putting aside the difficulties of trying to say anything definitive about the intent of 535 legislators and the executive, and putting aside as well the Fourth Circuit dissent and its powerful rejoinders about Congress's putative intent in this case), the law before us that survived the gauntlet of bicameralism and presentment couldn't be plainer. By its express terms, the statute does not authorize the government to imprison Mr. Games-Perez and people like him unless and until the government can show they knew of their felon status at the time of the alleged offense. The government did not attempt to prove as much here. And that is all we need to know. Congress could have written the law differently than it did, and it is always free to rewrite the law when it wishes. But in our legal order it is the role of the courts to apply the law as it is written, not some different law Congress might have written in the past or might write in the future.

Besides, even if the government could somehow manage to squeeze an ambiguity out of the plain statutory text before us, it faces another intractable problem. The Supreme Court has long recognized a "presumption" grounded in our common law tradition that a *mens rea* requirement attaches to "each of the statutory elements that criminalize otherwise innocent conduct." Our statute operates to criminalize the possession of any kind of gun. But gun possession is often lawful and sometimes even protected as a matter of constitutional right. The only statutory element separating innocent (even constitutionally protected) gun possession from criminal conduct is a prior felony conviction. So the presumption that the government must prove *mens rea* here applies with full force. Yet, for its part the government never explains how a much disputed legislative record can overcome this longstanding interpretive presumption.

In the end, I do not for a moment question that the standard for rehearing *en banc* is a high one or that the arguments one might muster against rehearing are thoughtful or principled. In my judgment, however, none of these arguments compels us to perpetuate the injustice of disregarding the plain terms of the law Congress wrote and denying defendants the day in court that law promises them. To the contrary, this case presents the surely exceptional situation where rehearing is appropriate to "give effect to [Congress's] plain command, even if doing that will reverse . . . longstanding practice." The Supreme Court has told us time and again that "[a]ge is no antidote to clear inconsistency with a statute." And while we must and do always take special care before expressing disagreement with other circuits and reversing our own panel precedents, sometimes these things are done because they must be done. The Supreme Court has not hesitated to give effect to the unambiguous meaning of a congressional command even when all circuits to have addressed the question have failed to abide the statute's express terms. Respectfully, I submit, this is a case where we should follow the Court's lead, enforce the law as Congress wrote it, and grant Mr. Games-Perez the day in court the law guarantees him.

United States v. Rentz

—

If Games-Perez highlights the problem with straying from the statutory text, here's an excerpt from a case that shows the virtues of sticking to it. Here, the Tenth Circuit faced (a different part of) the very same statute at issue in Games-Perez but used textualism rather than hidden legislative intentions to resolve the dispute. In the process, we used one of textualism's most basic tools: good old-fashioned sentence diagramming. My daughter's high school English teacher, a good friend of mine, appreciated this one.

FEW STATUTES HAVE PROVEN AS ENIGMATIC AS 18 U.S.C. §924(C). Everyone knows that, generally speaking, the statute imposes heightened penalties on those who use guns to commit violent crimes or drug offenses. But the details are full of devils. Originally passed in 1968, today the statute says that "any person who, during and in relation to any crime of violence or drug trafficking crime . . . uses or carries a firearm, or who, in furtherance of any such crime, possesses a firearm, shall, in addition to the punishment provided for such crime . . . be sentenced to a term of imprisonment of not less than 5 years." That bramble of prepositional phrases may excite the grammar teacher but it's certainly kept the federal courts busy. What does it mean to "use" a gun "during and in relation to" a drug trafficking offense? What does and doesn't qualify as a "crime of violence"? And then there's the question posed by this case: What is the statute's proper unit of prosecution? The parties before us agree that Philbert Rentz "used" a gun only once but did so "during and in relation to" two separate "crimes of violence"—by firing a single shot that hit and injured one victim but then managed to strike and kill another. In circumstances like these, does the statute permit the government to charge one violation or two?

This circuit and virtually every other has held that for each separate charge it pursues under the statute the government must prove a separate crime of violence or drug trafficking crime. The government admits this burden and no one asks us to revisit it. But what about the statute's discussion of uses, carries, and possessions? Must the government also prove a separate one of those for each separate charge it brings?

Cases like Mr. Rentz's are hardly unusual. In an age when the manifest of federal criminal offenses stretches ever longer, a parsimonious pleader can easily describe a defendant's single use of a firearm as happening "during and in relation to" multiple qualifying crimes. Like when a defendant shoots a potential witness against him—committing at once the separate crimes of murder and the killing of a witness. Or when a defendant brandishes a weapon to induce his victim to surrender a car and come with him—committing in the process the crimes of car-jacking and kidnapping. Or when a defendant points a gun at his victim and demands that she call relatives for cash—giving rise to both an unlawful ransom demand and attempted extortion. In all these circumstances and many more besides, deciding what is required to prove each charge matters greatly, determining whether the defendant will face five or ten years in prison or more like thirty years to life.

When seeking a statute's unit of prosecution—when asking what the minimum amount of activity a defendant must undertake, what he must do, to commit each new and independent violation of a criminal statute—the feature that naturally draws our immediate attention is the statute's verb. This comes as no surprise, of course, as the verb supplies the action or doing part of most any sentence, statutory or otherwise. True, in the business of statutory interpretation we do not always bow to linguistic rules. A court's job, after all, is to discern the statute's meaning not grade its grammar, and sometimes a law's meaning can be clear even when the grammar's downright awful. But until a clue emerges suggesting otherwise, it's not unreasonable to think that Congress used the English language according to its conventions. And in the statute's language we find three relevant verbs: uses, carries, and possesses. This alone supplies some evidence that each charge must involve an independent act of using, carrying, or possessing. After all, if a law's verb says it's a crime to kill someone, we usually think a defendant must kill more than one person to be found guilty of more than one offense. That's the action necessary to support each and every unit of prosecution. The statute's verbs make it a crime to use, carry, or possess a firearm in certain circumstances. So reading it like our homicide statute and in accord with the normal rules of statutory (and sentence) construction goes some way to suggest that every new conviction requires a new act falling into one of those three categories.

Another linguistic clue points in the same direction. The statute doesn't prohibit using or carrying or possessing a gun in isolation. Nor could it, for guns often may be lawfully used, carried, or possessed: the Constitution guarantees as much. Instead, the statute prohibits using or carrying a gun during and in relation to any crime of violence or drug trafficking crime, or possessing a gun in furtherance of any such crime. These adverbial prepositional phrases modify the verbs uses, carries, and possesses. They tell us which acts of using, carrying, or possessing Congress sought to punish—explaining that the statute doesn't seek to make illegal all such acts, only the narrower subset the phrases specify.

Simplified somewhat, the language looks like this:

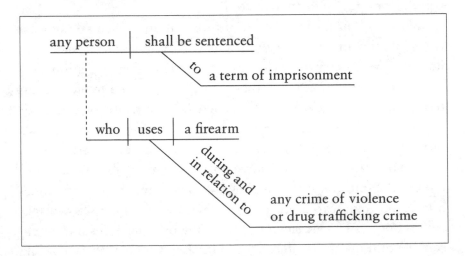

Visualized this way it's hard to see how the total number of charges might ever exceed the number of uses, carries, or possessions. Just as you can't throw more touchdowns during the fourth quarter than the total number of times you have thrown a touchdown, you cannot use a firearm during and in relation to crimes of violence more than the total number of times you have used a firearm. So it is we now have in hand a pair of textual clues, clues suggesting that each charge must involve both an act of using, carrying, or possessing and that such an act must come during and in relation to (or in furtherance of) a qualifying crime.

To the extent ambiguity remains, we don't default to the most severe possible interpretation of the statute but to the rule of lenity. Our job is always in the first instance to follow Congress's directions. But if those directions are unclear, the tie goes to the presumptively free citizen and not the prosecutor. Here that means the government must prove both a use, carry, or possession as well as a qualifying crime. The rule of lenity seeks to ensure legislatures, not prosecutors, decide the circumstances when people may be sent to prison. It seeks to ensure, too, that if a legislature wishes to attach criminal consequences to certain conduct—to deprive persons of their property, liberty, or even lives—it provides fair warning.

Of course, Congress is free if it wishes to amend the statute to state that a second conviction doesn't require a second use, carry, or possession. But unless and until it does, we will not relegate men and women to prison (or to decades more time in prison) because they did something that might—or might not—have amounted to a violation of the law as enacted. "In our legal order it is not the job of independent courts to bend ambiguous statutory subsections in procrustean ways to fit the prosecutor's bill."

4.

THE ART OF
JUDGING

WE OFTEN HEAR THESE DAYS THAT A JUDGE WHO rules for a criminal defendant is "soft" on crime, that a judge who rules against an employee "likes" corporations, and so many other things along those lines. And maybe talking or writing about cases in these simplistic ways is easier and more exciting than trying to communicate the underlying and often technical (and, yes, sometimes boring) legal reasons why one side won and the other lost a particular case. After all, a case that on its surface looks like it's about whether the accused should escape punishment or a worker can recover damages from his employer often winds up really being about a statute of limitations, the demands of precedent, or some essential rule of procedure that one side or the other neglected. And retelling these details is sure a lot less exciting (and a lot less likely to attract eyeballs and clicks).

Maybe, too, we hear so much about judges "liking" or "disliking" this or that group of persons because we've lost sight of the limited job judges are meant to perform under our Constitution. Maybe we've come to think of them like politicians who make law rather than neutral arbiters who are simply supposed to follow it. Yet judges in our constitutional order aren't supposed to act like philosopher-kings, care about their personal popularity, or spend time guessing whether their decisions will win acclaim or promote one cause or another. In the last chapter, I discussed some of the tools of interpretation that can help keep a judge safe from these pitfalls. But like any job, there's more to it than the tools; there's the art of how those tools are used, and that's the subject of this chapter.

When it comes to the art of judging, I've learned over the years from watching my mentors and heroes that a good judge knows a few things. A good judge knows that often the lawyers in the case have lived with it for months or years and thought deeply about it long before the judge enters the picture; they deserve the judge's respect as valuable colleagues whose thinking can be mined and tested to better the judge's own. A good judge recognizes that existing judicial precedents reflect the considered judgment of judges who have come before and sometimes embody the settled expectations of those in our own generation. A good judge listens carefully to colleagues, appreciating the different perspectives each brings to bear. A good judge always questions not only the positions espoused by the litigants but his own tentative conclusions as they evolve. Pride of position and fear of embarrassment associated with changing one's mind play no useful role; regular and healthy doses of self-skepticism always do.

While judging is meant to be a relatively humble business, that does not mean it's an easy one. In every case, someone must win and someone must lose and the only sure guarantee is that 50 percent of the parties before you will be unhappy with your decisions 100 percent of the time. Remaining faithful to the judicial oath to apply, and not to remake, the law means there will be many days when the judge finds himself bound to enforce statutes he personally dislikes or to hold unconstitutional ones he prefers. Often enough, the judge will find himself forced to rule against the "good guy" and in favor of the "bad" one because that is what the law and facts demand. Through it all, the judge can only take faith in the hope that, by enforcing the law's demands rather than his preferences, he is serving a larger purpose by helping make real the rule of law and passing down its vital protections from one generation to the next.

To do this and no more can be a lonely business. When a social crisis presses or a case becomes heated, the calls for that day's going conception of "justice" are sure to multiply loudly. People can easily forget that the law is meant to protect the beloved and the detested alike, and a judge who enforces the law equally for disfavored and favored persons alike will not usually win a popularity contest. But our founders knew, expected, and even demanded this. To secure the "inflexible and uniform adherence to the rights of the Constitution," they knew judges would need to show "fortitude" and "integrity" (*Federalist No. 78*). To encourage that kind of judicial courage—and to that end alone—they afforded judges extraordinary independence from the political branches and electoral pressures.

When I think of courageous judges, I sometimes think of Frank Johnson, whose story is beautifully told in his obituary and by Judge Kethledge and Michael Erwin in *Lead Yourself First: Inspiring Leadership Through Solitude*. Appointed to the bench by President Eisenhower, Judge Johnson served first as a district and later as a circuit judge in his home state of Alabama. Seeking to follow the original understanding of the Equal Protection Clause and Supreme Court precedents like *Brown v. Board of Education,* he issued one decision after another that protected the civil rights of African-Americans in a time and place that required high measures of both fortitude and integrity. Johnson once said that his "philosophy as a trial judge and as an appellate judge is to follow the law and the facts without regard to the consequences." Whether he meant "consequences" for the parties or for himself or both I don't know, but the fact is that ruling according to the law and the facts alone was no easy thing. As a result of his rulings, his community branded him a pariah. He was shunned on the street and snubbed in church. His life was threatened repeatedly; crosses were even burned on his front lawn. His circle of friends grew small. To be sure, as he became a villain to some he became a hero to others. *Time* magazine put him on its cover in 1967. But there's a lesson here too. For while in his day the judge was both hated and revered, the reality is that few remember him today. And that, I've learned, is exactly how it should be. For a good judge knows that flattery and scorn alike are fleeting and false guides.

I think that is exactly what Justice White was trying to teach me so many years ago as we walked that hallway filled with portraits of past justices, and what he was trying to teach me when he later shared one of his favorite poems, "If," which includes these lines:

> If you can trust yourself when all men doubt you,
> But make allowance for their doubting too . . .
>
> Or being hated, don't give way to hating . . .
>
> If you can meet with Triumph and Disaster
> And treat those two impostors just the same . . .
>
> Yours is the Earth and everything that's in it. . . .

ON COURAGE

———

After my first full term on the Supreme Court, Drake University invited me to speak to its incoming students. The new students were sure to learn plenty about the law in their upcoming classes. So I hoped to encourage them to think about something else they will need as they head into our profession and civic society: courage. This speech may be directed to aspiring lawyers and judges, but I hope its themes speak more broadly too.

T HANK YOU FOR INVITING ME. I AM DELIGHTED TO BE IN IOWA AT the home of one of the country's oldest law schools, in fact the second oldest west of the Mississippi. As a product of the West myself, I can only imagine the foresight and courage of those who decided to start a law school in Des Moines in 1865, when this half of the country was pretty rugged—and in many ways pretty proudly lawless too.

I understand most of you are incoming first-year students. Soon enough you will be neck deep in cases and statutes, rules and regulations. So today I want to take advantage of a quiet moment before all that begins to talk about something that cannot be easily learned by reading textbooks—something that's often given too little attention in the legal profession, and something the founders of your law school displayed.

That something is courage. Courage has been essential to the rule of law in this country from the beginning. The Declaration of Independence itself was, at heart, a complaint that the king had denied colonists the rule of law. As justification for their rebellion, colonists

cited the fact the king had withheld assent to duly enacted legislation, refused trial by jury, and prevented colonists from playing a
significant role in their own governance. About half of the fifty-six
colonists who signed the Declaration were lawyers. They quite literally put their lives on the line to secure a representative government
and one of just laws: By signing the Declaration, they became marked
men who faced certain death if their cause failed.

Courage remains as important in the legal profession today as it
was then. Through our history the lawyers who have made the greatest mark on this country haven't done so because they were smarter
or were born into better families or held more important positions;
it was because they were willing to stand firm for justice in the face
of immense pressure and often at grave personal costs.

The truth is, whatever role you wind up playing in this profession,
courage will be required of you. There will be times when you will be
tested by a client, an opposing party, or, yes, even a judge. When the
temptation to give in and go along rather than stand firm in aid of a
just cause will be great. These moments will come in large cases and
in small ones, when everyone seems to be looking and when no one
is around. Sometimes the need for courage will be obvious; sometimes it will be easy to overlook. But courage is a lawyerly virtue
every one of us needs to cultivate.

What do I mean by courage? Well, let's start with what I don't
mean. I don't mean blind bullheadedness or rudeness or incivility.
We have all too much of those things in our culture and in our profession. They are pretenders of courage, not the real thing. For true
courage will often require you to admit a mistake, hold your tongue,
or wait to fight another day. When it requires you to stand up against
the powers arrayed around you, it will also require you to do so with
not just respect but affection for your fellow citizen. What I mean by
courage is what Atticus Finch meant by it in *To Kill a Mockingbird*.
You may remember that Finch defended an African-American man
wrongly accused of raping a white woman in Alabama during the
Great Depression—and that in taking on the representation he faced
criticism and threats from his friends and community. As he told his
daughter in the book: "I wanted you to see what real courage is, instead of getting the idea that courage is a man with a gun in his

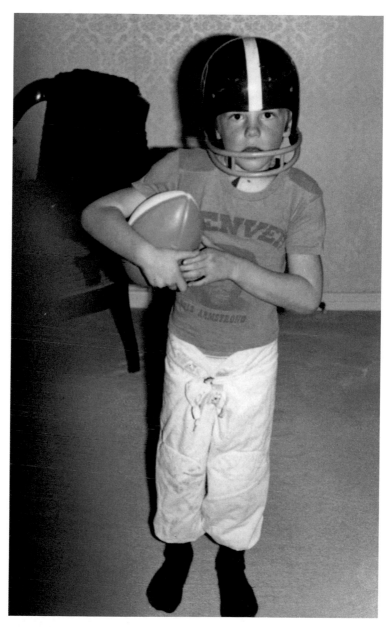

As a fourth-generation Coloradan, in my family most everything else came to a stop when the Broncos played.

My grandmother
Freda's family built
the Hotel Wolf
in Saratoga,
Wyoming. It remains
a regular stop on
summer family trips
through the
mountains.

My father, David,
and his father, John,
on their way to
go fishing in
the Colorado
mountains, the
favorite family
pastime
then and now.

My grandfather John as a young man in his law office during the
Great Depression, just down the street from where I later served
as a Tenth Circuit judge.

John (third from left) worked his way through school as a streetcar
operator. Here he is years later at a reunion. Even when he was
eighty-nine years old, he could still name all the streets east to west
across old Denver.

My grandfather and grandmother Joe and Dorothy McGill raised seven children, six of them girls. Mom is third from the left.

My mother, Anne, was the first woman in the Denver District Attorney's office. Can you spot her?

Life in Niwot,
Colorado.
From top to
bottom: Morris
and Nibbles;
Ponio; baby chicks
brought from the
barn by the girls
to "visit" my
home office.

Some of my happiest memories: fishing on the Colorado River with my daughters, Emma and Belinda.

With Justice White, October Term 1993. It was an honor to serve as a law clerk to the only other Supreme Court justice from Colorado. He was hardworking, even in retirement, and humble despite his achievements.

November 20, 2006, at the Byron R. White Courthouse in Denver. Emma and Belinda help me put on my robe for the first time, as Justice Kennedy (left) and my new colleagues look on.

In the Lincoln Bedroom preparing my remarks for the announcement of my nomination on the evening of January 31, 2017.

The East Room announcement begins. The next day, on what would've been my father's eightieth birthday, my nomination was formally filed with the U.S. Senate.

Immediately after the announcement of my nomination, Father Paul Scalia, on the far right, next to his mother, Maureen Scalia, offers a prayer in the Green Room.

On my arrival in Washington, my team had me walking miles through the Senate tunnels, meeting with every senator who asked, over eighty in all. I was fortunate to have the counsel and support of some remarkable people, including (left to right) Mary Elizabeth Taylor, Senator Kelly Ayotte, and Mike McGinley.

The confirmation process sometimes seemed lonely and overwhelming, but Louise and I were so grateful for the support of our family, our friends, and my former law clerks. Many came to Washington from across the country to help in any way they could. They made all the difference.

Justice Kennedy administers the Judicial Oath in the Rose Garden with Louise holding the family bible on April 10, 2017. It marked the first time a justice and his former clerk came to serve as colleagues.

On a date in England with Louise and Barnaby. Louise and I met at Oxford. Later, she moved to the United States with me and became an American citizen.

Investiture at the Supreme Court, June 15, 2017. I've learned that you may lose your balance from time to time, but the people who love you will set you right.

Leroy the Elk, as displayed in my chambers, courtesy of Maureen Scalia. His story is told on page 23.

A fishing adventure in Colorado with Justice Scalia, 2014.

Life at the Court, 2018 clerk skit. After working hard all term, the clerks let off some steam and take a few good-natured shots at their bosses.

The Court, at the time of my arrival.

The Old Granary Burying Ground, Boston, Massachusetts, where Increase Sumner lies. This is from the epitaph on his tomb; I keep a copy on my desk and turn to it often:

Here Repose the Remains of
INCREASE SUMNER.
He was born at Roxbury
November 27th, 1746
and died at the same place,
June 7th, 1799 in
the 53d year of his age. . . .

As a lawyer, he was faithful and able; as a judge, patient, impartial, and decisive; as a chief magistrate, accessible, frank, and independent. In private life, he was affectionate and mild; in public life, he was dignified and firm. Party feuds were allayed by the correctness of his conduct; calumny was silenced by the weight of his virtues; and rancor softened by the amenity of his manners.

hand. It's when you know you're licked before you begin but you begin anyway and see it through no matter what."

THE FACT IS, OUR Constitution depends on and presupposes courageous lawyers of this kind. Consider the Sixth Amendment. It provides that "[i]n all criminal prosecutions, the accused shall enjoy the right . . . to have the Assistance of Counsel for his defence." When all the might of the leviathan is turned on a person, when he stands alone with nowhere else to look, he is at least guaranteed a lawyer. A lawyer who is expected to represent the least powerful and the most unpopular; to do so often for little pay and without regard to his own professional advancement. In our adversarial system, courage is equally expected from those of you who will be on the other side of the courtroom. The powers of a prosecutor, and the discretion to turn the might of the government against anyone of his choosing, are vast. So, too, is the temptation to focus on easy and unpopular prey. The pressure to *win*—pressure from your community and your co-workers, and pressure to further your own career—can be immense.

Let me mention two models of lawyerly courage that might inspire you when times like these come. In March 1770, a grand jury indicted a British captain, Thomas Preston, and his men for the death of several colonists in what came to be called the Boston Massacre. If the soldiers were found guilty, they could face the death penalty. Yet the redcoats were so unpopular in the local community that they had a hard time finding a lawyer to represent them. It wasn't until they approached John Adams and Josiah Quincy that they found someone willing to lead their defense.

Adams, of course, went on to become president of the United States. But when he took on the case as a local lawyer, he was worried that it could harm his reputation, his political future, his financial well-being, and even the safety of his family. None of that stopped him. And in the end, he persuaded the jury to acquit most of the soldiers. Years later, he recalled: "The Part I took in Defence of Cptn. Preston and the Soldiers, procured me Anxiety, and Obloquy enough. It was, however, one of the most . . . disinterested Actions of my whole Life, and one of the best Pieces of Service I ever rendered my Country. Judgment of Death against those Soldiers would have been [a] foul . . . Stain upon this Country."

Quincy even had to fend off pressure from his father. The father criticized his son for "advocat[ing] for those criminals who are charged with the murder of their fellow-citizens." Yet Quincy didn't hesitate to reply: "[C]riminals . . . are entitled by the laws of God and man, to all legal counsel and aid; that my duty as a man obliged me to undertake; that my duty as a lawyer strengthened the obligation. . . . I never harboured the expectation, nor any great desire, that all men should speak well of me. To inquire my duty, and to do it, is my aim."

Of course, lawyerly courage hardly guarantees that you will prevail in courts of law, let alone in courts of public opinion. Take this example Neal Katyal has reminded us of from the *Korematsu* case where the Supreme Court wrongly upheld the mass internment of American citizens of Japanese descent during World War II. During the proceedings, senior Department of Justice officials prepared a brief representing to the Supreme Court that Japanese Americans were engaging in espionage on a large scale and posed a national security threat. But two relatively young Justice Department lawyers, Edward Ennis and John Burling, were aware of evidence from the Office of Naval Intelligence and the FBI undermining this claim and sought to have the government's brief amended. The pair appealed to an assistant attorney general for aid, writing that "it was highly unfair to this racial minority that these lies, put out in an official publication, go uncorrected. . . . The Attorney General should not be deprived of the present, and perhaps only, chance to set the record straight." In the end, the record was not set straight for many years, until well after Ennis and Burling died. In fact, it took until 2011 when Katyal, then serving as acting solicitor general, took the admirable step of acknowledging the government's failure to be fully forthcoming to the Court. The Court itself finally and formally disavowed *Korematsu* only in 2018.

Of course, Ennis and Burling were no less courageous because they failed—indeed, that is the essence of courage. To know that you face a choice that may harm you in concrete and meaningful ways.

To know that you may gain nothing but scorn in return for your risk, and that your decision may never be vindicated. And then, *knowing* all this, to step forward anyway.

HOW DO YOU CULTIVATE lawyerly courage? It starts right here, right now, in your first days in law school. "[Y]ou need to decide now," at the beginning, "what kind of lawyer you want to be," what kind of life story you want to be able to tell at the end of it all. After all, it's only by seeing the target that you have much chance of hitting it. Then, once you have your eyes on the destination, you must begin to behave in ways designed to take you there and see it through, no matter what. As my friend Judge Patrick Schiltz would say, you must live your ideals "[a]lways. Everywhere. In big things and small."

Make a daily habit of courage in small matters, and that habit will enable you to persevere when the big ones arrive. From your first day of law school, you must choose whether to volunteer your thoughts and insights in the classroom. You may be afraid of public speaking, or simply worry that you will look foolish. Remember what Patton said: Courage is just fear hanging on one minute longer. So hang on just a little longer and speak up. Next year, you will choose whether to take difficult classes or easy ones. Take the risk. Throughout your time in law school, remember, too, that while you will have many regrets in life—things done or said, things left undone or unsaid—you will never regret being kind to those around you. The easy path is to shun those with whom you disagree. Show the courage of kindness.

What does this daily habit require of you once you leave these halls and enter practice as a young lawyer? It might be to choose taking up a public-interest cause, to enter public service, or to take some other risk. It will always require you to avoid blindly taking the path of least resistance. To be civil and decent to opposing counsel when your client or boss wants you to act rudely or wrongly. To refuse to pad your time sheet, even when it's late at night, you're facing an hours shortage, and no one's looking. To tell a boss that you won't make an argument because it's untenable and unethical. To acknowledge your own mistakes rather than lay blame on a secretary, a paralegal, a colleague. Now, none of us is perfect. All of us falter and fail to live up to our own ideals. But when that happens, you cannot give up or give in. You must look at yourself squarely in the mirror, warts and all; make a full assessment; and then pick yourself up and begin again.

Some of the challenges you face will come only once you've become a more senior attorney. You may have to tell clients that they have no case or that hiring you to perform a task simply isn't worth the cost to them even though it would feather your nest. You may have to refuse to allow a client to testify falsely—even if no one would ever find out. You may have to tell clients to turn over responsive documents even when they would very much like to hide them and you can even tell yourself some not-implausible-but-not-wholly-persuasive story for giving in. Like John Adams, you may need to take on an unpopular representation. The challenges will only grow, but I hope your response will be the same. Hopefully by then, courage will be a well-practiced habit that comes naturally, if sometimes with real and heavy costs.

STILL DIFFERENT CHALLENGES COME your way when you become a judge. Joining the bench may seem a distant and remote possibility today. But I can tell you that day will be upon some of you sooner than you imagine.

Alexander Hamilton recognized the need for—but the difficulty of—encouraging judicial courage when defending the new Constitution in *The Federalist Papers*. He explained that the job of the judge is to enforce the supreme and enduring law of the Constitution over the current will of the majority even as embodied in duly enacted legislation. To encourage the sort of courage necessary to that unpopular and difficult task, Hamilton noted that the Constitution promised life tenure to judges. Yet even then, Hamilton acknowledged it would still "require an uncommon portion of fortitude in the judges to do their duty as faithful guardians of the Constitution," especially "where legislative invasions of it had been instigated by the major voice of the community." No one, after all, much relishes ridicule, castigation, or derision, even with life tenure.

Our history offers examples of both judges who displayed the kind of uncommon fortitude Hamilton hoped for, as well as those who did not. Consider the second of the famous *Chenery* cases, which concerned FDR's wildly popular New Deal. In the 1940s, the newly created Securities and Exchange Commission issued an order stripping a company's employees of stock they had acquired consistent with the laws at the time. Yet the SEC decided to make the acquisition unlawful retroactively, without any prior notice to the affected parties, penalizing them for past and entirely lawful conduct that they couldn't now change. A majority of the Court acquiesced, justifying the agency's retroactive lawmaking. But Justice Robert Jackson cried foul. Though he had served as FDR's attorney general only years before, though he was himself an architect of the administrative state, he could not see how any government official should be allowed to rewrite the law after the fact. He wrote that the Court's decision approved a naked exercise of "administrative authoritarianism, th[e] power to decide without law." This, he warned, threatened to weaken the very rule of law itself, for the "decision is an ominous one to those who believe that men should be governed by laws that they may ascertain and abide by, and which will guide the action of those in authority as well as of those who are subject to authority." Jackson had to know that his opinion would alienate his friends at 1600 Pennsylvania Avenue and win little popular support. But as he explained, "something does happen to a man when he puts on a judicial robe, and I think it ought to. The change is very great and requires psychological change within a man to get into an attitude of deciding other people's controversies, instead of waging them."

This brave, if lonely, dissent is at least recorded on the pages of the *United States Reports*. But many equal or greater acts of courage occur daily and often with little fanfare in the lower courts throughout our country. Consider what happened to J. Waties Waring. As John Cannon Few has reminded us, Judge Waring stood firm against popular pressures in early civil rights cases that deeply challenged segregated society in his home state of South Carolina. Because of his decisions, his friends and community shunned him and his home was damaged. Thousands of his fellow South Carolinians signed an impeachment petition against him. At one point, when lightning hit Judge Waring's neighbor's house, the neighbor responded with a sign that said: "Dear God, Judge Waring Lives Next Door." A mob even burned a cross in Waring's front yard. Years later, in a speech honoring Waring, a member of the bar observed that "[i]t takes real courage for a judge, in opposition to the deep-seated folkways of those with whom he lives . . . to say, 'This is the law. It is my duty to enforce the law and I will do my duty.' "

Acting in the face of pressure to abstain, though, is only one aspect of judicial courage. There's another and parallel aspect that flies more under the radar, is perhaps harder to accomplish, and may be even more praiseworthy. This form of courage is self-restraint in the exercise of power. It seems to me that the courageous judge recognizes that the Constitution doesn't afford him life tenure so he can invent new laws for which today's passing majority may be clamoring. Instead, he recognizes that his tenure exists for a more timeless purpose, to uphold and defend the Constitution as adopted—and to go no further.

To be sure, we've reached an odd point in our constitutional culture today that this latter form of courage is something we need even mention. But today it sometimes seems that many people in our society think that whatever is bad must be unconstitutional—and whatever is good the Constitution must compel. Some seem to assess judges based not on their technical competence, judicial demeanor, or logical consistency, but simply based on whether they're willing to find this or that popular idea in the Constitution. They do not want judges to decide cases impartially; they seem to want judges who are willing to pick and choose winners and losers based on their favorite policy results. They seek judges who care not about fair process, but who are instead all about ensuring certain favored policy outcomes.

It takes more than a little courage to stand up against this trend. Judge Robert Bork aptly put the point in this way:

> In law, the moment of temptation is the moment of choice, when a judge realizes that in the case before him his strongly

held view of justice, his political and moral imperative, is not embodied in a statute or in any provision of the Constitution. He must then choose between his version of justice and abiding by the American form of government. Yet the desire to do justice, whose nature seems to him obvious, is compelling, while the concept of constitutional process is abstract, rather arid, and the abstinence it counsels unsatisfying. To give in to temptation, this one time, solves an urgent human problem, and a faint crack appears in the American foundation. A judge has begun to rule where a legislator should.

What happens when these cracks appear? Consider *Dred Scott v. Sandford*—one of the darkest hours in the Supreme Court's history. There, the Court went out of its way to bend the Constitution's terms in an effort to try to quell unrest in the country over the question of slavery. The Court invented the legal doctrine of "substantive" due process and then proceeded to use it to hold that Congress had no power to regulate slavery in the Territories. This innovation, the Court thought, would solve a current social crisis. Of course, it did not. Only Justices Benjamin Robbins Curtis and John McLean dissented to explain that the Court's course had no basis in the constitutional text.

A more recent and hopeful example of this kind of judicial courage can be found in *Washington v. Glucksberg*. In that case, the Court was confronted with the question whether the Constitution contained a right to assisted suicide. You might think that assisted suicide is a very good idea as a matter of policy and morality. Or maybe you think that assisted suicide is a very bad idea as a matter of policy and morality. But whatever your personal opinion on these hard questions of *policy* and *morality,* the Court recognized that the question is easy as a matter of *law:* There's absolutely nothing in the Constitution to suggest that it dictates a right to assisted suicide or prevents a self-governing people from regulating the practice. Just as there was nothing in the Constitution that prohibited Congress from regulating slavery in the Territories in *Dred Scott.* Yet here, unlike there, the Court showed the courage of restraint and did not arrogate to itself a decision that the Constitution allowed a self-governing people to make.

———

WHETHER YOU SERVE ULTIMATELY AS a lawyer or judge, I hope as an officer of the court all the same you will help explain these virtues to your clients, your family, and your friends. In popular culture, we often see people deriding judges who issue unpopular rulings or lawyers who represent unpopular clients. We see those who confuse a judge's ruling or a lawyer's representation with support for the person's cause or personal favoritism or bias. They suggest that when a judge rules for a corporation, he loves corporations. Or that when a lawyer represents a criminal defendant, he loves criminals.

Attacks like these miss the mark. They misunderstand completely the roles of the judge and lawyer. I hope you will help remind those you encounter that if they want to secure their own liberty from oppression, they should want lawyers and judges who are unafraid to follow the law where it leads and enforce the law fearlessly, without bending to the passing whims and wishes of public opinion. For one day, too, you might remind your friends, they could find themselves braced against the prevailing winds of the day, in need of a lawyer and facing a judge. And when that day comes, I hope you will ask them, would they rather stand before a court of public opinion or a court of law?

(HOW) DO JUDGES THINK?

———

Early in my tenure as a Tenth Circuit judge, I was asked to participate in a lecture series before Oklahoma City lawyers and judges named in honor of Judge William Holloway. By that point, Bill Holloway had been a member of the Tenth Circuit for almost as long as I had been alive. His life and career were a model for all of us who had the privilege of serving with him, even if his deep and honest humility wouldn't ever allow him to admit it. I sought to honor his example that night by speaking about some of the judicial virtues I had watched him exemplify and some of the vices he took care to avoid.

IT IS A PLEASURE TO BE PART OF A LECTURE SERIES NAMED IN HONOR of my colleague Bill Holloway. Judge Holloway is universally admired by the members of the Tenth Circuit, as I know he is by members of the bar in Oklahoma. To be a part of a lecture series that is an ongoing, living tribute to Bill and Helen Holloway is a humbling privilege.

The organizers of tonight's event asked if I would share some reflections on what it's like to be a still-somewhat-new federal appellate judge. Though now three years into the job, I confess the memory of my first day on the bench won't soon fade. I donned the robe, shook hands with my colleagues, and headed into the courtroom. But as I ascended the steps to the bench, I stepped on the bottom of my robe, tripped, and just about sent my papers flying. I spent the remainder of the day's arguments red in embarrassment. When I finally made it back to chambers, my wife called to ask how my day went. After I sheepishly recounted my misadventure, she advised me, "Neil, you have to lift your hem as you climb stairs." So it was that my first lesson in judging was really a lesson in fashion. And so it is that tonight I will offer a peek inside the robing room and hazard a few early—and so necessarily tentative—reflections on how an appellate judge thinks.

In approaching this topic—how appellate judges think—I recognize it is a delicate one. One fraught with disagreement. One on which some harbor grave reservations. After all, many of our brothers and sisters on the district court doubt whether appellate judges think at all. Or whether appellate judges can only do so in groups of three or more. Or whether the deferential standards of review we appellate judges owe to district courts really mean appellate judges are best off not even trying to think. And there is something admittedly peculiar about the role of the appellate judge. As the saying goes, it is the duty of the district court judge to be quick in ruling and courteous to the litigants. But does that mean judges of the court of appeals always have to be slow and crapulous? I hope not, even if I suspect some of the district judges in the room may harbor a different opinion on that one.

In approaching the peculiar role of the intermediate federal appellate judge, let me begin in the same way, suggesting first what the judge hopefully is not before focusing on what the judge might aspire to be. Now, I realize this is a roundabout way to proceed. Still, I follow this route not only because it is easier, but also because I can't help it. After all, even now I remain a member of the only profession known to mankind that could call a ten-thousand-word document a "brief."

What is it that I want to exclude from the idea of the good appellate judge? It's the idea that the appellate judge should or does decide cases based on his views of social policy. It seems this view of judging is everywhere these days. Television, movies, and popular culture all reinforce the view of the judge as some autocrat issuing idiosyncratic orders from his armchair. Yet, somewhat surprisingly, this view of judging is also sometimes given a degree of credence, though in a much more sophisticated form, by members of our own tribe.

In particular, I have in mind here my Seventh Circuit colleague

Richard Posner. Judge Posner is among the most accomplished federal appellate judges in our country. He is renowned for his intellectual prowess and efficiency—I hear he can simultaneously write an opinion with his right hand and a book with his left. But my sincere respect (and even envy) of Judge Posner notwithstanding, I must respectfully dissent from the thesis of his recent book, entitled *How Judges Think,* a title on which I have played a bit in the title of my remarks tonight.

In his book, Judge Posner advocates what he calls judicial pragmatism. He tells us that, at least in hard cases where there isn't yet a clear legal rule, judges can and should assess the potential consequences of available outcomes, and choose the one that they think, based on their personal assessment, will yield the best consequences for society. As he puts it, "American appellate courts are councils of wise elders . . . and it is not completely insane to entrust them with responsibility for resolving these disputes in a way that will produce the best results in the circumstances rather than resolving them purely on the basis of rules created by other organs of government or by their own previous decisions."

But how is this supposed to work? By the time cases reach us in an appellate court, both sides usually have a good story about how deciding in their favor would advance the social good—especially in the hard cases Judge Posner discusses. In criminal cases, for example, we often hear arguments from the government about how its view would promote the goods of public security and finality. Meanwhile, from the defense we often hear about how its view would promote the goods of personal liberty and procedural fairness. How is the judge supposed to weigh or rank these radically different goods? How is the judge supposed to say one is more important or socially preferable to another? The problem is, the pragmatic model of judging offers us no value or rule to compare or rank which costs and benefits are to be preferred and which aren't. It's sort of like asking judges to decide which is better: the taste of steak or the look of a mountain? Both are good and maybe I can tell you which I prefer, but my preference is only that, a preference—not something based on any principled analysis. In a very real way, then, the pragmatic enterprise is senseless, impossible; or, to borrow a phrase, it is rationally indeterminate. It may help us identify the costs and benefits, but it doesn't offer any guide on which to choose.

This, in turn, brings into view a separate and maybe bigger problem with the pragmatic approach to judging. In a representative democracy, deciding which competing social good to choose and which to forgo generally isn't supposed to be left to judges. We are a nation governed by the consent of the people. It is usually they, through the Constitution they adopted or through the representatives they elect, who are supposed to choose between and prioritize the many competing goods that are worthy of our attention—deciding, say, how much of our collective social resources should be devoted this year to promoting education of the young versus caring for the elderly. Or how much to devote this year to guns versus butter. Or to take two more mundane but real examples of the sorts of things our Congress debates—whether to fund this year either barnyard fly control in Colorado or a sheep museum in Wyoming.

The point is that we are a nation under laws as adopted by the people, not a nation ruled by unelected elders. Federal legislation must survive the arduous procedures prescribed by the Constitution. Procedures that force compromise and thus ensure that at least some social consensus has been hammered out before a new law may bind the nation. How can it be "pragmatic" to say that a few unelected judges are entitled to do the job constitutionally assigned elsewhere? For that matter, are we really sure that we would do a better job? We lawyers and judges are trained in logical reasoning, not the social sciences, economics, business, sociology, or management. Even if pragmatism were permissible, as a matter of institutional competence would it be sensible to assign judges the job?

What's more, if hard and ambiguous cases liberate judges to act as councils of elders who tote up consequences and proceed to the result they consider socially optimal, no doubt judges will find a great many cases to be hard and ambiguous. Why would a judge want to spend hours parsing convoluted statutory and contractual language, or reviewing a voluminous administrative record, when he could just announce his own preferred rule? Sometimes I'd rather suffer an appendectomy than scour through a joint appendix. Legal clarity thus becomes the chain that binds the brilliant judge from fixing society. The clever judge has every incentive to wrest himself from that chain—to find the liberating ambiguities necessary to become a benevolent social engineer.

Of course, there are some truly hard cases, plenty of them. And judging is more of an art than some mechanical science always yielding a single obviously right answer. So, one might ask, what are judges supposed to do when faced with, say, a cryptic congressional statute whose meaning is genuinely ambiguous? *Federalist No. 78* long ago put its finger on the essential attribute of the good appellate judge when it called on members of the judicial branch to bear in mind the distinction between what it called the exercise of political will and the exercise of legal judgment, noting that judges in our constitutional system do well to avoid "the substitution of their pleasure to that of the legislative body." It is, in other words, the judge's job to employ not his own will but the traditional tools of legal analysis—the various canons of statutory construction, rules of grammar, analogies to precedent, and the like—in an effort to discern the meaning of Congress's commands. Of course, judges sometimes disagree about which tools of legal analysis are most helpful in the art of ascertaining Congress's meaning in hard cases. They also sometimes disagree over the order of priority we should assign to these competing tools. And they sometimes even disagree over the results these tools yield in particular cases. But debates like these reflect a genuine concern with how we can best reach or approximate Congress's will, not our own.

Many other features of our legal system do much to encourage this view of the good judge. One of them is the adversarial process. When I was his law clerk many years ago, Judge David Sentelle of the D.C. Circuit liked to remind me, in his North Carolina drawl, that "in this country, Neeeilll, we have a little thing called party control of litigation." It seems to me that the good judge recognizes that, in our adversarial process, many of the lawyers in the cases before us have lived with and thought deeply about the legal issues for months or years before the judge ever comes on the scene. Unlike continental Europe, where the judge often charts the course of litigation in an inquisitorial search for the truth, our common law system generally affords litigants the opportunity and duty to choose which arguments to advance and how to develop the record. We usually depend on the parties rather than a judicial bureaucracy to identify, limit, and sharpen the issues for our decision. The judges I have come to know generally have a healthy dose of skepticism about their capacities to arrive at the optimal legal answer in complex cases purely by self-direction. Instead, they rely heavily on members of the bar as partners in the process of identifying the issues and arguments for decision.

Another constraint on the judicial function lies in the collegial process of deciding appeals. We do not sit alone, but work in panels—or, as a veteran appellate attorney might put it, in packs. This process rewards efforts to reach consensus. To be sure, consensus isn't always possible, or even necessarily desirable. After all, who would have wanted Justice Harlan to forgo his dissent in *Plessy* calling on the Court to recognize the true meaning of the constitutional promise of equal protection of the laws due all persons? One of the most important aspects of the judge's role is to bear faith to the meaning of the Constitution or a statute in the face of criticism and majoritarian opposition. Ours is often a counter-majoritarian function, aimed at protecting the constitutional rights of every person, even (and perhaps especially) in the face of strong opposition.

At the same time, the process of at least trying to obtain consensus within the court often serves to illuminate the more subtle issues, sharpen the analysis, and help guard against individual biases, temptations, and willful preferences. It also means that a nuance one colleague may miss might be captured and corrected by another. The model here for me is again my first boss out of law school, David Sentelle. During the time I clerked for him, he first issued a panel opinion going one way but, later, changed his mind and wrote an *en banc* opinion (for the full court) reversing his own panel opinion. I admired the humility he showed, and the careful consideration he gave to his colleagues' views. In this respect, the Tenth Circuit may be particularly blessed. Even when we do not agree, our interactions and opinions are usually collegial and we do not hesitate to change our minds when a colleague sees something we may have missed. I think that serves the people of this part of the country well, and it is surely the envy of many of our appellate court colleagues elsewhere.

The role of precedent in our legal system also serves to constrain the good judge. While other legal systems afford little or no deference to precedent, in our system judges generally respect and follow precedents written by those who preceded us in the profession. We rightly treat these precedents as a form of intellectual inheritance, as learning handed down from those who have faced similar problems in the past, and we are obliged to give them the respect one well owes those who have come before, seen it, been there, and done that. And we remember that people often enough order their affairs around these precedents and these reliance interests count too.

There are also our standards of review. Though cynics question whether they have any meaning, they have real and important meaning to the good appellate judge. Take "abuse of discretion" review. That standard, music to the ears of many a district judge, implies a recognition that the district court frequently faces situations in which there will be a range of possible outcomes that the facts and law can fairly support. Rather than pick and choose among them ourselves, we defer to the district court's choice so long as it falls within the realm of those rationally available under the facts and law. So, for example, in sentencing we recognize that the district court is required to balance a host of disparate considerations, ranging from the degree of the defendant's cooperation and remorse to the need for deterring potential future offenders. And we recognize that the district court is in a far superior position to engage in this act of discretion, having had a chance to see and hear from the defendant, try the case, and listen to victims. At the same time, a district court's discretion is neither boundless nor bounded by appellate judges' personal preferences. We act as a backstop by, among other things, scrutinizing purely legal questions anew and by double-checking to make sure the factual findings of the district court enjoy some basis in the record. As appellate judges, then, we do not simply displace the jury's or the district court's judgment with our own. We serve a more modest backstop function that very often requires us to uphold decisions we would not ourselves make.

Ultimately, I can offer tonight only a few examples of the sorts of institutional constraints and personal characteristics of the good judge that help distinguish legal judgment from willful policymaking.

But there's one more feature I would like to comment on, given the individual we are here to honor tonight—a feature on which I think Judge Posner and I would agree.

It has to do with personal integrity. In my three years on the bench, I have served with judges who strive to leave aside their personal biases, who do not aspire to shake the earth as willful Legal Titans. I've witnessed men and women quietly working hard to be fair arbiters of the disputes placed before them, knowing they, like most of their cases, will be forgotten in the sweep of time. Judges who struggle to decide cases dispassionately, assiduously seeking to avoid the temptation to secure results they prefer. Judges who pause to ask whether the results they are reaching are self-indulgent or ones justified by the law and facts of the case. Ones who act independently, without fear of disfavor or desire for public plaudits. Men and women who do not thrust themselves into the limelight but who are patiently tending to the great promise of our legal system—that all litigants, whether popular or reviled, will receive equal protection under law and due process for their grievances. These are judges who realize that every case, no matter how small, matters monumentally to the people involved. And all this, I think, is what makes our jobs most meaningful. It is the timeless virtue of a life well lived in the service of others that matters.

I emphasize this particular trait of the good judge tonight because there can be few better models of it than the man we are here to honor. In the midst of the Great Depression, as Judge Holloway's father was wrapping up his term as governor of Oklahoma, some of you may know that he sat down and wrote a note to his son. It was January 12, 1931, the last day the governor was to serve in office. In his letter, the governor related that it was "the last instrument or message" he would sign while he was governor, and he went on to say to his son that "my prayer and greatest ambition is that you may have good health and live to become a useful and upright citizen. To the accomplishment of this high purpose for you I shall devote my life. I am as proud of you as it is possible for a father to be of a son."

I think it is safe to say that Judge Holloway has not just met, but amply exceeded, his father's aspirations for him. And how many better things than that can be said about any man's life?

OF INTENTIONS
AND CONSEQUENCES

———

Many years ago, I was lucky enough to receive a scholarship to pursue a doctorate at Oxford. It was a time when legal giants roamed that city. John Finnis, Joseph Raz, and Ronald Dworkin were all there, busy with their seminal works, their lectures and seminars open to any curious graduate student. As a student at the same college where Professor Finnis has spent almost a half century, I was fortunate to have him as my dissertation supervisor.

Many years later, on Professor Finnis's retirement from Oxford, I was asked to speak at a symposium at Notre Dame and contribute to a book in his honor. My assignment: discuss and develop one aspect of his many contributions to legal scholarship. What follows is an excerpt from my speech. In some sense it might seem a tribute to a professor—and it is certainly that. But I hope it also offers a glimpse into some of the reasons why I think our Anglo-American legal tradition and the role it gives the judge form such a special inheritance. It is a tradition, after all, that rests on fundamental convictions about treating individual persons as ends, not means; the importance of free will and individual liberty, not just social consequences and overall utility; and the equality of all human beings.

———

O THERS HAVE, AND WILL FOR YEARS TO COME, WRITE AND SPEAK about, learn from and debate, John Finnis's contributions to ethics, philosophy, even Shakespearean scholarship and theology. But as a workaday judge, my daily bread does not consist of such high cuisine. It is instead made up of a comparatively pedestrian—if wholesome and filling—stew of statutes and precedents, regulations and rules. Yet, from time to time, Professor Finnis has been kind enough to dine with those of us who subsist on such doctrinal fare— and here, too, he has applied his remarkable talents in important and enduring ways.

In crime and tort, legal liability has often and long depended on a showing that the defendant intended to do a legal wrong. When it comes to inchoate offenses (incomplete offenses, like attempt and conspiracy), the presence of an unlawful intent is frequently what separates criminality itself from legally innocuous behavior. The same holds true when it comes to accessory liability. The law of ho-micide, as well, "often distinguishes either in setting the 'degree' of the crime or in imposing punishment" between intended and unin-tended killings. And many of our most serious torts (say, battery and assault) are denominated intentional torts. Of course, what qualifies as "intentional" and thus sufficient to render the defendant liable in the civil context is broader than in the criminal context—embracing knowing as well as truly purposeful wrongs in American law. And perhaps this is so for good reason, given that in tort only money, not freedom, is on the line. But in the civil context it remains a fact that the nature of liability (punitive damages, for example) is generally more expansive and serious for what tort law deems an intentional wrong than for wrongs involving only lesser *mens rea*.

In comparatively recent years, some have argued for tearing down this traditional legal edifice. These theorists have suggested that the presence or absence of an intent to perform a legal wrong should be "neither here nor there" when it comes to assigning legal liability; that the common law's traditional reference to intention should be scrapped or revised; that a better way forward exists. Let me outline just two of the challenges to our received tradition and then high-light some of the defects associated with those efforts, defects that Finnis's scholarship has helped illuminate.

THE BOLDER OF THE TWO challenges is perhaps most emblematically identified with the prolific Judge Richard Posner. In Judge Posner's view, legal liability in tort should turn on a comparison of social costs and benefits. Whether a legal wrong is done intentionally is more or less beside the point. Intentional torts merit stiffer penalties than those done recklessly or negligently only if and to the extent that economic efficiency requires that outcome. To explain why this is so, Judge Posner asks us to consider the case of *Bird v. Holbrook*—a chestnut that many of us encountered in law school and that, as it happens, involved an actual bird and, perhaps even better still, a bed of tulips.

So let us begin with the facts of that case. In *Bird,* the defendant owned a walled garden where, as the court put it, he "grew valuable flower-roots, and particularly tulips, of the choicest and most expensive description." To protect the garden, the defendant-owner set up a hidden spring gun, a shotgun rigged to fire when any trespasser stumbled over a contact wire. The plaintiff, a William Bird, was a young man of nineteen who saw a neighbor's female servant in distress. She was in distress because a wandering peahen apparently belonging to her employer had escaped and "alighted in the defendant's garden." So Will Bird, a well-raised young man it would seem, volunteered to collect the bird. He clambered to the top of the defendant's garden wall and called out two or three times to see if anyone was around. Receiving no reply, he jumped into the garden. Once in the garden he saw that the peahen had taken shelter near a summer house and so he went to collect it. Seeking to pluck the bird, not pick the flowers, he was nonetheless rewarded for his troubles with a spray of swan shot from the defendant's hidden spring gun.

When his case for damages eventually made it to court, the English bench found the garden owner liable. The court did so on the basis that it is unacceptable (at least without notice) for anyone to maim others intentionally simply for picking tulips. The intentional harming of another's person is a grave thing and generally impermissible at law, even for the protection of property. Neither, the court pointed out, was the defendant really even seeking to defend his tulips. By leaving a hidden spring gun lying around, the owner demonstrated that he was just as happy to injure someone who had already picked his flowers as he was someone about to pick them. And no doubt in the owner's view punishing the completed picker was a useful deterrent, a way to dissuade other future would-be pickers from even trying. But this was a serious wrong because, as counsel for Mr. Bird put it, the sanction of law is required "to give effect to punishment, and pain [intentionally] inflicted for a supposed offence, at the discretion of an individual, without the intervention of a judicial sentence, is a mere act of revenge."

Now back to Judge Posner. For his part, Judge Posner encourages us to analyze *Bird,* and tort law generally, in a radically different way. In his view, the case can be and is perhaps better understood not as involving an intentional wrongdoing but as involving an effort to achieve the optimal social balance between two perfectly "legitimate activities, raising tulips and keeping peahens." Spring guns, Judge Posner suggests, may well be an efficient, perhaps even the most efficient, way of protecting tulips in a time and place where police protection is not readily available; conversely, spring guns may be inefficient in times and places where other means of protection are more accessible and accidental shootings more likely. The real trick, Judge Posner argues, and what he says judges already may be doing subconsciously, is "design[ing] a rule of liability [in tort] that maximize[s] the (joint) value of both activities, net of any protective or other costs (including personal injuries)." Neither does Judge Posner confine his critique to the realm of civil liability. In criminal law, too, he argues that intent has significance only as a proxy for other variables in an economic cost-benefit analysis. So it is that, under his approach, the fact that a defendant may have intended to kill or maim others is itself really "neither here nor there."

To those who might object that liability for intentionally killing or maiming another human being should not turn on a balancing of economic costs and benefits, Judge Posner offers this reply:

> It is surely not correct to say that society never permits the sacrifice of human lives on behalf of substantial economic values. Automobile driving is an example of the many deadly activities that cannot be justified as saving more lives than they take. Nor can the motoring example be distinguished from the spring-gun case on the ground that one who sets a spring-gun intends to kill or wound. In both cases, a risk of

death is created that could be avoided by substituting other methods of achieving one's ends (walking instead of driving); in both cases the actor normally hopes the risk will not materialize. One can argue that driving is more valuable and spring-guns more dangerous; but intentionality is neither here nor there.

A SECOND, PERHAPS MORE MODEST, challenge to our received legal tradition, though one headed in much the same direction, might be identified with Glanville Williams and his theory of "oblique intention." While Williams did not insist that intention (however defined at law) is entirely irrelevant to the assignment of legal liability, he argued for collapsing intent with foresight or knowledge and treating the two the same when it comes to determining culpability in the criminal law, much as American law typically does in tort.

To make his point, Williams once offered this example—a colorful and complex one in its own right. Suppose a spy is discovered to be ferrying a top secret and highly sensitive device to a hostile state by way of an international flight. Detected in air, the spy fears he will be prevented from completing his mission, so he seizes a hostage and demands that the flight steward prepare a parachute so that he can escape with the device intact. The steward (apparently steeped in national security matters himself) recognizes that the consequences will be dire if the secret device falls into the hands of the enemy, so he discreetly cuts the parachute's rip cord. In a rush, the spy fails to check the parachute, leaps from the plane, and the device (along with the spy) is destroyed upon hitting the ground. Applying his oblique theory of intention, Williams had this to say:

> It seems clear that, as a matter of law, the steward must still be credited with an intention to kill the criminal. He foresees the certainty of the criminal's death if the events happen as he sees they may, even though he does not desire that death.

Of course, the steward's homicidal act might be legally justified on other grounds, say perhaps because of the affirmative defense involving the defense of others. But Williams used his hypothetical to make a different point. He used it to argue that whether the steward intended the spy's death or merely knew it would happen should not matter when assessing his legal liability or access to any affirmative defense. In Williams's view, there is no point in distinguishing between at least intended and foreseen homicides because all that does is "involve the law in fine distinctions, and make it unduly lenient."

WITH JUDGE POSNER'S AND Glanville Williams's views now (albeit very briefly) sketched, we might begin to ask some analytical and normative questions about their project, questions that Finnis's scholarship has suggested and illuminated.

Let us begin with the analytical. Judge Posner rests his argument in large measure on the notion that intended harms (however defined) and purely negligent harms are much the same because both involve the imposition of a risk of harm on someone else. In particular, the automobile driver and the spring gun operator, he says, are essentially indistinguishable. Both take actions that create some risk of harm, even though both hope that harm will not materialize. Whether any harm is intended is beside the point, "neither here nor there," because the risk of the unhoped-for harm is just an inherent cost associated with performing two generally beneficial activities, driving and tulip growing.

But we might well question whether this line of analysis conflates two different things, hoping and intending. After all, as Finnis asks, can't one "intend to achieve a certain result without desiring it to come about"? Can't one "choose and intend to do what is utterly repugnant to one's dominant feelings"? Consider the spring gun owner. We can all agree with Judge Posner that the garden owner may well hope everyone stays away from the trap he sets. But if he thinks that many will be deterred and only a few will come, then doesn't he really intend to shoot those few? Isn't the whole point of a spring gun deterrent that the owner intends to injure or kill those who ignore or test it, however repugnant that result may be to the owner's hopes? In this way, doesn't the spring gun owner intend to maim or kill, even if he may hope not to have to do so? And, having observed this much, can we really say the negligent driver is in the same position as the spring gun owner? After all, the negligent driver neither hopes nor intends to hurt anyone when he takes to the road. He may hurt someone by accident, but killing or maiming is simply not part of his plan or intent—either as a means or as an end. Any injury he might cause would be grounds for serious regret, not the fulfillment of any intention he harbors. In this way, the cases of the spring gun owner and the driver come to us in very different postures analytically—not at all indistinguishable as Judge Posner's analysis would have us posit.

A similar analytical question attends Williams's effort to equate intent and knowledge or foresight. We might approach that question by asking whether it is really fair to say that Williams's steward is guilty of an intentional killing. To be sure, the steward knew the spy would die; but did he intend that death? Or might there be, as Finnis suggests, a strong argument that Williams's steward "did not intend to kill the spy, though he foresaw and accepted that his own choice would certainly bring about [the spy's] death"? Indeed, might it be a fairer view of the facts that the spy's "free-fall and death are side effects of the steward's plan to destroy the . . . device" that might do harm to his country? After all, and for all we know from Williams's hypothetical, if the steward could have destroyed the device without killing anyone he gladly would have done so.

And this leads us to the real analytical question confronting Williams's project: Is he right that no meaningful distinction exists between intent and foresight that the criminal law might recognize, at least sometimes? In answering this question, it is hard to do better than Finnis once did with this illustration:

> Those who wear shoes don't intend to wear them out [even though they may foresee that as an inevitable consequence]. Those who fly the Atlantic foreseeing certain jetlag [likewise] don't do so with the intention to get jetlag; those who drink too heavily rarely intend the hangover they know is certain. Those who habitually stutter foresee with certainty that their speech will create annoyance or anxiety, but do not intend

those side effects. Indeed, we might well call [Williams's] extended notion of [oblique] intent the Pseudo-Masochist Theory of Intention—for it holds that those who foresee that their actions will have painful effects on themselves intend those effects.

Plainly, a meaningful analytical distinction does exist between intending and foreseeing a consequence. Recognizing exactly this, the Model Penal Code acknowledges that a line can and sometimes should be drawn in American criminal law "between a [person] who wills that a particular act or result take place and another who is merely willing that it should take place." So, too, the Supreme Court, which has emphasized that, at least in the criminal law, the idea that "knowledge is sufficient to show intent is emphatically *not* the modern view." Tellingly, even Williams himself ultimately conceded that in certain areas of law—treason, for example—society should require proof of intention rather than knowledge before imposing liability. Yet, Williams notably failed to explain why this should be so or how it might be reconciled with his claim elsewhere that the intent-knowledge distinction lacks force. His ambiguity and equivocation seem the product of a largely unexplored (if ultimately correct) intuition that, at least sometimes, intent does matter.

NOT ONLY DOES FINNIS help us see that the traditional intent-knowledge distinction in law bears analytical power overlooked by its critics. He also helps expose the undergirding normative reasons for the law's traditional cognizance of intention. He reminds us, for example, that some of the law's harshest punishments are often (and have long been) reserved for intentional wrongs precisely because to intend something is to endorse it as a matter of free will—and freely choosing something matters. Our intentional choices reflect and shape our character—who we are and who we wish to be—in a way that unintended or accidental consequences cannot. Our intentional choices define us. They last, remain as part of one's will, one's orientation toward the world. They differ qualitatively from consequences that happen accidentally, unintentionally. Intending to do a legal wrong to another person is something special because, as Finnis puts it,

> [t]o intend something is to choose it, either for its own sake or as a means; and to choose is to adopt a proposal (a proposal generated by and in one's own deliberation). Once adopted, the proposal, together with the reasoning which in one's deliberation made that proposal intelligently attractive, *remains*, persists, in one's will, one's disposition to act.

This is a view that has long and deeply resonated through American and British jurisprudence, and indeed the Western tradition. It is precisely why the law treats the spring gun owner who maims or kills intentionally differently from the negligent driver whose conduct yields the same result. As Roscoe Pound once put it, our "substantive criminal law is," at least at minimum, "based upon a theory of punishing the vicious will. It postulates a free agent confronted with a choice between doing right and doing wrong." At bedrock, and whatever else it may require of citizens, our law rests on what Justice Robert Jackson called the "belief in freedom of the human will and [the] consequent ability and duty of the normal individual to choose between good and evil." Finnis reminds us of the normative power lurking behind familiar precepts and proclamations like these.

But there are still other normative justifications for the special emphasis the law places on intentional conduct. One has to do with human equality. When someone intends to harm another person, Finnis encourages us to remember, "[t]he reality and fulfillment of those others is radically subjected to one's own reality and fulfillment, or to the reality and fulfillment of some other group of persons. In *intending* harm, one precisely makes their loss one's gain, or the gain of some others; one to that extent uses them up, treats them as material, as a resource." People, no less than material, become means to another's end. To analyze *Bird v. Holbrook* as the challengers to extant law would have us, we ask merely whether superior collective social consequences are produced by ruling for the plaintiff or the defendant. On this account, there is nothing particularly special about the individual. Like any other input or good, it gives way whenever some competing and ostensibly more important collective social good is at stake. But it is exactly to prevent all this that the law has traditionally held, in both crime and tort, that one generally ought not choose or intend to harm another person, and that failing to observe this rule is a particularly grave wrong. This traditional rule "expresses and preserves each individual person's . . . *dignity* . . . as an equal." It recognizes that "to choose harm is the paradigmatic wrong; the exemplary instance of denial of right." It stands as a bulwark against those who would allow the human individual to become nothing more than another commodity to be used up in aid of another's (or others') ends.

Assigning legal liability based on intent can serve still other virtues. While Williams said that requiring a showing of intent rather than knowledge leads to unduly fine distinctions and too much leniency in criminal matters, lawmakers and courts have frequently found these distinctions necessary to avoid results they perceive as unjust. So, for example, when it comes to attempt and conspiracy crimes, a showing of intent is often required to establish criminal liability, even though a lesser *mens rea* may suffice to establish liability for the same completed offense. And even when criminal liability attaches to the primary criminal offenders on a lesser *mens rea* showing, proof of intent is typically required to hold liable those only tangentially involved with the illegal enterprise as accessories. While, of course, legislators are free to vary these rules and sometimes have, these rules largely persist and are no doubt what the Supreme Court has called a product of "an intense individualism . . . root[ed] in American soil" willing to attach criminal sanction for actions just indirectly (or not at all) responsible for harm befalling others only if a choice to do wrong is present. Attention to the defendant's intent can help address and prevent what Learned Hand once called a "drag net" effect of sweeping up "all those who have been associated in any degree whatever with the main offenders." The intent requirement in attempt, accessory, and conspiracy law ensures that there is no criminal prosecution, for example, when a utility provides telephone service to a customer "knowing it is used for bookmaking" or "[a]n employee puts through a shipment in the course of his employment though he knows the shipment is illegal." In this way, American law seeks to allow the liberty of normal commerce and communication between individuals without forcing them always to be on guard against Williams's "oblique" intentions.

In response to all this, one might imagine Judge Posner or Williams replying that all the doctrine of intent does could be done just as easily through a system that looks purely to social consequences. Or arguing that intent doctrine does, in some sense, serve to maximize collective social welfare because of the very features that distinguish it. But replies like these would, of course, only serve to demonstrate that the fine gradations of *mens rea* traditionally recognized in the common law are not beside the point ("neither here nor there") as both Judge Posner and Williams have suggested (albeit in their own different ways). In this respect, an argument along these lines would be nearly self-defeating. Neither would responses like these answer the objection that the common law's frequent focus on intent has meaning for the reasons the law has traditionally given (free will, equality, liberty)—reasons that seem to be justifiable on bases independent of any underlying social-welfare calculus. Nor would they address the objection that the common law's stated reasons for focusing on intent are its true and accurate reasons—that the law possesses an integrity and deep logic to it. And they would do little to confront the argument that the law's prohibition of intentional wrongs should sometimes trump even (and perhaps especially) when a utilitarian calculus suggests a different result.

To be sure, much more could be said about Finnis's contribution to the question of intention in crime and tort. There is a great deal more complexity and subtlety both to his arguments and to those of his antagonists than I can stitch out in these few pages. And many more difficulties to explore. Like the incommensurability problems Finnis argues can sometimes attend consequentialist explanations of the law. Or the complexities involved in trying to distinguish intended means and ends from unintended side effects. Or the question when exactly the law should take special cognizance of intent and distinguish intended consequences from those merely known or foreseen. After all, while Finnis reminds us that the law may take cognizance of an analytically and normatively meaningful distinction between intended and unintended conduct, he hardly suggests that the law always must do so or that other bases for legal liability should not exist—two positions that would themselves be plainly mistaken.

But let me leave those issues dangling. For our purposes here it is enough to note that Finnis has done much to remind us that the law's use of intention as a basis for liability is not always and wholly beside the point; that the law's focus on intent can, at least sometimes, be both analytically and normatively justified; and that all this can make a significant difference in the analysis of many legal questions across many fields and in many different ways. Finnis's work has helped explain and defend the thicket of the common law's traditional *mens rea* rules, reminding us of the intellectual pedigree of those rules and of the reasons why the law has often and for so long taken care with what sometimes seem complex and unduly fine distinctions. No doubt the debate will continue, with rejoinders made and new lessons learned. But no one seeking to raze or reimagine the law's protective *mens rea* forest in favor of some (surely well-intentioned) alternative vision will be able to do so without first confronting Finnis's defense. And that, though but a very small part of Finnis's body of work, represents a significant achievement indeed.

ON PRECEDENT

_____

When should judges follow—or overrule—a prior decision
they earnestly believe to be mistaken? Most everyone would
agree the answer isn't always or never; judgment is required.
Trying to tease out and assess the relevant considerations
took twelve distinguished collaborators and me two years
and nine hundred pages. What follows doesn't try to sum-
marize all we said but represents our introduction to the
book. This piece is adapted from Bryan A. Garner et al., The
Law of Judicial Precedent *(2016), and reprinted with permis-*
sion of Thomson Reuters. My co-authors included Carlos
Bea, Rebecca White Berch, Harris L Hartz, Nathan L. Hecht,
Brett M. Kavanaugh, Alex Kozinski, Sandra L. Lynch, Wil-
liam H. Pryor, Jr., Thomas M. Reavley, Jeffrey S. Sutton, and
Diane P. Wood.

ONE MIGHT BE TEMPTED TO SAY, AFTER LONG AND HARD STUDY,
that the law of judicial precedent amounts to no more than
this: All tribunals look at decisional precursors; all have at least some
discretion in deciding whether to follow those precursors (or to distinguish them); and the higher the court, the greater its discretion.
That's about it.

But that's gross reductionism. There's actually much more to it
than that. There are nuances and complications. It takes patience
and acuity to work through them. It's fair to say that "[l]ay people—
and, for that matter, more than a few lawyers and judges—have more
misunderstandings about the nature and role of precedents than

about any other aspect of legal reasoning." So let's start at the very beginning.

Judicial precedents are one of the two main sources of law in Anglo-American legal systems. Constitutions and statutes make up the other. Traditionally, statutes and precedents were considered to be very different types of law. Statutes have always been thought of as "written law." Because they are written, their text tends to be analyzed very closely.

Precedents contained in judicial opinions have traditionally been considered "unwritten law" because long ago judges simply read or announced their decisions from the bench, without writing them down. In fact, some English judges still do that.

It used to be widely thought—until about the end of the nineteenth century—that judicial precedents were merely *evidence* of the law, as opposed to a *source* of it. No serious legal thinker now believes this. Today, precedents are understood to make up part of the law.

Because all American appellate judges produce written opinions today, few commentators now refer to case law as unwritten law. Yet although judicial opinions are now written, reading case law differs fundamentally from reading statutes. Judges often say that they *construe* or *interpret* a statute, which means they try to determine the meaning of its language. By contrast, judges and lawyers often say that they *analyze* a judicial precedent. Although analyzing an opinion involves delving into the judge's words, you must go beyond the judge's words—which in themselves are of no great significance, as opposed to what they denote. You must also understand the opinion's legal background, the facts of the case, and the relationship between those facts and the outcome.

In other words, with case law you can't just interpret its language; you must also engage in legal reasoning to find what we call the case's *holding*—the rule or principle necessary to justify or explain the outcome. When lawyers and judges analyze a precedent, they're usually trying to determine just what its holding is. They're also trying to gauge how broadly or narrowly the holding sweeps—that is, how it will apply to future cases that present a similar issue but with different facts.

You begin the task of analyzing a precedent with the thought in mind that readers—yourself included—may find its meaning uncertain. Opinion writing isn't an exact science or a precise art. A judge might not reach a perfect understanding of the basis for the judgment. And even a judge who clearly grasps that basis might not be able to articulate it in ways that others will understand. That's why reading an opinion calls for careful thought and at times a tolerance for frustration. Different readers may come away from the same opinion with quite different versions of its meaning. And different meanings are even more likely to be found when different readers take various approaches to the analysis.

Finding the right approach depends partly on your purpose. Are you arguing an appeal from the opinion? Urging a lower court that its decision is or isn't controlled by a higher court's decision? Relying on the opinion—or distinguishing it—before the court that delivered it? Planning a transaction and hoping to find a secure basis for the deal? Offering general advice to a client who needs to plan how to act despite a set of legal principles that are still developing? Sitting as a judge and weighing the opinion's importance to your own decision? You may be looking for different things in each of these situations. At times a narrowly technical approach may be called for. Other occasions may demand a broader approach, one that relies more heavily on sensitivity, seasoned judgment, even intuition.

Whatever your purpose, you'll begin by trying to identify a holding that expresses a legal rule. Doing that requires you to master the facts and pay attention to the procedural context that frames the question. You might not need to go any further—the decision may reconfirm a well-settled proposition, or you may conclude that greater refinement is inappropriate for other reasons. But more often you'll need to draw on sophisticated analytic tools and various doctrines related to understanding precedent.

ENTRENCHED IDEAS

Let's consider some instances. Does major-league baseball engage in "interstate commerce" so that it must obey federal antitrust laws like other businesses operating across state lines? Should a farmer feel confident that he doesn't "take" wildlife in violation of the Endangered Species Act when he plows a field, even if in the process he unintentionally disturbs birds that have settled there? You might think the answer to these questions is yes. Surely professional baseball is a form of commerce—an interstate one at that. And it may seem odd to think of a farmer's "taking" wildlife by plowing a field. But in both cases your intuitions would be entirely wrong—legally speaking. And the reason they're wrong has to do with the nature of judicial precedent.

On behalf of the U.S. Supreme Court, Justice Oliver Wendell Holmes wrote nearly a century ago that "giving exhibitions of baseball" doesn't involve interstate commerce. In the years since then, the Supreme Court has reconsidered that decision, even admitting doubts about its soundness, but has adhered to it all the same. As for our farmer, the Court has more recently upheld regulations interpreting the statutory term *take* to apply to him. This despite the intuition that "taking" requires an act aimed at killing or capturing wildlife, an intuition that one dissenting judge expressed this way: "[I]f I were intent on taking a rabbit, a squirrel, or a deer, as the term 'take' is used in common English parlance, I would go forth with my dogs or my guns or my snares and proceed to 'harass, . . . pursue, hunt, shoot, wound, kill, trap, capture, or collect' one of the target species."

A judicial precedent does its most strenuous work when a later court thinks it's wrong. Let's assume it's pretty obvious that "exhibitions of baseball" do involve interstate commerce. If we lacked a system of precedent, courts faced with the issue would have to decide it on the merits in every case, and presumably they would get the outcome right more often than not. But in a system respectful of precedent, if an authoritative court holds that baseball isn't engaged in interstate commerce, later courts may be obliged to get the answer wrong in every case that follows. The power of precedent includes, then, the power to enshrine wrong decisions.

It's this very aspect of precedent that has proved such a rich source of material for the satirist. Take Jeremy Bentham, who called the art of judicial decisionmaking "the art of being methodically ignorant of what everybody knows." Or the inimitable Jonathan Swift:

"It is a maxim among these lawyers that whatever hath been done before may legally be done again: and therefore they take special care to record all the decisions formerly made against common justice and the general reason of mankind." Bentham and Swift were describing precedent at its worst; at its best it amounts to a prudent guide for future decisions.

The legal doctrine commanding deference to precedent derives its shorthand Latin name, *stare decisis,* from the maxim *stare decisis et non quieta movere*—"to stand by things decided and not disturb settled points." Under *stare decisis,* in short, a court must either follow or distinguish the controlling decisions of its predecessor court on a question of law. For *stare decisis* to apply, a decision must have been rendered by a majority of the voting judges of the hearing court; must involve an issue of law, not of fact; and usually must be in a published opinion. Most important, the court must have decided the issue for which the precedent is claimed; it cannot merely have discussed it in dictum, ignored it, or assumed the point without ruling on it.

Despite the age of the Latin phrase, *stare decisis* isn't well understood. To the contrary, the application of *stare decisis* remains remarkably uncertain. Perhaps that's because it's not so much a doctrine as a *method*. As Max Radin has explained, "As applied in the United States, the rule of *stare decisis* is a matter of technique. In whatever way courts reach their conclusion, they are expected to place the situation they are judging within the generalized class of some existing decision."

THE LEGAL BASIS FOR THE DOCTRINE

The Constitution does not mention the doctrine of precedent or *stare decisis.* Sometimes courts (including the U.S. Supreme Court) refer to *stare decisis* as a mere "judicial policy."

But can that be right? Not infrequently the Supreme Court reaffirms debatable decisions on the ground that they warrant deference as precedent. But by what power might judges favor a mere policy of their own hand over what (they are convinced) the Constitution commands or the legislature requires? And if precedent lacks constitutional grounding, might Congress have the power to compel courts to disregard it, to decide cases without reference to precedent? Could courts even choose to disregard precedents and abandon *stare decisis*?

Perhaps some degree of respect for precedent may be required for federal courts to exercise the "judicial Power" endowed by Article III, or to comply with other constitutional commands like due process. By the time of the founding, William Blackstone reported that it was "an established rule" that English courts should "abide by former precedents." In *The Federalist*, Alexander Hamilton emphasized that "[t]o avoid an arbitrary discretion in the courts, it is indispensable that they should be bound down by strict rules and precedents." And Justice Joseph Story maintained in his *Commentaries on the Constitution* that the "conclusive effect of judicial adjudications, was in the full view of the framers."

In fact, it was in the founding era that the modern concept crystallized. In his celebrated *Commentaries on American Law,* James Kent traced the doctrine of precedent to the formative years of American law: "The inviolability of precedents was . . . inculcated at a period which we have been accustomed to regard as the infancy of our law, with as much zeal and decision as at any subsequent period." Today, the Supreme Court's occasional references to *stare decisis* as a "judicial policy" rather than an "inexorable command" should be read as suggesting not that the doctrine lacks constitutional provenance but that the doctrine doesn't demand obedience to precedent without exception. It leaves room for courts to distinguish and overrule. But even if that's true, other intriguing questions remain—not least how much respect for precedent the Constitution requires or, put differently, how far courts may go in distinguishing and overruling precedent consistently with the Constitution or in declaring what counts as precedent and what doesn't.

THE PRACTICAL JUSTIFICATIONS
FOR THE DOCTRINE

Why do we bother with precedent? How is it that a system devoted in part to preserving *wrong* decisions has proved so durable in Anglo-

American law and come to be thought of by many as central to our conception of justice?

Five discrete arguments are frequently advanced here. Some depend on the consequences associated with respecting precedent. Other arguments are rule based, grounded on the conviction that a just judicial system requires at least some degree of deference to precedent. And some suggest that it's simply better than all the alternatives. Let's consider each of the five practical arguments in defense of our system of precedent.

First, the past can teach valuable lessons inherently worthy of our respect. Precedent is a way of accumulating and passing down the learning of past generations, a font of established wisdom richer than what can be found in any single judge or panel of judges. Sometimes it is also said that past cases are worthy of consideration by virtue of the very fact that they *are* our past. Or to put it negatively, a judge who departs from a precedent without rationally distinguishing it is necessarily, though perhaps only implicitly, criticizing it. Hewing to past decisions isn't just a matter of inertia. It's also a matter of professional honor and fealty.

Second, cases are decided one at a time, and rules often take shape only slowly and from the accumulation of case-specific decisions pointing in the same direction. Our system deals with questions of law by increment, by degree, and on specific facts litigated from the bottom up. This system allows for a greater degree of fine-tuning and refinement—and constant improvement.

Third, efficiency benefits are often claimed for precedent. Just as citizens benefit from having some idea what law will apply to their cases, so too courts, litigants, and the public at large gain something from a system that doesn't require each case to be litigated anew and instead allows resort to rules already at hand. As Justice Benjamin Cardozo put it: "[T]he labor of judges would be increased almost to the breaking point if every past decision could be reopened in every case, and one could not lay one's own course of bricks on the secure foundation of the courses laid by others who had gone before him."

Fourth, by seeking to ensure some consistency in outcomes among decisionmakers, the doctrine of precedent may simultaneously promote respect for the judiciary as a neutral source. In this way, the doctrine might be thought to be thoroughly utilitarian.

Fifth, a respect for precedent is said to advance notice and reliance interests. To a society aspiring to live under the rule of law, it's no small thing to ensure that citizens can determine in advance what the law will require of them and have the chance to conform their conduct to it.

In this enterprise, then, the right answer to a legal question is sometimes less important than a clear one. Does it matter more which side of the road the law says we should drive on, or that everyone follows the same rule? To facilitate social coordination, the answer we choose may be less important than that an answer simply be chosen and be clear. A system of precedent—the promise that future cases will be decided as similar past cases were decided—helps ensure that people can know what the law will be when applied to them, their actions, and their enterprises. Productive social coordination stands strong on the basis of (relatively) ascertainable ground rules.

The Con Arguments

To be sure, our system of precedent, perhaps like anything else constructed by imperfect humans, guarantees costs along with its benefits. One we've already seen: Deference to precedent can wind up ensconcing not just wise decisions but wrong ones. In the name of obedience to precedent, judges may pass judgment without giving much thought to the merits of the case at hand, inviting a sort of "judicial somnambulism."

Justice Holmes expressed this risk shortly before becoming a judge: "It is revolting to have no better reason for a rule of law than that so it was laid down in the time of Henry IV. It is still more revolting if the grounds upon which it was laid down have vanished long since, and the rule simply persists from blind imitation of the past." But eighteen years later, as chief justice of Massachusetts, he seemed more cautious: "[P]recisely because I believe that the world would be just as well off if it lived under laws that differed from ours in many ways, and because I believe that the claim of our especial code to respect is simply that it exists, that it is the one to which we have become accustomed, and not that it represents an eternal principle, I am slow to consent to overruling a precedent."

Respect for precedent may also create abiding injustice as the cost of ensuring consistency and predictability more systemically. In the words of Jerome Frank, courts may "feel obligated to consecrate their former blunders." A precedent may yield not just wrong results (as with the baseball holding) but gravely wrong ones (as with *Dred Scott*—the infamous pre–Civil War case in which the U.S. Supreme Court held that no black person, enslaved or free, could be a citizen of the United States, nor of any individual state, and therefore had no standing in federal court). While unjust judicial decisions can be overruled, that change can come slowly—very slowly. Radical system-wide reform by way of legislation can be more difficult in an incremental case-or-controversy process respectful of precedent.

One can question, too, how well precedent ever fulfills the goals it is said to serve. Take, for example, the goal of predictability. Looking up precedents has never been easy or cheap. At one time, precedents were accessible only in expensive and rare law books. Now precedents are ubiquitous—easy to produce and store, thanks to the computer. Yet that very ubiquity can make it more difficult than ever to know what the controlling law is—a sort of information overload. The accelerating speed with which cases have filled the *Federal Reporter* illustrates the problem. The *Reporter*'s first series, which contained but 300 volumes, spanned 1880 to mid-1924—meaning that on average it covered a year's worth of opinions in just shy of 7 volumes. The second series contained 999 volumes covering mid-1924 to mid-1993—more than 14 volumes a year. The current third series has taken well over 600 volumes to cover just the time between mid-1993 and the present day—a pace approaching 30 volumes a year. Lawyers have a hard time staying abreast of developments even in specialized fields. Nonlawyers have little chance.

But weighty as such criticisms are, our system doesn't lack counterbalances to them. The American judiciary doesn't treat precedent as an ironclad edict. Not every decision offered by one court binds every other court. By dividing our courts into parallel systems (federal and state) and even limiting precedential effect horizontally within those parallel systems (federal circuits, for example, generally aren't bound by one another's decisions), we have achieved a significant degree of flexibility in the system. Nor, as we have seen, is every word in every judicial opinion binding even on those courts generally obliged to follow the source's dictates. And to be sure, most courts have the power to overrule their own precedents.

Like most other social arrangements, a system of precedent can hope to achieve only some roughly workable accommodation between competing goals—in our case, between interests like predictability and equality on the one hand, and adaptability and individual justice on the other. It has been well said by Neil Duxbury that "[t]he doctrine of precedent entails both constraint and creativity. If precedents bound absolutely, . . . judges would have very little capacity and opportunity to develop the common law; but if judges could ignore precedents completely, the doctrine would not exist in any meaningful sense." Unsurprisingly, even as harsh a critic of the doctrine of precedent as Jerome Frank conceded that "no sensible person suggests that *stare decisis* be abandoned."

Henson v. Santander

We move now to some excerpts from judicial opinions. This one discusses the temptation to allow policy pleas to prevail over a statute's language—and the importance of resisting it. It comes from the first opinion I authored as a Supreme Court justice. A new justice's first assignment isn't usually a block-buster and this one surely addressed an obscure question. Everyone agreed that in the Fair Debt Collection Practices Act Congress didn't regulate loan originators who sought to collect debts owed to them. Instead, Congress sought to reg-ulate the sometimes abusive practices of third-party debt collection agencies hired by loan originators. But in the years after the act's adoption some loan originators had begun sell-ing debts, and these new owners had begun trying to collect those loans for their own account. That development raised this question: Does the statute treat loan purchasers like loan originators or like third-party debt collectors? In the end, the Court unanimously agreed that loan purchasers do not meet the statute's written test for "debt collectors." Anticipating the Court would reach that conclusion, the petitioners sought to persuade the Court to rule for them anyway based not on the law's terms but on policy concerns. We refused and this excerpt explains why.

FACED WITH OBSTACLES IN THE TEXT AND STRUCTURE OF THE FAIR DEBT Collection Practices Act, petitioners ask us to move quickly on to policy. Indeed, from the beginning that is the field on which they seem most eager to pitch battle. Petitioners assert that Congress passed the

Act in large measure to add new incentives for independent debt collectors to treat consumers well. In their view, Congress excluded loan originators from the Act's demands because it thought they already faced sufficient economic and legal incentives to good behavior. But, on petitioners' account, Congress never had the chance to consider what should be done about those in the business of purchasing defaulted debt. That's because, petitioners tell us, the "advent" of the market for defaulted debt represents "'one of the most significant changes'" to the debt market generally since the Act's passage in 1977. Had Congress known this new industry would blossom, they say, it surely would have judged defaulted debt purchasers more like (and in need of the same special rules as) independent debt collectors. Indeed, petitioners contend that no other result would be consistent with the overarching congressional goal of deterring untoward debt collection practices.

All this seems to us quite a lot of speculation. And while it is of course our job to apply faithfully the law Congress has written, it is never our job to rewrite a constitutionally valid statutory text under the banner of speculation about what Congress might have done had it faced a question that, on everyone's account, it never faced. Indeed, it is quite mistaken to assume, as petitioners would have us, that "whatever" might appear to "further[] the statute's primary objective must be the law." Legislation is, after all, the art of compromise, the limitations expressed in statutory terms often the price of passage, and no statute yet known "pursues its [stated] purpose[] at all costs." For these reasons and more besides we will not presume with petitioners that any result consistent with their account of the statute's overarching goal must be the law but will presume more modestly instead "that [the] legislature says . . . what it means and means . . . what it says."

Even taken on its own terms, too, the speculation petitioners urge upon us is far from unassailable. After all, is it really impossible to imagine that reasonable legislators might contend both ways on the question whether defaulted debt purchasers should be treated more like loan originators than independent debt collection agencies? About whether other existing incentives (in the form of common law duties, other statutory and regulatory obligations, economic incentives, or otherwise) suffice to deter debt purchasers from engaging in certain undesirable collection activities? Couldn't a reasonable legislator endorsing the Act as written wonder whether a large financial institution that purchases defaulted debt is any more or less likely to engage in abusive conduct than another large financial institution that originates that debt? Especially where (as here) the institution says that its primary business is loan origination and not the purchase of defaulted debt? We do not profess sure answers to any of these questions, but observe only that the parties and their *amici* manage to present many and colorable arguments both ways on them all, a fact that suggests to us for certain but one thing: that these are matters for Congress, not this Court, to resolve.

In the end, reasonable people can disagree with how Congress balanced the various social costs and benefits in this area. We have no difficulty imagining, for example, a statute that applies the Act's demands to anyone collecting any debts, anyone collecting debts originated by another, or to some other class of persons still. Neither do we doubt that the evolution of the debt collection business might invite reasonable disagreements on whether Congress should reenter the field and alter the judgments it made in the past. After all, it's hardly unknown for new business models to emerge in response to regulation, and for regulation in turn to address new business models. Constant competition between constable and quarry, regulator and regulated, can come as no surprise in our changing world. But neither should the proper role of the judiciary in that process—to apply, not amend, the work of the people's representatives.

A.M. v. Holmes

As much as I am sure they didn't like it, my Tenth Circuit colleagues thought the law allowed the unlikely arrest in this case. I dissented because I believed precedent fairly warned police that their conduct was unlawful. At the same time, though, I hoped to make clear that I admired my colleagues for their willingness to follow the law faithfully where they thought it led rather than take the all-too-tempting path of rewriting the law themselves.

IF A SEVENTH GRADER STARTS TRADING FAKE BURPS FOR LAUGHS IN gym class, what's a teacher to do? Order extra laps? Detention? A trip to the principal's office? Maybe. But then again, maybe that's too old school. Maybe today you call a police officer. And maybe today the officer decides that, instead of just escorting the now compliant thirteen year old to the principal's office, an arrest would be a better idea. So out come the handcuffs and off goes the child to juvenile detention. My colleagues suggest the law permits exactly this option and they offer ninety-four pages explaining why they think that's so. Respectfully, I remain unpersuaded.

The simple fact is the New Mexico Court of Appeals long ago alerted law enforcement that the statutory language on which the officer relied for the arrest in this case does not criminalize "noise[s] or diversion[s]" that merely "disturb the peace or good order" of individual classes. Instead, the court explained, the law requires "a more substantial, more physical invasion" of the school's operations—proof that the student more "substantially interfered" with the "actual functioning" of the school. What's more, other state courts have interpreted similar statutes similarly. They've sustained criminal convictions for students who created substantial disorders across an entire school. But they've also refused to hold students criminally liable for classroom antics that "momentarily divert[ed] attention from the planned classroom activity" and "require[d] some intervention by a school official." Even when the antics required a teacher to leave her class for several minutes, or otherwise "divert[ed] the teacher or the principal from other duties for a time." Respectfully, I would have thought this authority sufficient to alert any reasonable officer in this case that arresting a now compliant class clown for burping was going a step too far.

As Charles Dickens once wrote, often enough the law can be "a ass—a idiot"—and there is little we judges can do about it, for it is (or should be) emphatically our job to apply, not rewrite, the law enacted by the people's representatives. Indeed, a judge who likes every result he reaches is very likely a bad judge, reaching for results he prefers rather than those the law compels. So it is I admire my colleagues today, for no doubt they reach a result they dislike but believe the law demands—and in that I see the best of our profession and much to admire. It's only that, in this particular case, I don't believe the law happens to be quite as much of a ass as they do. I respectfully dissent.

Direct Marketing Association v. Brohl

———

This concurrence illustrates the struggle a lower court judge can sometimes face in seeking to apply precedent. The case involved the intersection of two forces. First, a Colorado law that sought to collect taxes from in-state citizens who purchased goods from out-of-state Internet retailers. Second, a Supreme Court precedent that forbade states from directly taxing out-of-state retailers but that had been undermined itself by later Supreme Court teachings. How should a judge navigate these tricky waters? (Later, during my first full term on the Supreme Court, it resolved the confusion by formally overruling its precedent in South Dakota v. Wayfair.*)*

IN OUR LEGAL ORDER PAST DECISIONS OFTEN CONTROL THE OUTCOME of present disputes. Some criticize this feature of our law, suggesting that respect for judicial precedent invests dead judges with too much authority over living citizens. They contend, too, that it invites current judges to avoid thinking for themselves and to succumb instead in "judicial somnambulism." But in our legal order judges distinguish themselves from politicians by the oath they take to apply the law as it is, not to reshape the law as they wish it to be. And in taking the judicial oath judges do not necessarily profess a conviction that every precedent is rightly decided, but they must and do profess a conviction that a justice system that failed to attach power to precedent, one that surrendered similarly situated persons to wildly different fates at the hands of unconstrained judges, would hardly be worthy of the name.

At the center of this appeal is a claim about the power of precedent. In fact, the whole field in which we are asked to operate today—dormant commerce clause doctrine—might be said to be an artifact of judicial precedent. After all, the Commerce Clause is found in Article I of the Constitution and it grants Congress the authority to adopt laws regulating interstate commerce. Meanwhile, in dormant commerce clause cases Article III courts have claimed the (anything but dormant) power to strike down some state laws even in the absence of congressional direction. And the plaintiffs' attempt in this case to topple Colorado's statutory scheme depends almost entirely on a claim about the power of a single dormant commerce clause decision: *Quill Corp. v. North Dakota.*

Everyone before us acknowledges that *Quill* is among the most contentious of all dormant commerce clause cases. Everyone before us acknowledges that it's been the target of criticism over many years from many quarters, including from many members of the Supreme Court. But, the plaintiffs remind us, *Quill* remains on the books and we are duty-bound to follow it. And about that much the plaintiffs are surely right: we are obliged to follow *Quill* out of fidelity to our system of precedent whether or not we profess confidence in the decision itself.

With that much plain enough, the question remains what exactly *Quill* requires of us. Later (reading) courts faced with guidance from earlier (writing) courts sometimes face questions how best to interpret that guidance. And the parties before us today offer wildly different accounts of *Quill*. Most narrowly, everyone agrees that *Quill's* holding forbids states from imposing sales and use tax collection duties on firms that lack a physical presence in-state. And everyone agrees that Colorado's law doesn't quite go that far. While Colorado requires in-state brick-and-mortar firms to collect sales and use taxes, it asks out-of-state mail order and internet firms only to supply reports designed to enable the state itself to collect the taxes in question. Indeed, Colorado suggests that its statutory scheme carefully and consciously stops (just) short of doing what *Quill's* holding forbids.

But as the plaintiffs note, that is hardly the end of it. Our obligation to precedent obliges us to abide not only a prior case's holding but also to afford careful consideration to the reasoning (the "ratio decidendi") on which it rests. And surely our respect for a prior decision's reasoning must be at its zenith when the decision emanates from the Supreme Court. Indeed, our court has said that it will usually defer even to the dicta (not just the ratio) found in Supreme Court decisions. And building on this insight the plaintiffs argue that respect for *Quill*'s ratio, if not its holding, requires us to strike down Colorado's law. After all, the plaintiffs note, Colorado's regulatory scheme seeks to facilitate the collection of sales and use taxes by requiring out-of-state firms to satisfy various notice and reporting obligations—burdens comparable in their severity to those associated with collecting the underlying taxes themselves.

It's a reasonable argument, but like my colleagues I believe there's a reason it's wrong. The reason lies in the exceptional narrowness of *Quill*'s ratio. If the Court in *Quill* had suggested that state laws commanding out-of-state firms to collect sales and use taxes violated dormant commerce clause doctrine because they are too burdensome, then I would agree that we would be obliged to ask whether Colorado's law imposes a comparable burden. But *Quill*'s ratio doesn't sound in the comparability of burdens—it is instead and itself all about the respect due precedent, about the doctrine of *stare decisis* and the respect due a still earlier decision.

This distinction proves decisive. Some years before *Quill*, in *National Bellas Hess, Inc. v. Department of Revenue of Illinois*, the Supreme Court held that states could not impose use tax collection duties on out-of-state firms. In *Quill*, the Court openly reconsidered that decision and ultimately chose to retain its rule—but it did so only to protect the reliance interests that had grown up around it. Indeed, the Court expressly acknowledged that *Bellas Hess* very well might have been decided differently under "contemporary Commerce Clause jurisprudence." The Court also expressly acknowledged that states can constitutionally impose tax and regulatory burdens on out-of-state firms that are more or less comparable to sales and use tax collection duties. And the Court expressly acknowledged that this dichotomy—between (impermissible) sales and use tax collection obligations and (permissible) comparable tax and regulatory burdens—is pretty "artificial" and "formalistic." Given all this, respect for *Quill*'s reasoning surely means we must respect the

Bellas Hess rule it retained. But just as surely it means we are under no obligation to extend that rule to comparable tax and regulatory obligations. In fact, this much is itself a matter of precedent for this court and many others have already held *Quill* does nothing to forbid states from imposing regulatory and tax duties of comparable severity to sales and use tax collection duties.

It may be rare for Supreme Court precedents to suffer as highly a "distinguished" fate as *Bellas Hess*—but it isn't unprecedented. Take baseball. Years ago and speaking through Justice Holmes, the Supreme Court in *Federal Baseball* held baseball effectively immune from the federal antitrust laws and did so reasoning that the "exhibition[] of base ball" by professional teams crossing state lines didn't involve "commerce among the States." Since then the Supreme Court has recognized that other organizations offering "exhibitions" in various states do engage in interstate commerce and are subject to antitrust scrutiny. But though it has long since rejected the reasoning of *Federal Baseball*, the Supreme Court has still chosen to retain the holding itself—continuing to rule baseball effectively immune from the antitrust laws, if now only out of respect for the reliance interests the *Federal Baseball* decision engendered in that particular industry. And, of course, Congress has since codified baseball's special exemption. So it is that the baseball rule now applies only to baseball itself, having lost every away game it has played.

Accepting at this point that *Quill* doesn't require us to declare Colorado's law unconstitutional, the question remains whether some other principle in dormant commerce clause doctrine might. For their part the plaintiffs identify (only) one other potential candidate, suggesting that Colorado's law runs afoul of the principle that states may not discriminate against out-of-state firms, a principle often associated with *West Lynn Creamery, Inc. v. Healy.* And to the extent that there's anything that's uncontroversial about dormant commerce clause jurisprudence it may be this anti-discrimination principle, for even critics of dormant commerce clause doctrine often endorse it even as they suggest it might find a more textually comfortable home in other constitutional provisions.

But any claim of discrimination in this case is easily rejected. The plaintiffs haven't come close to showing that the notice and reporting

burdens Colorado places on out-of-state mail order and internet retailers compare unfavorably to the administrative burdens the state
imposes on in-state brick-and-mortar retailers who must collect
sales and use taxes. If anything, by asking us to strike down Colorado's law, out-of-state mail order and internet retailers don't seek
comparable treatment to their in-state brick-and-mortar rivals, they
seek more favorable treatment, a competitive advantage, a sort of
judicially sponsored arbitrage opportunity or "tax shelter."

Of course, the mail order and internet retailer plaintiffs might
respond that, whatever its propriety, they are entitled to a competitive advantage over their brick-and-mortar competitors thanks to
Bellas Hess and *Quill*. And about that much (again) I cannot disagree. It is a fact—if an analytical oddity—that the *Bellas Hess*
branch of dormant commerce clause jurisprudence guarantees a
competitive benefit to certain firms simply because of the organiza-
tional form they choose to assume while the mainstream of dormant
commerce clause jurisprudence associated with *West Lynn Creamery* is all about preventing discrimination between firms. And the
plaintiffs might well complain that the competitive advantage they
enjoy will be diluted by our decision in this case. Indeed, if my colleagues and I are correct that states may impose notice and reporting
burdens on mail order and internet retailers comparable to the sales
and use tax collection obligations they impose on brick-and-mortar
firms, many (all?) states can be expected to follow Colorado's lead
and enact statutes like the one now before us.

But this result too seems to me, as it does to my colleagues, entirely
consistent with the demands of precedent. After all, by reinforcing an
admittedly "formalistic" and "artificial" distinction between sales and
use tax collection obligations and other comparable regulatory and
tax duties, *Quill* invited states to impose comparable duties. In this
way, *Quill* might be said to have attached a sort of expiration date for
mail order and internet vendors' reliance interests on *Bellas Hess*'s rule
by perpetuating its rule for the time being while also encouraging
states over time to find ways of achieving comparable results through
different means. In this way too *Quill* is perhaps unusual but hardly
unprecedented, for while some precedential islands manage to survive

indefinitely even when surrounded by a sea of contrary law (e.g., *Federal Baseball*), a good many others disappear when reliance interests never form around them or erode over time (e.g., *Montejo v. Louisiana*). And *Quill*'s very reasoning—its ratio decidendi—seems deliberately designed to ensure that *Bellas Hess*'s precedential island would never expand but would, if anything, wash away with the tides of time.

American Atheists v. Davenport

————

To honor its fallen troopers, the Utah Highway Patrol erected road-side crosses near the spots where they were mortally injured. The crosses bore each trooper's name and badge number. Just below the name appeared the Utah Highway Patrol's beehive symbol, along with biographical details about the trooper. Did this violate the Constitution's Establishment Clause, which prohibits laws "respecting an establishment of religion"?

This Tenth Circuit case presented us with a difficult job when it came to trying to follow precedent. In Lemon v. Kurtzman, *the Supreme Court offered a three-part test for determining when a law violates the Establishment Clause. But a decade later, Justice Sandra Day O'Connor modified that test and sought to require courts to ask whether an objective, reasonable observer would view the government's action as "endors[ing]" religion. Still later Supreme Court decisions called into question both* Lemon *and Justice O'Connor's modification of it and suggested that in some disputes neither should control. In this case, my colleagues and I sought to make sense of these various precedents as best we could. For my part, I suggested in this dissent that we should review our own lower court precedents in light of the most recent intervening Supreme Court developments. And I submitted that if we were still bound to apply Justice O'Connor's reasonable observer modification of the* Lemon *test, our reasonable observer should at least be reasonable. (Eventually, during my second full term, the Supreme Court grappled with some of the issues discussed here, in* The American Legion v. The American Humanist Association *[2019].)*

OUR COURT HAS NOW REPEATEDLY MISAPPLIED THE "REASONABLE observer" test, and it is apparently destined to continue doing so until we are told to stop. Justice O'Connor instructed that the reasonable observer should not be seen as "any ordinary individual, who might occasionally do unreasonable things, but . . . rather [as] a personification of a community ideal of reasonable behavior." Yet, our observer continues to be biased, replete with foibles, and prone to mistake.

In this case, according to the panel opinion, our observer starts with the biased presumption that Utah's roadside crosses are unconstitutional. He does so despite the fact that a plurality of the Supreme Court only this year held that "[a] cross by the side of a public highway marking, for instance, the place where a state trooper perished need not be taken as a statement of governmental support for sectarian beliefs." Our observer takes no heed of this direction. And when he looks to see whether he might overcome his initial bias, the task proves impossible because he disregards the very secularizing details—such as the fallen trooper's name inscribed on the crossbar—that might allow him to change his mind. He misses these integral components of the display, we're told by the panel, because "a motorist driving by one of the memorial crosses at 55-plus miles per hour may not notice, and certainly would not focus on, the biographical information." So it is that we must now apparently account for the speed at which our observer likely travels and how much attention he tends to pay to what he sees. We can't be sure he will even bother to stop and look at a monument before having us declare the state policy permitting it unconstitutional.

But that's not the end of things. It seems we must also take account of our observer's selective and feeble eyesight. Selective because our observer has no problem seeing the Utah Highway Patrol insignia and using it to assume some nefarious state endorsement of religion is going on; yet, mysteriously, he claims the inability to see the fallen trooper's name posted directly above the insignia. And feeble because our observer can't see the trooper's name even though it is painted in approximately 8-inch lettering across a 6-foot cross-bar—the same size text used for posting the words "SPEED LIMIT" alongside major interstate highways. What's more, many of Utah's memorials aren't even on highways: four of the thirteen are adjacent to side-streets where "55-plus" speeds aren't common—including two in front of a Utah Highway Patrol field office. All the same, our observer plows by, some combination of too blind and too fast to read signs adequate for interstate highway traffic. Biased, selective, vision impaired, and a bit of a hot-rodder our observer may be, but the reasonable observer of Justice O'Connor's description he is not.

Still, if this case could be dismissed as a "one off" misapplication of the reasonable observer test, that might make it less worthy of review. But it can't be so easily shrugged off. Two years ago we applied a similar misconstruction of the reasonable observer test in *Green v. Haskell* to become the only circuit court since the Supreme Court's decision in *Van Orden v. Perry* to order the removal of a Ten Commandments display that was admittedly erected without a religious purpose and in the context only of a larger secular historical presentation. There, like here, we did so only by employing an observer full of foibles and misinformation. Now we become the only circuit since *Van Orden* to order the removal of memorial highway crosses to fallen public servants, using this same strikingly unreasonable observer who bears none of the traits Justice O'Connor described. Thus, the pattern is clear: we will strike down laws other courts would uphold, and do so whenever a reasonably biased, impaired, and distracted viewer might confuse them for an endorsement of religion.

And this raises an even larger question. The court's holding does and must rest on the view that anything a putatively "reasonable observer" could think "endorses" religion is constitutionally problematic. Indeed, the result in this case could hardly be achieved under any different test. It is undisputed that the state actors here did not act with any religious purpose; there is no suggestion in this case that Utah's monuments establish a religion or coerce anyone to participate in any religious exercise; and the court does not even render a judgment that it thinks Utah's memorials actually endorse religion. Most Utahans, the record shows, don't even revere the cross. Thus it is that the court strikes down Utah's policy only because it is able to imagine a hypothetical "reasonable observer" who could think Utah means to endorse religion—even when it doesn't.

But whether even the true reasonable observer/endorsement test remains appropriate for assessing Establishment Clause challenges is far from clear. A majority of the Supreme Court in *Van Orden* declined to employ the reasonable observer/endorsement test in an Establishment Clause challenge to a public display including the Ten Commandments. Following the Supreme Court's cue, at least three of our sister circuits seem to have rejected the test, at least when it comes to passive public displays like Utah's. And this year a plurality of the Supreme Court questioned whether even the true "reasonable observer" framework is always appropriate for analyzing Establishment Clause questions.

The court today, however, declines to consider any of these developments, much as it declined to do so in *Green*. So it is that our opinions in this field continue to apply (or misapply) a reasonable observer/endorsement test that has come under much recent scrutiny—and, worse, our opinions do so without stopping to acknowledge, let alone grapple with, the questions others have raised about the test. It is a rare thing for this court to perpetuate a circuit split without giving due consideration to, or even acknowledging, the competing views of other courts or recent direction from the High Court. But that's the path we have taken.

Neither is this any humdrum disagreement where uniformity of federal law may not be a pressing concern. Where other courts permit state laws and actions to stand, we strike them down. And the test we use to do so rests on an uncertain premise—that this court possesses the constitutional authority to invalidate not only duly enacted laws and policies that actually "respect[] the establishment of religion," but also laws and policies a reasonable hypothetical observer could think do so. And, in this circuit's case, to go even a step further still, claiming the authority to strike down laws and policies a conjured observer could *mistakenly* think respect an establishment of religion. That is a remarkable use of the "awesome power" of judicial review, and it would have been well worth our while at least to pause to consider its propriety before rolling on.

5.

TOWARD JUSTICE
FOR ALL

THE RULE OF LAW IN THIS COUNTRY IS SOMETHING
every American can rightly take great pride
in. As my friend Judge John Kane likes to say, the
greatest proof of any society's commitment to the
rule of law may be whether the government can and
does lose in its own courts and then respects those
judgments. That doesn't happen everywhere, but it
happens in the United States day in and day out.

Still, complacency isn't part of the American spirit.
In the last few chapters, I've raised some questions and
offered some arguments about things we might improve in our system of justice. But there's an even
larger question still lurking here: What good is any
system of justice, even an otherwise perfect one, if it is
too often practically inaccessible? While the promise

of "Equal Justice Under Law" is chiseled into marble above the entrance to the Supreme Court, the hard truth is that that promise remains unrealized in the lives of too many today. Often enough, justice proves out of reach because of the prohibitive expense associated with our justice system and the intractable delays it sometimes invites.

The law's shortcomings on these scores are nothing new. As Professor Arthur Miller has observed, "In ancient China, a peasant who resorted to the courts was considered ruined, no matter what the eventual outcome of the suit. Hamlet rued 'the law's delay.' Goethe quit the legal profession in disgust over cases that had been languishing in the German courts for three hundred years." As a product of the American West, though, one story that speaks to me about this enduring challenge is the Johnson County War. It's a story that has achieved almost mythic status as a symbol of the early days on the western frontier. There are many versions of the story, but one I particularly enjoyed and benefited from is Christopher Knowlton's *Cattle Kingdom: The Hidden History of the Cowboy West*. The Johnson County War saga is often told as a story about land, growth, and class tensions. But to me it's also a story about why the rule of law depends on access to justice.

JOHNSON COUNTY IS BEAUTIFUL country. It lies next to the Bighorn National Forest in Wyoming. The county seat, Buffalo, sits a little west of Gillette and a couple hundred miles north of Saratoga, where my grandmother's family settled. In the second half of the nineteenth century, cattle barons roamed its open range with huge herds destined for nearby railroad depots and the slaughterhouses back East, where demand for beef had skyrocketed as the country grew prosperous after the Civil War. The cattle barons didn't own the range, but they often acted like they did. Many were rich eastern heirs or sons of British aristocrats more in love with the myth of the cowboy than the reality of the cow.

Trouble erupted when homesteaders arrived from the East and began parceling up the open range. Enticed by the federal government's offer of cheap and plentiful land, thousands began pouring into Wyoming, settling the land and tilling the soil. Thanks to the advent of barbed wire, these "sodbusters" fenced in their lands and fenced out the cattle barons' ranging herds. The land belonged to them. Or so the government told many of them and so they thought.

The cattle barons had different ideas. Squeezed by the new settlements, they decided to strike. After accusing (probably falsely) a couple of settlers of stealing their cattle, they began drawing up a "dead list" of those who had offended them. They used the newspapers to spread the rumor that Johnson County suffered from a rustler problem. They hired vigilante gunmen from Texas. And soon enough they and their hired guns set out for Buffalo to attack their enemies.

But the barons weren't ones to stick to plans. On their way to town, they heard that some of the men on their dead list were holed up at a small farmhouse. So the barons detoured there and managed to kill two men and capture others. But things went awry when homesteaders spotted the siege and fled to town to warn others. When the sheriff learned what was happening, he assembled a posse and eventually surrounded the cattle barons and their men.

What the cattle barons may have lacked in foresight they made up for in well-placed friends. During the fighting that ensued, one of their men escaped the encircling forces and managed to send a telegram to the governor, who was sympathetic to their cause. In turn, the governor scrambled to send his own telegrams to the president of the United States and Wyoming's two U.S. senators. The president, awakened in the middle of the night by the senators and the assistant secretary of war, issued an order for military intervention. So it was that the cattle barons were rescued by politicians (and the U.S. Army) from near-certain death.

Though the fight on one front ended, it soon began on another. Johnson County sought to prosecute the cattle barons and their Texas gunslingers for murder. But the barons turned to a powerful and very able lawyer: Willis Van Devanter (who much later, as it turns out, served as a justice of the Supreme Court). And Van Devanter used every one of his many legal wiles to advance his clients' cause. He insisted that the invaders should be tried together, which promised to strain the courts. He sought to ensure that the trial would take place in Cheyenne, a long distance from Buffalo. He managed to win months of delay—all while his clients and their friends worked to secure the disappearance of the gunmen and key witnesses. Some melted away back to Texas; others were ferreted into a hotel in Rhode Island, all expenses paid, and promised a bonus if they kept quiet (appropriately enough, it seems the checks bounced once it came time to pay). Van Devanter also helped ensure favorable press coverage from Wyoming's most influential newspapers. And when a smaller rival paper dared to take Johnson County's side, Van Devanter threatened it with claims of slander, demanded the postmaster to stop its distribution, and seems even to have had the editor arrested. Maybe most shrewdly of all, Van Devanter ensured that Johnson County would have to house and feed the defendants, a strategy well designed to bankrupt the county.

Even when the time for trial arrived at last, Van Devanter still had cards left to play. Reportedly, something like a thousand men were called for jury selection—a startling number for almost any trial in any time or place. And then Van Devanter made sure the jury selection proceedings dragged on almost impossibly. Eventually, Johnson County was forced to give up. By now, the county coffers were more or less empty, many of the key witnesses had evaporated, and even after an interminable jury selection process an empty seat still remained to fill in the jury box. The prosecutor realized he was beaten. The county filed a motion to dismiss.

But the cattle barons and their lawyer *opposed* the motion. Why? If the court ordered dismissal of the case before a full jury could be empaneled, the cattle barons knew that the county could try them another day. So what did Van Devanter do? After dragging out jury selection for so long, he now turned tactics. He quickly persuaded a courtroom spectator to sit in the last jury seat, allowed the full jury panel to be sworn, and *then* invited another motion to dismiss. Now, the constitutional right against double jeopardy would prevent any second trial. No doubt, the cattle barons laughed all the way home.

I WISH I COULD say this is a story only of frontier justice. But it's not. Many of the challenges that faced the people of Johnson County in seeking justice still face those in our courts today. While the world has never seen a perfect legal system, that's no excuse. We should not hide from our shortcomings or shirk from the job of trying to correct them. So, it seems to me, any book about the rule of law in this country today wouldn't be complete without some candid conversation about some of the ways in which we still fall short in our aspirations. That's what this chapter is about.

Take our civil justice system today. Few Americans can afford a lawyer. I couldn't afford my own services when I was in private practice; today's law school graduates can't either. According to Professor Luz Herrera, the average person who needs a lawyer makes $25 an hour while the average hourly rate of a lawyer hovers between $200 and $300—more in many markets. Why are lawyers so staggeringly expensive? I cannot help but think some of the problem has to do with the expense of legal education. To provide legal services most anywhere in the United States today, no matter how routine or easy, you must attend a four-year college and then three years of law school and sit for a bar exam. If you have to pay your way, as so many students do, you can easily walk out of school deeply in debt. No wonder lawyers must charge so much for their services.

Then there's the expense and delay of it all. In criminal cases, prosecutors are automatically required to produce relevant exculpatory material to the other side. But no similar duty exists today in most civil cases in our federal courts. So before you can reach trial, you must often endure months or years of wrangling over the production of documents and fighting repetitive rounds of motions. The lawyers call this "civil discovery," but too often the process produces little civility and less discovery. The federal rules and their official commentary that govern the civil discovery process now span more than seventy single-spaced pages, all in nine-point font. They have become the centerpiece of contemporary civil litigation. Lawyers who in another age would have been masters of cross-examination are now more likely to be masters of discovery disputes. Where in our civil justice system we used to have trials without discovery, today we have discovery without trials. The whole process is so complex and expensive and takes so long that many meritorious suits aren't filed and many nonmeritorious ones settle for more than they're really worth. For one, I cannot see why we allow this. The Constitution guarantees everyone a trial before a jury—not the right to keep from that trial the relevant facts.

Some say the answer to these problems is to allow individuals more easily and frequently to represent themselves *pro se* (with no help from a legal professional). I'm not convinced. Time and again on the Tenth Circuit I saw *pro se* cases with real merit face daunting odds because the litigant didn't know how to navigate the wildly complex rules of modern civil litigation. My colleagues and I did our best to catch cases like these and seek willing attorneys to take them on without pay. With competent legal help, at least these individuals stood a chance. Almost always, the help of some competent lawyer, or even a nonlawyer licensed professional in the field, is better than no help at all.

Our criminal justice system suffers from its own grave problems. According to the Heritage Foundation, the federal statutory books today contain more than an estimated 4,500 criminal laws, most of very recent vintage. And that doesn't even begin to account for criminal laws at the state and local levels—or, for that matter, the hundreds of thousands of criminal penalties federal agencies impose through their regulations. Out of curiosity I asked my law clerks one day to find out how many of those regulations are floating around; they reported back that most scholars gave up trying to count them all back in the 1990s. *The Wall Street Journal* has quoted one government official who made an attempt, Ronald Gainer, as saying that "you will have died and resurrected three times" before you will count them all. John Baker, a law professor, even told the paper that "[t]here is no one in the United States over the age of 18 who cannot be indicted for some federal crime."

With so many potential charges available to the prosecutor, often carrying such long sentences, it's little surprise, too, that criminal defendants routinely feel no choice but to plead guilty. When the available criminal charges on the books were few and their corresponding sentences relatively short, a trial was worth the risk. But in an age when the charges on the books have grown legion and a prosecutor can stack charge upon charge on a defendant for the same underlying course of conduct, a trial becomes a luxury few dare. So just as we've witnessed the death of the civil trial, we've witnessed the death of the criminal trial: Today, only about 1.5 percent of civil cases are decided by jury trial, and more than 97 percent of federal convictions come through plea bargains.

These facts, I think, should worry anyone who fears the arbitrary exercise of power. The idea that a jury of your peers should decide your fate—not a prosecutor holding all the cards, not an opposing lawyer versed in discovery games—is a core principle of our democracy. Just as the framers divided Congress into two houses, they balanced the judiciary between judges—the least democratic participants in our legal order and responsible for questions of law—and juries— the most democratic participants in our system and responsible for questions of fact. One of the leading trial lawyers of his era, John Adams considered the role of juries essential to the "liberty and security of the people." For him, as for so many of our founders, the right to a jury trial in civil cases, enshrined in the Seventh Amendment, was vital to ensure that "[n]o man's property or liberty can be taken away from him till . . . men in his neighborhood have said upon oath, that by the laws of his own making it ought to be taken away." As Adams put it, the right to vote and the right to trial by jury represented democracy's "heart and lungs, the mainspring and the centre wheel, . . . without [which] the body must die, the watch must run down, the government must become arbitrary."

In my own career as a trial lawyer, I saw time and time again the same wisdom of juries Adams did. Twelve people working together in good faith can see and hear more of what's happening in a courtroom than any single person might. They bring the common sense of the sovereign people to bear, cutting through legalese to the heart of the matter. They take their oaths seriously. They witness the judicial system up close and usually come away with a new appreciation of it. Experience on a jury is often the closest most people ever get to participation in their own government. All that is lost when trial by jury dies.

This chapter seeks to shine a light on some of the access to justice challenges we face today. The stories in the pages that follow sometimes have happy endings; often they do not. The Johnson County War may seem from a time long past, but as you read these stories I suspect it will follow you as it does me.

LAW'S IRONY

———

In this speech to the Federalist Society's annual lawyers' convention in 2013, I tried to sum up some of my concerns about our civil and criminal justice systems today: Our civil justice system is too expensive for most to afford; our criminal code is too long for most to comprehend; and our legal education system is too monolithic to allow lawyers to serve clients as affordably and well as we might.

LET ME BEGIN BY ASKING THE LAWYERS IN THE ROOM IF YOU'VE ever suffered through a case that sounds like this one:

> [I]n [the] course of time, [this suit has] become so complicated, that no man alive knows what it means. . . . [A] long procession of [judges] has come in and gone out; the legion of bills in the suit have been transformed into mere bills of mortality [but still it] drags its dreary length before the Court, perennially hopeless.

How familiar does that sound? Could it be a line lifted from a speaker at an electronic discovery conference? From a brief in your last case? Or maybe from a recent judicial performance complaint?

The line comes from Dickens's *Bleak House,* published in 1853. It still resonates today, though, because the law's promise of deliberation and due process sometimes—ironically—invites the injustices of delay and irresolution. Like any human enterprise, the law's crooked timber occasionally produces the opposite of its intended effect. We turn to the law earnestly to promote a worthy idea and sometimes wind up with a host of unwelcome side effects and find ourselves ultimately doing more harm than good. In fact, the whole business is something of an irony: We depend on the rule of law to guarantee freedom but we have to give up freedom to live under the law's rules.

In a roundabout way, that leads me to the topic I'd like to discuss with you tonight: law's irony. Dickens had a keen eye for it. But, the truth is, Demosthenes plied similar complaints two thousand years ago. And if we're honest, we should expect lawyers and judges to carry on similar conversations about the law's ironies two thousand years from now.

But just because unwelcome ironies may be as endemic to law as they are to life, Dickens would remind us that's hardly reason to let them go unremarked and unaddressed. So it is I would like to begin by discussing a few of the law's ironies that I imagine he would consider worthy of attention in our time.

CONSIDER FIRST TODAY'S VERSION of the *Bleak House* irony. Yes, I am referring to civil discovery.

The adoption of the "modern" rules of civil procedure in 1938 marked the start of a self-proclaimed "experiment" with expansive pre-trial discovery—something previously unknown to the federal courts. More than seventy years later, we still call them the "new" and the "modern" rules of civil procedure.

Now, that's a pretty odd thing, when you think about it. Maybe the only thing that really sounds new or modern after seventy years is Keith Richards of the Rolling Stones. Some might say he looks like he's done some experimenting too.

In any event, our 1938 forefathers expressly rested their "modern" discovery "experiment" on the assumption that with ready access to an opponent's information, parties to civil disputes would achieve fairer and cheaper merits-based resolutions.

Now, how is *that* working out for you?

Does modern discovery practice *really* lead to fairer and more efficient resolutions based on the merits? I don't doubt it does in many cases. Probably even most. But should we be concerned when

80 percent of the American College of Trial Lawyers say that discovery costs and delays keep injured parties from bringing valid claims to court? Or when 70 percent also say attorneys use discovery costs as a threat to force settlements that *aren't* based on the merits? Have we maybe gone so far down the road of civil discovery that—ironically enough—we've begun undermining the purposes that animated our journey in the first place?

What we have today isn't your father's discovery. Producing discovery no longer means rolling a stack of bankers' boxes across the street. We live in an age when every bit and byte of information is stored seemingly forever and is always retrievable—if sometimes only at a steep price. Today, the world sends fifty trillion emails a year. An average employee sends or receives more than one hundred every day. That doesn't begin to account for the billions of instant messages shooting around the globe. This isn't a world the writers of the discovery rules could have imagined in 1938—no matter how "modern" they were.

No surprise, then, that many people now simply opt out of the civil justice system. Private alternative dispute resolution (ADR) abounds. Even the federal government has begun avoiding its own courts. Recently, for example, it opted to employ ADR to handle claims arising from a massive oil spill in the Gulf of Mexico. These may be understandable developments given the costs and delays inherent in modern civil practice. But they raise questions, too, about the transparency and independence of decisionmaking, the lack of development of precedent, and the future role of courts in our civic life. For a society aspiring to live under the rule of law, does this represent an advance or perhaps something else?

We might even ask what part the rise of discovery has played in the demise of the trial. Surely other factors are at play here, given the disappearance of criminal trials as well. But we've now trained generations of attorneys as discovery artists rather than trial lawyers. They are skilled in the game of imposing and evading costs and delays; they are poets of the nasty gram, able to write interrogatories in iambic pentameter. Yet they are terrified of trial.

The founders thought trials were a bulwark of the rule of law. As Hamilton saw it, the only room for debate was over whether jury trials were "a valuable safeguard to liberty" or "the very palladium of free government." But is that still common ground today? No doubt, our modern discovery experiment is well-intentioned. Yet one of its effects has been to contribute to the death of an institution once thought essential to the rule of law.

WHAT ABOUT OUR CRIMINAL justice system, you might ask? It surely bears its share of ironies too. Consider just this one.

Without question, the discipline of writing the law down, codifying it, advances the rule of law's interest in fair notice. But today we have about 4,500 federal criminal statutes on the books, most added in the last few decades. And the spigot keeps pouring, with hundreds of new statutory crimes inked every few years. Neither does that begin to count the (literally) hundreds of thousands of additional *regulatory* crimes buried in the *Federal Register*. There are now so many crimes cowled in the numbing fine print of those pages that scholars *debate* their number. When he led the Senate Judiciary Committee, Joe Biden worried that we have assumed a tendency to "federalize everything that walks, talks, and moves." Maybe we should say hoots, too, because it's now a federal crime to misuse the likeness of Woodsy Owl or his immortal words "Give a hoot; don't pollute!" Businessmen who import lobster tails in plastic bags rather than cardboard boxes can be brought up on charges. Mattress sellers who remove that little tag: yes, they're probably federal criminals too. Whether because of public choice problems or otherwise, there appears to be a ratchet clicking away relentlessly, always in the direction of more—never fewer—federal criminal laws.

Some reply that the growing number of federal crimes isn't out of proportion to our growing population. Others suggest the recent proliferation of federal criminal laws might be mitigated by allowing the mistake (or ignorance) of law defense to be more widely asserted. Others still suggest prosecutorial discretion can help with the problem.

However that may be, isn't there still a troubling irony lurking here? Without written laws, we lack fair notice of the rules we must obey. But with too many written laws, don't we invite a new kind of fair notice problem? And what happens to individual freedom and equality—and to our very conception of law itself—when the criminal code comes to cover so many facets of daily life that prosecutors can almost choose their targets with impunity?

The sort of excesses of executive authority invited by too few written laws helped lead to the rebellion against King John and the sealing of the Magna Carta—one of the great advances in the rule of law. But history bears warnings that too much and too much inaccessible law can lead to executive excess as well. Caligula sought to protect his authority by publishing the law in a hand so small and posted so high no one could be sure what was and wasn't forbidden. (No doubt, all the better to keep everyone on their toes. Sorry . . .) In *Federalist No. 62*, Madison warned that when laws become just a paper blizzard, citizens are left unable to know what the law is and cannot conform their conduct to it. It is an irony of the law that either too much or too little can impair liberty. Our aim here has to be for a golden mean. And it may be worth asking how far we might have strayed from it.

BEYOND THE LAW ITSELF, there are the ironies emanating from our law schools. A target-rich environment, you say? Well, let's be kind and consider but one example.

In our zeal for high standards, we have developed a dreary bill of particulars every law school must satisfy to win the American Bar Association's accreditation. Law schools must employ a full-time librarian (dare not a part-timer). Their libraries must include microform printing equipment. They must provide extensive tenure guarantees. They invite trouble if their student-faculty ratio reaches 30:1, about the same ratio found in many public schools. Keep in mind, too, under ABA standards adjunct professors, many of whom have decades of practical experience in the law, count as only one-fifth of an instructor.

Might it be worth pausing to ask whether commands like these contribute enough to learning to justify the barriers to entry—and the limits on access to justice—they impose? A legal education can cost students $200,000 today. That's on top of an equally swollen sum for an undergraduate degree—yet another ABA requirement. In

England, students are allowed to earn a law degree in three years as undergraduates or in one year of study after college, all of which must be followed by extensive on-the-job training. None of this is thought a threat to the rule of law there. One might wonder whether the sort of expensive and extensive homogeneity we demand is essential to the rule of law here.

SO FAR, WE'VE BRIEFLY visited ironies where the law aims at one virtue and risks a corresponding vice. But it seems to me that maybe the law's most remarkable irony today comes from the opposite direction—a vice that hints at virtues in the rule of law.

These days our culture buzzes with cynicism about the law. So many see law as the work of robed hacks and shiny-suited shills. Judges who rule by personal policy preferences. Lawyers who seek to razzle-dazzle them. On this view, the only rule of law is the will to power. Maybe in a dark moment you've fallen prey to doubts along these lines.

But I wonder whether the law's greatest irony might just be the hope obscured by the cynic's shadow. I wonder whether cynicism about the law flourishes so freely only because—for all its blemishes—the rule of law in our society is so successful that sometimes it's hard to see. I wonder if we're like David Foster Wallace's fish: surrounded by water, yet somehow unable to appreciate its existence.

Now the cynicism surrounding law is easy enough to see. When Supreme Court justices try to defend law as a professional discipline, when they explain their jobs as interpreting legal texts, when they echo the traditional *Federalist No. 78* conception of judging, they are mocked, often viciously. Leading media voices call them "deceiving." Warn that behind their "benign beige facade[s]" lurk "crimson partisan[s]." Even law professors venture to the microphones to express "complete[] disgust[]" and accuse them of "perjur[y]" and "intellectual vacuity." Actual quotes all.

If this bleak picture I've sketched were an accurate one, if I believed judges and lawyers regularly acted as shills and hacks, I'd hang up the robe and hand in my license. But even accounting for my native optimism, I just don't think that's what a life in the law is about.

As a working lawyer, I saw time and again that creativity, intelligence, and hard work applied to a legal problem could make a profound difference in a client's life. I saw judges and juries that, while human and imperfect, strove to hear earnestly and decide impartially. I never felt my arguments to courts were political ones, but ones based on rules of procedure and evidence, precedent, and standard interpretive techniques. The prosaic but vital stuff of a life in the law.

As a judge now, I see colleagues striving every day to enforce the Constitution, the statutes passed by Congress, the precedents that bind us, the contracts adopted by the parties. Sometimes with quiet misgivings about the wisdom of the regulation at issue. Sometimes with concern about their complicity in enforcing a doubtful statute. But enforcing the law all the same, believers that ours is an essentially just legal order.

This is not to suggest that we lawyers and judges bear no blame for our age's cynicism about the law. Take our self-adopted model rules of professional conduct. They explain that the duty of diligence we lawyers owe our clients doesn't "require the use of offensive tactics or preclude . . . treating [people] with courtesy and respect." Now, how's that for a professional promise? A sort of ethical commandment that, as a lawyer, you should do unto others before they can do unto you. No doubt we have reason to look hard in the mirror when our profession's reflected image in popular culture is no longer Atticus Finch but Saul Goodman.

In defending law as a coherent discipline, I don't mean to suggest that every hard legal question has a single right answer. That some Platonic form or Absolute Truth exists for every knotty statute or roiled regulation—if only you possess the superhuman power to discern it. I don't know about you, but I haven't met many judges who resemble Hercules. Well, maybe my old boss Byron White. But how many of us will lead the NFL in rushing? When a lawyer claims Absolute Metaphysical Certainty about the meaning of some chain of ungrammatical prepositional phrases tacked onto the end of a run-on sentence buried in some sprawling statutory subsection, I start worrying. For questions like these, my gospel is skepticism—though I try not to make a dogma out of it.

But to admit that disagreements do and will always exist over hard and fine questions of law doesn't mean those disagreements are the products of personal will or politics rather than the products of diligent and honest efforts by all involved to make sense of the legal materials at hand.

The first case I wrote for the Tenth Circuit to reach the Supreme Court involved a close question of statutory interpretation, and the Court split 5 to 4. Justice Breyer wrote to affirm. He was joined by Justices Thomas, Ginsburg, Alito, and Sotomayor. Chief Justice Roberts dissented, with Justices Stevens, Scalia, and Kennedy. Now that's a lineup the public doesn't often hear about, but it's the sort of thing that happens—quietly—day in and day out throughout our country.

As you know but the legal cynic overlooks, the vast majority of disputes coming to our courts are ones in which all judges do agree on the outcome. The intense focus on the few cases where we disagree suffers from a serious selection effect problem. More than 90 percent of the decisions issued by my court are unanimous; that's pretty typical of the federal appellate courts. Forty percent of the Supreme Court's cases are unanimous, too, even though that court faces the toughest assignments and nine, not just three, judges have to vote in every dispute. In fact, the Supreme Court's rate of dissent has been largely stable for the last seventy years—this despite the fact that back in 1945, eight of nine justices had been appointed by a single president and today's sitting justices were appointed by five different presidents.

Even in those few cases where we *do* disagree, the cynic also fails to appreciate the nature of our disagreements. We lawyers and judges may dispute which tools of legal analysis are most appropriate in ascertaining a statute's meaning. We may disagree over the order of priority we should assign to these competing tools and their consonance with the Constitution. We may even disagree over the results our agreed tools yield in a particular case. These disagreements sometimes break along familiar lines, but sometimes not. Consider, for example, the debate between Justices Scalia and Ginsburg, on the one hand, and Justices Thomas and Breyer, on the other hand, over the role the rule of lenity should play in criminal cases, or similar disagreements between Justices Scalia and Thomas about the degree of deference due precedent. Debates like these are hugely consequential. But they are disputes of legal judgment, not disputes about politics or personal will.

In the hardest cases, as well, many constraints narrow the realm of admissible dispute: closed factual records; an adversarial process where the parties usually determine the issues for the court's decision; standards of review that command deference to finders of fact; the rules requiring appellate judges to operate on collegiate panels where we listen to and learn from one another; the discipline of writing reason-giving opinions; and the possibility of further review. To be sure, these constraints sometimes point in different directions. But that shouldn't obscure how they serve to limit the latitude available to all judges, even the cynic's imagined judge who would like nothing more than to impose his policy preferences on everyone else. And on top of all that, what today appears a hard case tomorrow becomes an easy one—an accretion to precedent and a new constraint on the range of legally available options in future cases.

NOW, MAYBE I EXAGGERATE the cynicism that seems to pervade today. Or maybe the cynicism I see is real but endemic to every place and time—and it seems something fresh only because this is our place and time. After all, lawyers and judges have never been much loved. Shakespeare wrote the history of King Henry VI in three parts. In all those three plays there is only a single joke. Jack Cade and his followers come to London intent on rebellion, and offer as their first rallying cry: "Let's kill *all* the lawyers." As, in fact, they pretty much did.

But maybe, just maybe, cynicism about the rule of law—whatever the place and time—is its greatest irony. Maybe the cynicism is so apparent in our society only because the rule of law here—for all its problems—is so successful. After all, who can make so much fun of the law without being very sure the law makes it safe to do so? Don't our friends, neighbors, and we ourselves expect and demand—not just hope for—justice based on the rule of law?

Our country today shoulders an enormous burden as the most powerful nation on Earth and the most obvious example of a people struggling to govern itself under the rule of law. Our mistakes and missteps are heralded by those who do not wish us well, and noticed even by those who do. Neither should we try to shuffle our problems under the rug: We have too many to ignore. The fact is, the law can be a messy, human business, a disappointment to those seeking Truth in some Absolute sense and expecting more of the Divine or Heroic from those of us wearing the robes. And it is easy enough to spot examples where the law's ironies are truly bitter.

But it seems to me that we shouldn't dwell so much on the bitter that we never savor the sweet. It is, after all, the law that permits us to resolve our disputes without resort to violence, to organize our affairs with some measure of confidence. It is through the careful application of the law's existing premises that we are able to generate new solutions to changing social coordination problems as they emerge. And, when done well, the law permits us to achieve all of this in a deliberative and transparent way.

Here, then, is the irony I'd like to leave you with. If sometimes the cynic in all of us fails to see our nation's successes when it comes to the rule of law, maybe it's because we are like David Foster Wallace's fish that's oblivious to the life-giving water in which it swims. Maybe we overlook our nation's success in living under the rule of law only because, for all our faults, that success is so obvious it's sometimes hard to see.

ACCESS TO
AFFORDABLE JUSTICE

―――

Legal services are so expensive today that the United States ranks near the bottom of developed nations when it comes to access to counsel in civil cases. The question is what to do about it. In this essay, written originally for an exchange between U.S. and U.K. judges, I sought to explore some possibilities.

THIS PAPER EXPLORES THREE POSSIBLE AVENUES FOR CIVIL JUS-tice reform. All three lie within the power of the legal profession to effect. They include revisions to our ethical codes, civil justice rules, and legal education accreditation requirements—possibilities that in turn challenge each of the main elements of our profession: bar, bench, and academy. Each of these avenues of reform holds the promise of either reducing the cost or increasing the output of legal services—in that way making access to justice more affordable. And for that reason, you might think of them as (sort of) market-based solutions. Now, you might wonder why this paper doesn't address some other possible paths for change—perhaps most obviously the possibility of increased public financing for legal aid. One reason is that, whatever challenges may be associated with asking a self-regulating profession to reconsider its self-imposed barriers to entry and output restrictions, entering that political and fiscal thicket appears likely to pose even more. Maybe more important, though, on the road to change it seems to me that before asking others for help we should ask whether and to what degree our own self-imposed rules increase the cost of legal services and decrease access to justice in unwarranted ways.

THE REGULATION OF LAWYERS

We lawyers enjoy a rare privilege. We are largely left to regulate our own market, often through rules of our own creation and sometimes through statutes effectively of our own hand too. Of course, and no matter the industry, even the most well-intentioned regulations can bear negative unintended consequences. Sometimes even the intended consequences of regulations can only be described as rent-seeking. And it seems hard to think our profession might be immune from these risks. Surely many of our self-imposed regulations represent well-intentioned efforts to prevent and police misconduct that risks harm to clients. But you might also wonder if a profession entrusted with the privilege of self-regulation is at least as susceptible as (or maybe even more susceptible than) other lines of commerce to regulations that impose too many social costs compared to their attendant benefits. Consider two examples.

UNAUTHORIZED PRACTICE OF LAW. Marcus Arnold presented himself as a legal expert on AskMe.com, a website that allows anyone to volunteer answers to posted questions. Users of the site rate those who offer advice, and in time they came to rank Arnold as the third most helpful volunteer of legal answers out of about 150 self-identified legal experts. When Arnold later revealed that he was but a high school student, howls emerged from many quarters and his ranking dropped precipitously. Still, his answers apparently continued to satisfy the website's users because soon enough he went on to attain the number one ranking for legal advice, ahead of scores of lawyers. Like a Rorschach test, both supporters and opponents of unauthorized practice of law regulations see in this case support for their positions.

When approaching questions about the unauthorized practice of law, you might think a natural place to begin is to ask what exactly constitutes the practice of law. But that turns out to be a pretty vexing question. While the American Bar Association offers a set of model rules of professional conduct governing those who engage in the practice of law, it is surely a curiosity that those rules don't attempt to define what constitutes the practice of law in the first place. After all, it's no easy thing to regulate an activity without first defining what that activity is.

The fact is the job of defining what does and doesn't constitute the practice of law has largely been left to state statutes. And history reveals that the definitions states have adopted, usually at the behest of local bar associations, are often breathtakingly broad and opaque—describing the practice of law as, and prohibiting non-lawyers from participating in, the "represent[ation]" of others, or (even more circularly) any "activity which has traditionally been performed exclusively by persons authorized to practice law." More than a few thoughtful people have wondered if these sorts of sweeping and opaque restrictions may be subject to constitutional challenge on vagueness, First Amendment, or due process grounds.

But however that may be, about one thing there can be little doubt. In recent years, lawyers have used these rules to combat competition from outsiders seeking to provide routine but arguably "legal" services at low or no cost to consumers. Indeed, by far and away most unauthorized practice of law complaints come from lawyers rather than clients and involve no specific claims of injury. Take recent cases involving Quicken Family Lawyer and LegalZoom. Those firms sell software with forms for wills, leases, premarital agreements, and dozens of other common situations. When Quicken entered the Texas market, an "unauthorized practice of law committee" appointed by the Texas Supreme Court quickly brought suit, a fight that eventually yielded a federal court decision holding that Quicken had violated state regulations (though, happily, a result the legislature later effectively undid). Similarly, when LegalZoom entered the market in North Carolina, the state bar declared its operations illegal, a declaration that eventually induced the company to settle and promise to revise some of its business practices.

Neither are challenges of this sort aimed only at for-profit firms. The federal Individuals with Disabilities Education Act (IDEA) affords parents the right to be "accompanied and advised" in agency proceedings by nonlawyers who have special training or knowledge "with respect to the problems of children with disabilities." Yet even here, where (supreme?) federal law seems clear, state authorities have sought (sometimes successfully) to use unauthorized practice of law rules to forbid lay advocacy by nonprofit firms with expertise in IDEA procedures. To be sure, efforts like these to thwart competition from commercial and nonprofit advocates have proven only partially successful—LegalZoom and companies like it continue to expand. But surely, too, the threat and costs of litigation deter entry by others and raise costs for those who do enter, costs the consumer must ultimately bear.

It seems well past time to reconsider our sweeping unauthorized practice of law prohibitions. The fact is, nonlawyers already perform— and have long performed—many kinds of work traditionally and simultaneously performed by lawyers. Nonlawyers prepare tax returns and give tax advice. They regularly negotiate with and argue cases before the Internal Revenue Service. They prepare patent applications and otherwise advocate on behalf of inventors before the Patent and Trademark Office. And it is entirely unclear why exceptions should exist to help these sort of niche (and, some might say, financially capable) populations but not be expanded in ways more consciously aimed at serving larger numbers of lower- and middle-class clients.

Some states are currently experimenting with intriguing possibilities. California now licenses "legal document assistants" who may help consumers before certain tribunals. Colorado permits nonlawyers to represent claimants in proceedings involving unemployment benefits. And Washington allows legal technicians to assist clients in domestic relations cases provided they meet certain requirements— like obtaining an associate's degree, passing an exam, completing three thousand hours of supervised paralegal work, and taking certain legal courses. The ABA itself recently partnered with one of LegalZoom's competitors, Rocket Lawyer, to help the association's members connect with potential clients online, in the process seemingly granting its imprimatur to a company that some argue engages in the unauthorized practice of law.

Consistent with the law of supply and demand, increasing the supply of legal services can be expected to lower prices, drive efficiency, and improve consumer satisfaction. And, in fact, studies suggest that lay specialists who provide representation in bankruptcy and administrative proceedings often perform as well as or even better than attorneys and generate greater consumer satisfaction. The American Law Institute has noted, too, that "experience in several states with extensive nonlawyer provision of traditional legal services indicates no significant risk of harm to consumers." And the Federal Trade Commission has observed that it is "not aware of any evidence of consumer harm arising from [the provision of legal services by nonlawyers] that would justify foreclosing competition." In the United Kingdom, where nonlawyers can win government contracts to provide legal advice and appear before some administrative tribunals, nonlawyers significantly outperform lawyers in terms of results and satisfaction when dealing with low-income clients. Indeed, studies there show that the best predictor of quality appears to be "specialization, not professional status."

Of course, the potential for abuse cannot be disregarded. Many thoughtful commentators suggest that unauthorized practice of law restrictions are necessary to protect the public from fraudulent or unqualified practitioners. And surely many laypersons, and perhaps especially the most underserved, are not well equipped to judge legal expertise. But do these entirely valid concerns justify the absolute bans found today in so many states? That seems a hard case to make in light of an increasing amount of evidence suggesting that, at least in specified practice areas, a more nuanced approach might adequately preserve (or even enhance) quality while simultaneously increasing access to competent and affordable legal services.

CAPITAL INVESTMENT. All else being equal, market participants with greater access to capital can increase output and lower price. So, for example, optometry, dental, and tax preparation services are no doubt cheaper and more ubiquitous today thanks to the infusion of capital from investors outside those professions. Indeed, consumers can often now find all these services (and more) in their local "superstores." Yet Rule 5.4 of the ABA's Model Rules of Professional Conduct—adopted by most states—prohibits nonlawyers from obtaining "any interest" in a law firm. So while consumers may obtain basic medical and accounting services cheaply and conveniently in and thanks to (say) Walmart, they can't secure similar assistance with a will or a landlord-tenant problem. With a restricted capital base (limited to equity and debt of individual partners), the output of legal services is restricted and the price raised above competitive levels, for as Professor Stephen Gillers has put it, "lay investors might be willing to accept a lower return on their money" than lawyers shielded by Rule 5.4.

Rule 5.4 bears a curious history. After thoroughly studying the issue, the commission that created the first draft of the model rules back in 1982 suggested that lawyers should be allowed to work in firms owned or managed by nonlawyers. But this suggestion was defeated in the ABA House of Delegates and replaced by the present rule effectively preventing nonlawyers from acquiring "any interest" in a law firm. Since then, ABA committees have repeatedly proposed changes to Rule 5.4 but every proposal has, like the first, gone down to defeat in the House of Delegates. Most recently, in 2009 an ABA commission supported serious consideration of three alternatives to the rule. The most modest option would have (1) required a firm to engage only in the practice of law, (2) prohibited nonlawyers from owning more than a certain percentage (e.g., 25 percent) of a firm, and (3) demanded that nonlawyer owners pass a "fit to own" test. Another approach would have allowed lawyers to engage in partnerships of this sort without the cap on nonlawyer ownership or the fit-to-own test. And the third and final option would have done away with all three requirements and permitted firms to offer both legal and nonlegal services.

Notably, the United Kingdom has permitted multidisciplinary firms and nonlawyer investment since 2007. In the first two years of the program, 386 so-called "alternative business structures" (ABSs) were established. Six years into the experiment, the Solicitors Regulation Authority analyzed ABSs and found that while these entities accounted for only 3 percent of all law firms, they had captured 20 percent of consumer and mental health work and nearly 33 percent of the personal injury market—suggesting that ABSs were indeed serving the needs of the poor and middle class, not just or even primarily the wealthy. Notably, too, almost one-third of ABSs were new participants in the legal services market, thus increasing supply and presumably decreasing price. ABSs also reached customers online at far greater rates than traditional firms—more than 90 percent of ABSs were found to possess an online presence versus roughly 50 percent of traditional firms, again suggesting an increased focus on reaching individual consumers. Given the success of this program, it's no surprise that some U.S. jurisdictions have appointed committees to study reforms along just these lines.

To be sure, supporters of the current ABA ban contend that allowing nonlawyers to participate in firms with lawyers might allow nonlawyers to influence adversely the decisions of their attorney colleagues, inducing them to act in ways inconsistent with the rules of professional ethics. But it is again worth asking whether these entirely legitimate concerns justify a total ban on associations between lawyers and nonlawyers. After all, we routinely address similar independence concerns in the model rules without resort to total bans. So, for example, we permit third parties (e.g., insurance companies) to pay for an insured's legal services but restrict their ability to interfere with the attorney-client relationship. We allow in-house counsel to work for corporations where they must answer to executives but require them sometimes to make noisy withdrawals. And we increasingly permit law firms to manage client and personal financial conflicts by screening affected lawyers rather than by banning the firm from representing a client. Of course, in each of these cases lawyers stand to benefit from rules that permit an engagement that might otherwise be forbidden while here, by contrast, they may stand to lose financially. But surely it shouldn't be the case that we will forgo or lift outright bans in favor of more carefully tailored rules only when it's in our financial interest.

CIVIL PROCEDURE REFORMS

The Federal Rules of Civil Procedure aim to shepherd parties toward "the just, speedy, and inexpensive determination of every action and proceeding." But it seems the rules sometimes yield more nearly the opposite: expensive and painfully slow litigation that is itself a form of injustice. After years of study, the federal rules committees advanced a package of amendments (the "Duke Package") seeking to address the problem. The Duke Package made three important changes. It emphasized proportionality as the governing principle for discovery. It tightened discovery deadlines and so shortened the opportunities for delay. And it sought to reduce costs by increasing certainty about parties' obligations to preserve electronically stored information.

While these changes are no doubt a start, it's hard to imagine they'll finish the job of realizing the promise of just, speedy, and inexpensive civil proceedings. After all, our so-called "modern" rules of civil procedure are now almost eighty years old, written for an age in which discovery involved the exchange of mimeographs, not metadata. Neither do you have to look far to see promising models of change. In recent years, at least thirty states and federal district courts have implemented pilot projects testing various amendments to our long-in-the-tooth rules, all with an eye on increasing the efficiency and fairness of civil justice administration. Not every project has proven a resounding success, but the results suggest at least two other possible avenues for reform, and the federal rules committees are contemplating pilot projects to test both in the federal system.

EARLY AND FIRM TRIAL DATES. A study of the federal judicial system in the 1990s found (perhaps to no litigator's surprise) that setting a firm and early trial date is the single "most important" thing a court can do to reduce time to disposition. A more recent study found the same thing: a strong positive correlation between time to resolution and the elapsed time between the filing of a case and the court's setting of a trial date. Studies of recent experiments in Oregon, Colorado, and other state court systems have shown, as well, that firm and early trial dates contribute to reducing litigation costs and increasing client and lawyer satisfaction. And in light of so much data like this, many groups have endorsed the setting of an early and firm trial date as a best practice in civil litigation. Yet, despite this mounting evidence, and while some federal districts today adhere to the practice of setting a firm and early trial date in every case (e.g., the Eastern District of Virginia), system-wide in our federal courts more than 92 percent of motions to continue trial dates are granted and fewer than 45 percent of cases that go to trial do so on the date originally set by the court.

Naturally, the possibility of mandating the practice of setting early and firm trial dates will raise some legitimate concerns. Like the worry that reducing time for trial preparation may not afford complicated cases the time and attention they require. Or the worry that deadlines set early in a case may prove too rigid to account for developments that arise only later. No doubt concerns like these suggest the importance of accounting for a case's complexity when setting a trial date (perhaps examining empirical data regarding how long certain classes of cases take to prepare would be helpful here, data the federal courts now collect and share with judges routinely). Concerns like these may suggest as well the need to preserve a measure of flexibility to respond to new developments—perhaps by permitting continuances in "extraordinary circumstances." But just as important is what concerns like these don't suggest: reason to ignore the proven empirical benefits of setting an (appropriately) early and (normally quite) firm trial date in every single case.

MANDATORY DISCLOSURES. In 1993, the federal rules committees experimented with a rule requiring parties to disclose evidence and documents both helpful and harmful to their respective causes at the outset of discovery. As the committees reasoned, lawyers and parties are rightly expected to fight over the merits but that doesn't necessarily mean they should be permitted to fight (sometimes seemingly endless) collateral battles over what facts they must share with the other side. Just as a prosecutor must reveal exculpatory *Brady* material before proceeding to a vigorous fight on the merits, so too civil parties should have to disclose the good and the bad of their evidence before proceeding to litigate its significance.

The proposal met with swift criticism. Some argued that requiring lawyers to produce discovery harmful to their clients asks them to violate their clients' trust. Others questioned whether a lawyer for one side is well positioned to know what might be helpful to the other. In response to criticisms like these, the rules committees permitted districts to opt out of the initial disclosure requirement, and a number did so, resulting in a patchwork of practices nationwide. And then, responding to complaints about this development, the committees in 2000 narrowed the mandatory-disclosure rule to require only the production of evidence helpful to the producing party.

That might have seemed the end of it. Except that since 2000 a number of states have returned to the idea of mandating early and broad disclosures. And in that time a good deal of evidence has emerged suggesting these disclosures allow parties to focus more quickly and cheaply on the merits of their litigation. For example, Arizona requires parties to disclose all documents they believe to be "relevant to the subject matter of the action" within forty days after a responsive pleading is filed. In 2009, a survey found Arizona litigators preferred state to federal court practice on this score by a 2-to-1 margin. Respondents confirmed that Arizona's rule "reveal[s] the pertinent facts early in the case" (76 percent), "help[s] narrow the issues early" on (70 percent), and facilitates agreement on the scope and timing of discovery (54 percent). Similarly, respondents disagreed with the notion that the disclosure rule either adds to the cost of litigation (58 percent) or unduly front-loads investment in a case (71 percent). Important, too, counsel for plaintiffs and defendants responded in largely the same way on all these issues.

Other states and even an experiment in the federal system have reported similar results. A pilot project in Colorado requiring robust early disclosures in business disputes appears to have resulted in cases with fewer discovery motions and costs more proportionate to case type and the amount in controversy. Meanwhile in Utah, broad initial disclosure rules have seemingly led to quicker case dispositions, fewer discovery disputes in most types of cases, and, according to most attorneys, lower costs. Now decades removed from the backlash against the 1993 amendments, many federal district courts have begun experimenting with requiring parties in certain employment disputes to provide certain disclosures automatically and early. And a study by the Federal Judicial Center shows that motions practice in these cases has fallen by more than 40 percent.

Given all this evidence, it's hard not to wonder if the real problem with the 1993 experiment was simply that it was ahead of its time. Maybe we just needed to wallow a little longer in collateral discovery disputes and watch them become ever more complicated and exasperating with the exponential growth of electronically stored information before we could appreciate this potential lifeline. At the least, it would seem churlish to ignore all that's happened since 1993 and not bother with a pilot project to test in the federal system more broadly what seems to be working so well in so many states and in a discrete set of cases in federal court.

LEGAL EDUCATION

The skyrocketing costs of legal education are no secret. Since the 1980s, private law school tuition in the United States has increased by 155.8 percent and public law school tuition by 428.2 percent (yes, in real, inflation-adjusted terms). And with rising tuition costs come other costs too. Increased debt loads reduce students' incentives and ability to take on lower-paying public service or "main street" legal jobs. No doubt, as well, some of these increased costs are ultimately borne by consumers, as lawyers pass along as much of their "overhead" expenses (student loans) as they can. Which raises the question: Why is a legal education so expensive?

It's hard to ignore the possibility that our legal education accreditation requirements are at least partly to blame. Take California's suggestive experience. In deference to the ABA, most states require anyone sitting for the bar to graduate first from an ABA-accredited law school. But in California it's possible for graduates of state-accredited or unaccredited law schools to take the bar exam. And the cost differential is notable: Average tuition runs $7,230 at unaccredited schools, $19,779 at California-accredited schools, and $44,170 at ABA-accredited schools in the state. No doubt the increased marketability of an ABA-accredited degree is responsible for some of the difference here. But isn't it worth asking whether at least some of our often well-intended accreditation requirements are actually worth the costs they impose?

Consider first and perhaps most ambitiously the mandate that most everyone must attend three years of law school after the completion of a college degree. We've come a long way from Abraham Lincoln's insistence that "[i]f you wish to be a lawyer, attach no consequence to the place you are in, or the person you are with; but get books, sit down anywhere, and go to reading for yourself. That will make a lawyer of you quicker than any other way." For much of our nation's history, President Lincoln's advice held true: The only requirement to become a lawyer in most states was to pass the bar exam. Even some of the law's luminaries as late as the mid-twentieth century didn't attend three years of law school, greats like Justices Robert Jackson and Benjamin Cardozo and Harvard Law School dean Roscoe Pound.

Where did the idea of three years of graduate education come from? It appears most states adopted the requirement at the behest of the ABA. In pushing states to adopt this requirement, the ABA emphasized that legal education must develop in students a mind attuned to the common law—an argument arguably not specific to three years as opposed, say, to two or four. The ABA also invoked the fact that the American Medical Association had proposed a four-year standard for physicians and reasoned that, because law, like medicine, is a complex field, legal studies should last for a comparable period—an argument that seems to have stemmed more from professional pride than empirical proof.

Even if these doubtful rationales once seemed sufficient to persuade states to mandate a monolithic three-year graduate course of study, do they really remain persuasive today? Competitive and consumer-friendly markets are usually characterized by a diversity of goods specialized to fit consumer needs and preferences—and markets with just one good of uniform character are often the product of a producer-friendly monopoly or some similar competitive failure. And while it would be wrong to suggest that all law school educations are identical, it might be worth asking whether three years (with a largely prescribed first year) is necessary for each and every law student. Recently, the ABA acknowledged the need for greater heterogeneity in legal education. And one starting place might be to permit students to sit for the bar after only two years of study, allowing students and employers alike to determine the value of an optional third year of law school. President Obama, himself a Harvard-trained lawyer, has promoted this concept.

Consider that in the United Kingdom the legal education market is a good deal more heterogeneous than ours. To qualify for practice, a student may either take a three-year undergraduate course or a one-year graduate conversion course. Meanwhile, further graduate educational options are available in a variety of fields (e.g., criminal justice, intellectual property, and human rights) for those seeking specialized skills. But none of this is essential. After the basic academic instruction, a student may decide to become a barrister or a solicitor. Depending on his or her choice, the student will then have to undertake additional training, often a one-year specialized educational course followed by a hands-on apprenticeship during which he or she will usually receive only modest compensation. But even the minimum wage presents a substantial swing from expending $50,000 or more on a year of formal legal education in the United States. This diversity of legal education options does not appear to be a threat to the rule of law in the United Kingdom—and it is difficult to see how it might be here.

Beyond that, we might also ask about the value of some of the more discrete accreditation requirements we impose on law schools today. In our zeal for high educational standards, we have developed a long list of requirements that every law school must satisfy to win ABA accreditation and it's often unclear whether these many and various requirements can be justified on the basis of evidence of improved outcomes. Take just a few illustrations. Schools must extend extensive tenure guarantees to faculty, and full-time faculty must teach "substantially all" of a student's first-year courses, even if adjuncts would prove just as good. If an American law school wants to offer something other than a traditional JD program, it must receive a special dispensation from the ABA council responsible for legal education. Then, too, there are the restrictions on the number of credits a student may take at any given time, and the rule that no more than a third of credit hours can be earned for study or activity outside the United States. And beyond even that don't forget that while students usually may receive credit for unpaid internships, they generally may not earn credit for the very same internship if it offers pay and helps reduce their debt load.

Naturally, any revisions to our rules governing law schools would raise complicated cost-quality trade-offs. Some believe that the current American legal education regime is necessary to permit future lawyers to develop sufficient knowledge of legal doctrine and capacity for legal analysis. Justice Antonin Scalia, for example, once argued that "the law-school-in-two-years proposal rests on the premise that law school is—or ought to be—a trade school," a premise he believed erroneous. Others defend the current system by citing familiar consumer-protection concerns. And others still point out that the third year offers opportunities to take elective courses in specialty areas of the law.

Admittedly, these seem good enough arguments to persuade a reasonable mind that at least some lawyers should undertake three years of graduate education. These also may be good enough arguments to justify imposing some significant restrictions on those who opt out of a third year (e.g., requiring on-the-job training for a period of years under the tutelage of a supervisor). But it's far less clear whether these are sufficient grounds for concluding that everyone needs three years of graduate legal training, or legal training shaped by so many and such detailed accreditation requirements.

Commendably, a 2014 ABA white paper explored some of these questions and concluded that many current accreditation requirements do indeed increase cost without conferring commensurate educational benefits. As a result, the paper encouraged a shift from a regulatory scheme controlling so many detailed aspects of the educational process to a scheme focused more on outcomes and empirical cost-benefit analyses. And true to its word, the ABA's section on legal education has begun relaxing at least some of its more extraordinary accreditation requirements. First steps, maybe, but steps in the right direction.

CONCLUSION

Lowering barriers to entry, ensuring judicial resolutions come more quickly and at less cost, and making legal education more affordable share the common aim of increasing the supply and lowering the price of legal services. All of these potential changes, too, are uniquely within our profession's power to effect. Of course, meaningful change rarely comes easily, let alone when it requires a self-regulating profession to undertake self-sacrifice. But estimates suggest that inefficient policies and our professional regulations result in a roughly $10 billion annual "self-subsidy," in the form of higher prices lawyers may charge their clients compared to what they could charge in a more competitive marketplace. Might not our willingness to confront candidly just how much of that self-subsidy is warranted prove a good test of our commitment to civil justice reform—and whether we as a profession wish to do good or merely do well?

A NOTE ON
JURY TRIALS

———

The Sixth and Seventh Amendments guarantee the right to a jury trial, yet we have almost no trials anymore. Today, not even 2 percent of civil cases see a jury. Plenty of factors have contributed to this development. But one may lie in our own self-imposed rules. Today, for example, if people neglect to assert their right to a jury trial at the outset of a case, they are deemed to have waived it. This rule struck me and Judge Susan Graber, a former colleague on the standing committee that reviews federal rules of procedure, as odd. Our rules should encourage people to exercise their constitutional rights, not create barriers to their doing so. So when Judge Graber asked me to join her in sending the following note asking an advisory committee on the rules of civil procedure to consider a change, I was happy to say yes.

W E WRITE TO SUGGEST THAT THE ADVISORY COMMITTEE ON THE Rules of Civil Procedure consider a significant revision to the rules concerning demands for a jury trial.

The idea is simple: As is true for criminal cases, a jury trial would be the default in civil cases. That is, if a party is entitled to a jury trial on a claim (whether under the Seventh Amendment, a statute, or otherwise), that claim will be tried by a jury unless the party waives a jury, in writing, as to that claim or any subsidiary issue.

Several reasons animate our proposal. First, we should be encouraging jury trials, and we think that this change would result in more jury trials. Second, simplicity is a virtue. The present system, especially with regard to removed cases, can be a trap for the unwary.

Third, such a rule would produce greater certainty. Fourth, a jury-trial default honors the Seventh Amendment more fully. Finally, many states do not require a specific demand. Although we have not looked for empirical studies, we do not know of negative experiences in those jurisdictions.

We recognize that this would be a huge change, and we also recognize that problems could result, especially in *pro se* cases. Nevertheless, we encourage the advisory committee to discuss our idea. Thank you.

Alejandre-Gallegos v. Holder

———

*This Tenth Circuit case illustrates the sadly familiar prob-
lems that arise when lawyers fail to provide even basic assistance for their clients. In this case, the government sought to
deport Mr. Alejandre-Gallegos on the ground that he had
committed a crime of "moral turpitude." Mr. Alejandre-
Gallegos went to the expense of hiring a lawyer to argue that
he wasn't guilty of such a crime. But the lawyer failed to
provide anything approaching competent legal representation. Too often people get only as much justice as they can
afford; sometimes they don't even get that much.*

WORRIED THAT HE COULD BE DEPORTED FOR HIS UNLAWFUL
presence in this country, Santiago Alejandre-Gallegos sought
discretionary relief under a statute that allows the Attorney General
to "cancel" a deportation that would result in "unusual hardship" to
an alien's U.S. citizen family members. An Immigration Judge denied
the request and so did the Board of Immigration Appeals. No matter
how hard the hardship, the Board noted, an applicant can't win can-
cellation of removal if he has been convicted of a crime involving
moral turpitude. And, the Board observed, Mr. Alejandre-Gallegos
has pleaded guilty to at least one such offense.

Now before us, Mr. Alejandre-Gallegos seeks to undo this decision but his attorney fails to give us any grounds on which we might.
Counsel suggests the Board relied on improper evidence but doesn't
supply any citations to the record where it went wrong on the facts.
He suggests that the Board applied the wrong legal standards but
doesn't cite any legal authority that might remotely support his

claim. He even spends pages discussing another criminal charge against his client irrelevant to the one on which the Board relied. Neither are counsel's shortcomings confined to such important things. His statement of related cases includes argument. He does not "cite the precise reference in the record where [each of his issues] was raised and ruled on" and his statement of the case includes no record citations at all. His brief contains no "summary of the argument." He hasn't even bothered to "alphabetically arrange[]" his table of authorities. We could go on.

Essentially, counsel pronounces that the Board mistook the facts and acted in defiance of law and leaves it to the court to go fish for facts and law that might possibly support his claim. This, of course, the court has no obligation and is poorly positioned to do. In our adversarial system, neutral and busy courts rely on lawyers to develop and present in an intelligible format the facts and law to support their arguments and "[t]he adversarial process cannot properly function when one party ignores its obligations under the rules." For that reason it's within the court's power "to dismiss an appeal when the appellant has failed to abide by the rules of appellate procedure." That's the course we find ourselves forced to take in this case.

We confess reluctance about having to proceed so summarily and about having to chastise a professional colleague in this way. Everyone makes mistakes, and surely judges no less than lawyers. But the shortcomings here don't just suggest a mistake, a few, or even a thoroughgoing disinterest in the rules of procedure. They suggest a lack of competent representation. For all we know from counsel's garbled submission before us, his client may have a good claim or at least an arguable one: we just cannot tell. That worry occupied us so much that we decided to review counsel's past filings in this court to see if his conduct here was (hopefully) anomalous. But the results proved even more disquieting. They revealed that for at least a decade counsel has represented in this court immigrants seeking relief from removal—and that for at least that long his filings in this court have consistently suffered from the sort of shortcomings present in this one. It turns out that this court has noted the problem time and again. It has reminded counsel of his professional obligations. It has admonished him. All to no effect.

At some point, this court has a duty to do more than observe, record, and warn. It has a duty to act. After reviewing the record before us, we are confident that time has more than come. Because we believe sanctions—including suspension from this court's bar and restitution—may be appropriate, we direct the Clerk to initiate a disciplinary proceeding.

Mathis v. Shulkin

Access to justice problems sometimes come in more disguised form. Sometimes it's not just the obvious cost or the difficulty of obtaining a good lawyer. Take this case. Under the laws passed by Congress, our veterans are supposed to receive affirmative assistance from the Department of Veterans Affairs when they apply for disability benefits. But in this case, the agency developed a presumption against veterans that seemingly appears nowhere in the law—all apparently for its own administrative convenience. This piece was the first dissent I wrote from the denial of certiorari (refusal to hear a case) after joining the Supreme Court.

L OWER COURTS OFTEN PRESUME THAT DEPARTMENT OF VETERANS Affairs medical examiners are competent to render expert opinions against veterans seeking compensation for disabilities they have suffered during military service. The VA appears to apply the same presumption in its own administrative proceedings.

But where does this presumption come from? It enjoys no apparent provenance in the relevant statutes. There Congress imposed on the VA an affirmative duty to assist—not impair—veterans seeking evidence for their disability claims. And consider how the presumption works in practice. The VA usually refuses to supply information that might allow a veteran to challenge the presumption without an order from the Board of Veterans' Appeals. And that Board often won't issue an order unless the veteran can first supply a specific reason for thinking the examiner incompetent. No doubt this arrangement makes the VA's job easier. But how is it that an administrative agency may manufacture for itself or win from the courts a regime that has no basis in the relevant statutes and does nothing to assist, and much to impair, the interests of those the law says the agency is supposed to serve?

Now, you might wonder if our intervention is needed to remedy the problem. After all, a number of thoughtful colleagues on the Federal Circuit have begun to question the presumption's propriety. And this may well mean the presumption's days are numbered. But I would not wait in hope. The issue is of much significance to many today and, respectfully, it is worthy of this Court's attention.

Hester v. United States

———

The Sixth Amendment guarantees that a jury will find all the facts necessary to support any prison sentence you receive. But today courts often issue massive financial restitution orders rather than mandate prison time. Can the government avoid the demands of the Sixth Amendment by seeking financial penalties rather than prison time? This excerpt, from a dissent from denial of certiorari, discusses that question.

I F YOU'RE CHARGED WITH A CRIME, THE SIXTH AMENDMENT GUAR-antees you the right to a jury trial. From this, it follows that the prosecutor must prove to a jury all of the facts legally necessary to support your term of incarceration. Neither is this rule limited to prison time. If a court orders you to pay a fine to the government, a jury must also find all the facts necessary to justify that punishment too.

But what if instead the court orders you to pay restitution to victims? Must a jury find all the facts needed to justify a restitution order as well? That's the question presented in this case. After the defendants pleaded guilty to certain financial crimes, the district court held a hearing to determine their victims' losses. In the end and based on its own factual findings, the court ordered the defendants to pay $329,767 in restitution. The Ninth Circuit affirmed, agreeing with the government that the facts supporting a restitution order can be found by a judge rather than a jury.

Respectfully, I believe this case is worthy of our review. Restitution plays an increasing role in federal criminal sentencing today. Before the passage of the Victim and Witness Protection Act of 1982, restitution orders were comparatively rare. But from 2014 to 2016 alone, federal courts sentenced 33,158 defendants to pay $33.9 billion in restitution. And between 1996 and 2016, the amount of unpaid federal criminal restitution rose from less than $6 billion to more than $110 billion. The effects of restitution orders, too, can be profound. Failure or inability to pay restitution can result in suspension of the right to vote, continued court supervision, or even reincarceration.

The ruling before us is not only important, it seems doubtful. The Ninth Circuit itself has conceded that allowing judges, rather than juries, to decide the facts necessary to support restitution orders isn't "well-harmonized" with this Court's Sixth Amendment decisions. Judges in other circuits have made the same point in similar cases. Nor does the government's defense of the judgment below dispel these concerns. This Court has held that the Sixth Amendment requires a jury to find any fact that triggers an increase in a defendant's "statutory maximum" sentence. Seizing on this language, the government argues that the Sixth Amendment doesn't apply to restitution orders because the amount of restitution is dictated only by the extent of the victim's loss and thus has no "statutory maximum." But the government's argument misunderstands the teaching of our cases. We've used the term "statutory maximum" to refer to the harshest sentence the law allows a court to impose based on facts a jury has found or the defendant has admitted. In that sense, the statutory maximum for restitution is usually *zero*, because a court can't award *any* restitution without finding additional facts about the victim's loss. And just as a jury must find any facts necessary to authorize a steeper prison sentence or fine, it would seem to follow that a jury must find any facts necessary to support a (nonzero) restitution order.

The government is not without a backup argument, but it appears to bear problems of its own. The government suggests that the Sixth Amendment doesn't apply to restitution orders because restitution isn't a criminal penalty, only a civil remedy that "compensates victims for [their] economic losses." But the Sixth Amendment's jury trial right expressly applies "[i]n all criminal prosecutions," and the government concedes that "restitution is imposed as part of a defendant's criminal conviction." Federal statutes, too, describe restitution as a "penalty" imposed on the defendant as part of his criminal sentence, as do our cases. Besides, if restitution really fell beyond the reach of the Sixth Amendment's protections in *criminal* prosecutions, we would then have to consider the Seventh Amendment and its independent protection of the right to a jury trial in *civil* cases.

If the government's arguments appear less than convincing, maybe it's because they're difficult to reconcile with the Constitution's original meaning. The Sixth Amendment was understood as preserving the " 'historical role of the jury at common law.' " And as long ago as the time of Henry VIII, an English statute entitling victims to the restitution of stolen goods allowed courts to order the return only of those goods mentioned in the indictment and found stolen by a jury. In America, too, courts held that in prosecutions for larceny, the jury usually had to find the value of the stolen property before restitution to the victim could be ordered. And it's hard to see why the right to a jury trial should mean less to the people today than it did to those at the time of the Sixth and Seventh Amendments' adoption.

6.

ON ETHICS
AND THE
GOOD LIFE

S OME TIME AFTER I JOINED THE TENTH CIRCUIT, the University of Colorado Law School asked me to teach a course on legal ethics. Now, I know, some may wonder whether the course's very title amounts to an oxymoron. But my immediate reaction was a little different. I believed the course important to the development of sound professional values. At the same time, though, I thought the class was supposed to be taught by some graying, battle-worn practitioner who could tell war stories to scare students straight. But then I looked in the mirror . . . and I signed up.

I went on to teach that course for many years. At some point each semester I'd ask the students to participate in this exercise. Imagine you've graduated, finally won entry to the bar, and are now busy working as a lawyer. You're thumbing through documents a client gave you and you come across one that's a smoking gun against your client's interests. The other side has filed a discovery demand that clearly aims to secure the production of this very information. Lawyers are supposed to honor discovery requests, but this one's poorly written and there's a color-able argument that the document doesn't fall strictly within its terms. Should you turn over the document? Or do you hide it, keep your client happy, and hope no one finds out the truth? Each year, about three-quarters of the class told me they'd withhold the document. Even if it meant a gravely disabled person on the other side wouldn't win a warranted recovery. The students didn't necessarily think hiding the document was the morally upright thing to do; these were wonderful students, good people, with strong values. But somehow, they thought, it was a professionally acceptable thing for a lawyer to hide the document. Some even thought a lawyer had a professional *duty* to act this way. No wonder so many lawyers are so unhappy these days and rates of depression, anxiety, alcoholism, suicide, and divorce for lawyers stand at about twice the national average. The law tends to breed workaholics and sometimes disconnection from family, friends, community, and even (true) ethics.

How have we gotten here? It's a complicated story. But if there's one thing I sought to pass along to my students, it's that a life in the law doesn't have to look like this. After the document production discussion, I would ask the class to spend five quiet minutes drafting their own obituaries; how would they like them to read? Each year, there'd be an understandable amount of groaning at the start of this exercise. But after a minute or two the room would grow silent, even somber. When the time was up, I'd ask a few brave students to read their drafts aloud. Not once did their obituaries brag about how many hours they worked, what their billable hourly rate was, how many clients they lured, whether they had argued one or a hundred cases, what kind of car they drove, how big their house was, or whether they wound up with their name on their law firm's front door. Each one spoke of hoping to be remembered as kind; loved by family and friends; someone who left the world a little better, or at least no worse off, for their presence.

At the end of the session I would read my students a tombstone inscription I found when I was a law student walking through colonial Boston. It spoke of a lawyer and statesman who is largely forgotten today but who was obviously loved by family and friends during his time. (You can find it on page 321.) I would tell the class that I keep a copy of the epitaph on my desk as a sort of moral compass, a reminder of true north when the horizon seems hard to see, and as a source of encouragement to try again when I falter and fall short. I would then suggest to my students that they keep their own obituary drafts in their desk drawers and return to them every now and then so they might assess how their conduct is measuring up to their aspirations.

This chapter collects a sample of reflections I've offered over the years on the challenge of being a good lawyer and a good person.

A TRIBUTE

———

One of the special parts of my first year on the Supreme Court was the chance to serve beside my former boss Anthony Kennedy. When Justice Kennedy decided to retire at the end of our first full term together—after thirty years of service on the Supreme Court and another decade as an appellate judge on the Ninth Circuit—the Harvard Law Review *asked me to contribute a few words to its next edition. I was delighted to have the opportunity not only to offer my personal tribute of thanks but also to discuss some of the lessons his example holds for me.*

WITH JUSTICE KENNEDY'S RETIREMENT, THE SUPREME COURT has lost one of the most consequential justices in its history. His formidable legal legacy is the focus of other tributes in this edition of the *Harvard Law Review*. For my part, though, the editors have asked me to focus not so much on *Justice* Kennedy as on *Anthony* Kennedy. That assignment is a particular honor and a very happy one. For as much as the justice has touched the life of the law, the man has touched the lives of those around him in ways that hold rich lessons all their own.

There is this man's deep civility and respect for all persons. I first came to know Justice Kennedy as his "step clerk." Justice White had hired me to serve him in his first year in retirement, sitting by designation on the Tenth Circuit. But Justice Kennedy also "adopted" me and treated me as every bit a member of his law clerk family. The year began when the justice asked all of us to come to his home on the weekend to discuss the first set of merits cases. His only instruction: bring the whiteboard. So we trucked out to Virginia in a clunker with the whiteboard stashed in the trunk. We spent the day hunkered down debating cases, covering the whiteboard with arguments and diagrams. From that moment to the end of the year, I witnessed a gentle man who never raised his voice, who treated every lawyer he saw in the courtroom and every person he encountered in the halls as he would wish to be treated, and who afforded the most routine case with the same care as the (seemingly) most important. In his already long and distinguished judicial career, the justice had encountered before many of the issues we clerks faced for the first time. But all the same, he would follow the judicial process scrupulously from start to finish in every case—carefully reading the briefs, listening to the parties, talking over the issues with clerks and colleagues, and only then deciding. His enthusiasm, his level of attention to detail, and his interest in hearing different views was infectious. When at last he reached his final judgment and found himself at odds with a colleague or clerk, he would not hesitate to disagree, but he would never do it disagreeably.

There is his humility and his love of country and our courts. When years later I became a circuit judge, I asked the boss to come to Colorado to swear me in. Of course, he came. And, of course, I took the chance to seek his advice. His answer? Listen. Listen to your colleagues, to the parties, to scholars in the field. There's a reason federal courts of appeals sit on panels of three, he reminded me, and a reason why we engage in such a painstaking process before we announce our judgments. Do all you can, he said, to carry on the traditions of our independent judiciary and recognize always that, to those involved, the case before you may be the most important thing in their lives. Know, too, that you are part of something much greater than yourself, the promise of the rule of law in our time. This nation's independent courts may not be perfect but their promise of equal justice under law for all persons represents one of the noblest of human aspirations in any place or age. Justice Kennedy could say these things because he lived these things.

There is his kindness. After Justice Kennedy swore me in for a second time, now as his colleague on the Court, my family moved to Washington. It was the first time in our history that a justice and his former clerk had the chance to serve together on the Court. No surprise by now, the justice and his wife, Mary, offered us a welcome that could not have been more gracious. For as everyone who knows them knows, Mary Kennedy is every bit as special as her husband. The Kennedys were among the first to invite us to dinner and to introduce us to their friends. They even helped with our house hunt. When I circulated a draft of my first opinion for the Court, Justice Kennedy raced to join before anyone else. Even the fickleness of less-than-modern technology couldn't keep him from that object. I circulated my draft late in the day, after Justice Kennedy had gone home. When his clerk tried to fax the opinion to him, the machine wouldn't cooperate. But Justice Kennedy didn't want to risk waiting to get a copy until the next morning, so he requested that someone drive a hard copy out to his house. Before the open of business the next morning I received a handwritten "join memo"—one I keep in the top drawer of my desk and will always treasure.

As great as Justice Kennedy's legal legacy may be, I cannot help but wonder if today the person may have as much to teach us as the jurist. I've offered only a few (among so many) examples of the man I've known; the truth is, everyone who knows Tony and Mary Kennedy is blessed with an overabundance of memories like these. But what we've all witnessed perhaps boils down to this. The rules Tony Kennedy has chosen to follow in his life he's chosen carefully and worked hard to abide. They are timeless, tested, and true. They represent what is best, if these days too often missing, in our profession and our culture. Treat others as you would have them treat you, remembering that those with whom you disagree love this country every bit as much as you do. Strive for humility in argument and in making decisions, knowing that everyone around you has something to offer and teach. Accept praise and criticism with equal equanimity, realizing that life's real joy lies in serving something greater than yourself. Don't dwell on this nation's imperfections so much that you forget that its aspirations to the rule of law and to the equal protection of all persons are among the most worthy ambitions in human history. Along the way in life, too, try to be kind, for whatever regrets you may have in life you'll never regret being kind. Of course, no one is perfect, we all stumble and struggle, so learn to dust yourself off, hold fast, and aim again at getting it right. These are the simple but enduring truths this man has sought to honor in his life. It is a life that is a grace to our profession and our nation and a model for those who follow.

WHITE AND MURRAH

———

I've given variations of this speech to different groups of students and young lawyers in the Tenth Circuit over the years. It's a tribute to two great men from my part of the country. Some readers may have heard of one, though I'd guess that most haven't heard of the other. But the lives of both have much to offer—and not just about how to live a life in the law. Each achieved professional success without abandoning the qualities that made them good persons. Really, it was that very quality that made them such great lawyers and judges. They practiced a fearless integrity everywhere in their daily lives.

THE PUBLIC HAS ALWAYS HELD COMPETING PERCEPTIONS OF THE legal profession. On the one hand, there is the ideal of Clarence Darrow, Daniel Webster, and Louis Brandeis. Honorable men of the law. On the other hand, there are the classic scoundrels—the lawyers who seek to buy judges and the judges who are eager to be bought. In fact, it often seems that the scoundrel image overshadows the ideal. Even Judge Laurence Silberman of the D.C. Circuit, one of this nation's most respected judges, has observed that a great many lawyers today "hate what the practice of law has become." Another leading federal judge, Patrick Schiltz, has documented just how unhealthy, unhappy, and (yes) unethical our profession has become, pointing to alarmingly high rates of depression, alcoholism, divorce, and suicide.

I cannot dispute the grim numbers or the wisdom of my colleagues. But I'd like to suggest to you that this sad picture need not define the profession—that you can be both an ethical person *and* an ethical lawyer. In fact, it seems to me that you must be one to be the other. In the words of one favorite former professor of mine, Charles Fried, "Lawyers are people too!" There is no distinction between the professional you and the personal you.

To illustrate this point, I share a few stories about two of this country's greatest lawyers. The first, Byron White, sat on the Supreme Court for over three decades, and remains at least somewhat in the public consciousness. The second man, a former chief judge of the Tenth Circuit, Alfred Murrah, also served on the federal bench for over thirty years but is less recognizable today—although this certainly wasn't the case in his time, and most certainly wasn't the case in his home state of Oklahoma.

Both of these men had a hardscrabble upbringing in the West of the early twentieth century. Byron White grew up during the Great Depression and went to work on a sugar beet farm on the Colorado plains at age seven. He described his hometown of Wellington as a town of "350 God-fearing souls," where "[e]verybody worked for a living. Everybody. Everybody." From an early age, White excelled at everything. As valedictorian of his high school, he earned a scholarship to the University of Colorado. Once there, he became maybe the most celebrated college football player of his time, an All-American and a Heisman Trophy runner-up. But White hardly ignored his studies. He was elected to Phi Beta Kappa and graduated first in his class. From there, he earned a Rhodes Scholarship and later enrolled in Yale Law School. But even that wasn't all; he also played professional football to make some extra money. He led the league in rushing and was famously the highest-paid player of his day ($15,000, I think). He found time, too, to serve in the South Pacific during World War II and was twice decorated with the Bronze Star. Following law school, White clerked for the Supreme Court, worked in private practice in Denver, then joined the Kennedy administration as the deputy attorney general. Only about a year later, President Kennedy appointed him to the Supreme Court at age forty-four.

Judge Murrah was born in rural Oklahoma. His mother died when he was seven and his father took the family to Alabama to find work. Just eight years later, when Murrah was fifteen, his father passed away too. Now an orphan, Murrah decided to make his way back to Oklahoma. He did it by riding freight cars and doing odd jobs along the way. Back in his home state, a family agreed to care for him in exchange for work on their ranch. Like White, Murrah emerged from his rough-and-tumble childhood to graduate first in his high school class and go on to the state university. And like White, Murrah came to the federal bench at a very young age. President Franklin Roosevelt appointed him to the district court at age thirty-two and to the Tenth Circuit at age thirty-five. Judge Murrah went on to serve on the circuit for thirty years, and as the chief judge for eleven of those. After retiring, Murrah didn't just disappear to Fort Lauderdale either. Instead, he led the Federal Judicial Center, where he spearheaded the movement toward using pre-trial conferences, a development that has greatly streamlined federal litigation.

These short biographies and the accomplishments they chronicle, as interesting as they are, are not the real reason I bring up these men. Instead, I want to talk about how these men approached their jobs—how they viewed their role as lawyers and persons.

One thing that Justice White's former colleagues and clerks remember about him was his dedication to work. This is a man who by age forty-four had achieved about all one could, yet he never took his nose off the grindstone. In his time on the Court, Justice White was famous for dissenting from denials of certiorari—he authored more than two hundred. In these dissents, he identified disagreements over the law between circuits. And he argued that the Court had an obligation to take and resolve these disagreements so that people in one part of the country weren't treated differently from those elsewhere only because of the happenstance of geography. In his view, it was the judge's job to resolve even the most seemingly mundane of these disputes and he never shied away from doing his job. No matter that it meant (a lot) more work.

Even after three decades on the Supreme Court, Justice White worked as hard—and often harder—than his young law clerks. I can attest. When I clerked for him in his "retirement," he was continuing to work on the Tenth Circuit. When he'd get an opinion to write, he would race me to see who could finish a draft first. If I lost, he would toss my hard work straight into the trash can and we'd start editing his draft. About halfway through each race, he would come into my office and jokingly ask, "The Great Justice Gorsuch, how goes the opinion?" At first, I thought these playful questions were just small talk, but later I realized that they were his way of sizing up the competition. And so I quickly learned that I'd have to hold my cards a little closer if I was ever to have a chance. Once, when he was asked what he had learned from his time on the playing field, he said, "When the whistle blows you have only a limited amount of time to do what you have to do. You either do it then, or you don't do it at all." I think that this is how he viewed each day as a lawyer and a judge.

Beyond Justice White's hard work ethic and his sterling résumé, what clerks and colleagues most remember about him was his humility. Justice White's office at the Supreme Court provided no hint of the occupant's fame. There were no certificates of accomplishment hanging on the walls, simply photos of his family and paintings of his beloved Colorado. On a mantel in his office, there was a well-worn football, but no plaque proclaiming its significance or celebrating his past athletic accomplishments. One former clerk once shared the story of when he and the justice joined a tour of the then new Hart Senate Office Building. Justice White began asking a uniformed guard questions about the building—How high was the ceiling? How long had it taken to construct the building? The guard answered question after question, enjoying the opportunity to display his knowledge. At the end of the conversation, Justice White asked whether he could go up and see the gym, and the guard responded that the area was not open to the general public. Rather than identify himself, Justice White assured the guard that he understood and thanked him for taking the time to answer his questions. As this former clerk noted, Justice White was not one to use the prestige of his position to gain favors, even small ones. More important, he wasn't a person who would pull rank on a hardworking guard just to prove he could.

Like Justice White, Judge Murrah was known for his tireless work ethic. As his colleague Judge Holloway once recounted, Judge Murrah "was always encouraging us to do our best, to re-dedicate ourselves to the increasing tasks ahead, to deal with the mounting case load with innovation, and still to keep the quality of justice up to the standard worthy of the rich traditions of this court." And like Justice White, Judge Murrah loved his job. One day, Judge Murrah was attending a conference where he met David Lewis, then a state judge. Lewis told Murrah that he was not planning to run for reelection because the salary was too low for him to provide for his family as he wanted. To this, Judge Murrah responded, "Don't give it up. If you love to be a judge, you will always be good." Judge Lewis was inspired to reconsider his decision and ran for reelection. Years later, Lewis himself was appointed to the Tenth Circuit, ultimately succeeding Murrah as chief judge.

Judge Murrah was also famous for emphasizing that our system of justice—the best system in the world, he believed—is only as good as the people who work in it. Not just the judges and the lawyers, but the clerks and the employees. One of his former clerks once noted that Judge Murrah "would be entirely uncomfortable at the suggestion that his professional efforts were devoted to something as impersonal as the [justice] system." Rather, "the whole of his living was directed to people—to the individual people with whom he lived, and not an abstract system." Judge Murrah's career and beliefs remind me of Abraham Lincoln's exhortation that the nation's continued success depends on good men who toil quietly in the service of the common good, not those who ambitiously seek the throne; it is these good men who support and maintain the edifice erected by those who came before.

What I find most compelling about White and Murrah, though, is how these two great lawyers achieved professional success without ever abandoning the humility and integrity and simple hard work that made them great men. In fact, I'd venture to say that they achieved what they did precisely *because* they never distinguished between their lives as lawyers and their lives as people. They viewed the practice of law as a profession, as a calling to work for the benefit of others. Being a lawyer, to them, was not some instrumental means toward wealth or fame. Both gave up profitable careers and considerable riches to serve for decades as public servants. To them, being a lawyer meant pursuing and cultivating an ideal of hard work,

humility, and good judgment in the service of others—whether litigants, clients, family and friends, their communities, or the nation.

This, I think, is a worthy model for you to consider as you start
your own careers. It's a model with a very distinct and, yes, demanding view on ethics. Just as these men never distinguished between
who they were as lawyers and who they were as people, I suggest that
you cannot distinguish between professional ethics and personal ethics. As Judge Schiltz has thoughtfully explained, "Practicing law
ethically will depend primarily on the hundreds of little things that
you will do almost unthinkingly every day. . . . You are going to have
to act almost instinctively. What this means, then, is that you will not
practice law ethically—you cannot practice law ethically—unless
acting ethically is habitual for you." If you find yourself lying to opposing counsel, you might soon find yourself lying to your friends
and family. You can pretend there's a line between the office and the
home, but you are the same person in both places, and ethical behavior is not something you can turn on only sometimes in some places.
Good habits formed in your personal life will influence the split-
second judgments you make every day as an attorney; bad habits will
follow you too. Your habits will influence your character and, ultimately, form your own life's story. As White and Murrah teach us,
too, these habits take hard work and if you fail today, you have to try
again tomorrow; never tire and never give up. We only have a limited
amount of time once the whistle blows. Make it count.

BUT MY CLIENT
MADE ME DO IT

––––––

The Struggle of Being a Good Lawyer
and *Living a Good Life*

> *While I was a Tenth Circuit judge, Oklahoma City University*
> *asked me to visit, teach classes, and give a speech to the law*
> *school community. By that point, I had been teaching legal*
> *ethics at the University of Colorado for some time and in my*
> *speech I decided to offer a few reflections on the subject.*

MAYBE THE ISSUE MY ETHICS STUDENTS STRUGGLE WITH MOST CON-
cerns how far they should go to pursue a client's interest. The
Model Rules of Professional Conduct tell us that a lawyer has a
duty to represent the client's interests "diligent[ly]." But that doesn't
really answer my students' question. They know they have to be diligent. But what does that *mean*? The comments to the rules offer a
little more guidance, exhorting members of the profession to act
with zeal for their clients. But what the comments giveth, they also
taketh away. Immediately after telling us to act zealously, the comments add that lawyers may choose not to employ what they call
"offensive tactics." The comments likewise tell us that lawyers don't
have to "press for every advantage" for their clients.

Note how the comments are worded. We are told lawyers may
choose not to use offensive tactics. Now . . . that's not exactly a ringing endorsement of taking the high road, is it? Doesn't it intimate
that a lawyer may *also* choose to use offensive tactics? In fact, could

it even subtly suggest that most lawyers will employ such offensive tactics, and you're a bit of a coward if you don't?

These are questions my students struggle with.

As it happens, many students seem to come to my class with the conviction that they have an obligation to use zealously every lawful means available to vindicate their client's interests, whether offensive or not. They view litigation as a somewhat more dignified (or at least better-groomed) version of a Rambo movie. How is it that so many law students, so early in their professional lives, already harbor this view about our profession? My law clerks suggest that popular culture is a contributing, though not exclusive, cause. And it's easy to see their point.

When I was growing up, the leading TV lawyer was Perry Mason, and no doubt he inspired a lot of future lawyers to high professional standards. Today, who is modeling the profession for our future lawyers? Maybe Denny Crane of *Boston Legal*? Or Lionel Hutz of *The Simpsons*? I confess I enjoy watching them, but they're not quite Perry Mason, are they? Denny Crane tells us that the first rule of thumb in practicing law is this: "Always, always promise the client millions . . . and millions of dollars—It's good business." Meanwhile, Lionel Hutz's ads read: "Lionel Hutz, Attorney at Law, as Seen on TV . . . Your Case Won in 30 Minutes, or Your Pizza's Free."

If you think I'm picking on lawyers, consider how we judges are viewed. In addition to Lionel Hutz, *The Simpsons* features Judge Constance Harm. What a name. And she's so tough that, when she sentences a defendant, she likes to tell them that they will be in jail "'til frogs can do fractions." And that's a step up from the judge on *Boston Legal* who's so senile he seems close to drooling while issuing erratic orders. In a dispirited moment, one might worry that the term "legal ethics" has, at least as it is viewed in popular culture, become something close to a contradiction in terms.

Of course, we can't blame the media for our professional image. The media holds the mirror. The reflection is our own. So, where does this lawyer-as-land-shark view of legal ethics come from? Dean Lawrence Hellman wrote an influential and thoughtful article in the *Georgetown Journal of Legal Ethics* in which he documented a couple possible answers. He pointed to evidence suggesting that many law students get their ethical cues during internships, summer associate work, or their early years in practice. What the student learns about ethics in the workplace tends to overshadow whatever is taught in the classroom. At the same time, Dean Hellman also pointed to evidence suggesting that law school itself tends to have a corrosive effect on students' values—in some ways, law school seems to be leaving students with lower standards than those they arrived with. But wherever students get the idea from, it does seem as if today we enjoy a superabundance of lawyers—both in practice and in the academy—who defend the view that a client's immoral command should be followed.

I hope to persuade you to think again about this and about what kind of lawyer and person you might wish to become in the practice of law. Though we lawyers are fiduciary agents generally bound to assist our principals, we are also people too (popular mythology and many jokes notwithstanding). Saying "but my client made me do it" doesn't mean we always escape moral culpability for our actions. Yes, it is possible to be both a good lawyer and a good person, but it takes work. And I want to suggest that it's work well worth your attention.

When my students raise their "my client made me do it" hired-gun view of the lawyer's role, I ask them about the aftermath of World War II when certain Nazi war criminals sought to defend their actions on the basis that their superiors made them do it. The Nuremberg principles and charter governing the conduct of the Nazi war trials rejected this defense, explaining that "[t]he fact that the Defendant acted pursuant to order of his Government or of a superior" would not, categorically at least, "free [the defendant] from responsibility." So Nazi generals couldn't escape culpability for their actions just because some superior officer "told them to do it." And that's in the military, where chain of command principles are very strong, maybe even stronger than the fiduciary duty lawyers owe their clients. And in light of that, I ask my students: Where does that leave you? By the end of my ethics class, I hope I have convinced at least a few students that there are some circumstances when a good lawyer should not blindly follow a client's orders.

Now, to be clear, I don't mean to suggest a lawyer should lightly disregard a client's orders and simply do whatever the lawyer thinks best. Some, to be sure, have advocated for such a view of the lawyer's role. In Soviet systems, for example, it was often said there was to be "no division of duty between the judge, prosecutor, and defense counsel" because defense counsel was required "to assist the prosecution" in a purported search for the "truth" to promote overall social welfare. According to this vision, the lawyer owes his or her client's wishes no particular deference because the society's collective interests outweigh the individual's. But such a regime can work serious injustices. A just legal order seeks, among other things, to assure equal treatment for individuals and to ensure that an individual receives due process. Lawyers serve a critical instrumental function in our adversarial legal system by ensuring that their clients' positions are presented and heard. To usurp the client's voice, to become not just the client's advocate but also the judge and jury of the client's cause, is to do serious damage to the integrity of our adversarial legal order and, with it, to the dignity of the individual.

Nor is there anything immoral in preferring the interests of one's client to the interests of others. We do just this all the time in our daily lives. Your choice to spend this weekend with your children may preclude you from spending time volunteering. But that doesn't make it immoral. We live in a world where there are many upright ways to live life, and choosing one good often unavoidably means you will do incidental, if not intentional, harm to other goods. So I agree that we can and should generally prefer our clients' interests to other interests. But, just as with the case of the Nazis at Nuremberg, we shouldn't always do so.

In an effort to capture this balance of duties, Professor Charles Fried once famously offered this comparison. He suggested that a lawyer should act as a sort of friend. A friend generally prefers his friend's interests to the wider population's. In all sorts of ways, we give our friends loyalty and preference that we would not give a stranger. This is natural, human, and appropriate. At the same time, this doesn't mean that we will or should do anything for a friend. A line must be and is drawn somewhere. So, for example, we often say we won't kill or tell hurtful lies for friends. Respect for ourselves and others normally precludes us from following friendship to the point that we do intentional wrongs to ourselves or others. Fried argues that the lawyer-client relationship works in much the same way. We generally prefer our clients' interests to those of nonclients, but there are some things we just won't, and shouldn't, do.

Some have argued that the lawyer-as-friend metaphor has its problems. On close inspection, they say, the lawyer-client relationship doesn't compare well to a true friendship. Lawyers and clients premise their relationship on money, not true affinities. Also, there is often an inequality in power in the lawyer-client relationship, one that is not typical of true friendships based on mutual admiration. Lawyers and clients sometimes might not like each other and still have a professionally satisfactory relationship. All these and similar criticisms may well have something to them. But even if the lawyer-as-friend metaphor is imperfect, I wonder whether it at least captures the one important truth—namely, while lawyers generally should prefer their clients' interests, sometimes they should not do so.

Of course, the question remains *when* a lawyer should say no to a client. Professor Fried has sought to answer this question by distinguishing between what he calls institutional and personal harms. If in helping a client you happen to harm another person through the use of a legally approved rule, Fried would say you bear no moral culpability for the harm that follows. This permissible type of harm he calls an institutional harm because it is the legal institution, not the lawyer personally, that he believes is accountable for the harm that results. As an example, Fried points to statutes of limitations. Asserting a statute of limitations defense might extinguish a meritorious legal claim, but it is a defense the law allows. And Fried would say that it is the statute of limitations, not you, that is harming the plaintiff, so you may feel free to assert it. By contrast, Fried condemns what he terms personal harms—wrongs a lawyer does by his person to the person of another that are beyond what is sanctioned by the legal institution. These are things a lawyer should not do even if a client demands it. By way of example, Fried points to a client's request that you lie to opposing counsel. This, he says, is a moral act aimed at an individual, so the lawyer bears culpability for it and should refrain from doing it.

I confess I am not sure whether this account is totally satisfying. Consider, first, the claim that a lawyer bears no moral culpability for institutional harms. What if the law says, as it did in antebellum America, that you can use legal process to compel a person hiding a runaway slave to return that slave to your client? That's a claim or defense permitted by the legal institution and so at least arguably permissible according to Fried. Yet are we really confident a lawyer would bear no moral culpability for intentionally invoking such an obviously unjust law?

Next, let's take Fried's claim about personal harms. Here, consider a vigorous cross-examination that you know will undermine the witness's character and general credibility. This undoubtedly will benefit your client, but it will also upset the witness and cause emotional harm. Fried suggests that such questioning may be a personal harm to the extent it implies that the witness "is unworthy of respect." But it isn't clear why this harm is properly characterized as a personal rather than an institutional one. Isn't the very institutional purpose of cross-examination to test the worthiness of a witness's testimony? The same question can be asked about Fried's example of lying to counsel. He characterizes that as a personal harm. But such lies are also often forbidden by institutional rules because they impose a wrong on the justice system itself by misleading the tribunal and interfering with its truth-finding functions.

Instead of trying to distinguish between institutional and personal harms, I wonder whether it might be more useful, at least as a tentative starting point, to focus on whether the action involves the lawyer intentionally doing harm to other persons and goods. As we've discussed, the lawyer generally serves a morally upright function by helping ensure that a client can access our justice system. In this way, the lawyer usually intends to help realize important ends for his client, including equal treatment and due process. To be sure, in vindicating a client's lawful interests the lawyer also often does damage to someone else's interests. Litigation is often a zero-sum game. But in acting to vindicate the client's lawful interests, the lawyer does not intend to do any harm to the client's opponent—this is merely an unintended consequence, if one that is foreseen or even inevitable.

Consider, for example, a client who comes to you contending she was injured by the defendant and seeking compensation for her medical bills. In seeking compensation from the other party, no doubt you will injure the other party's interests and perhaps cause the other party serious emotional as well as financial trauma. But in doing all this you hardly intend to hurt the opposing party. You only intend to help vindicate your client's lawful interest. That this is true is suggested by the following counterfactual hypothetical: If you could fully vindicate your client's interest, obtain full compensation for her injuries, without hurting anyone else in the process, would that satisfy your purposes just as well? The answer here is emphatically yes. Injuring others, though it may be a consequence of your actions, is not part of your intent. And this occurs, as I alluded to before, because we live in a world where there are many upright ways to live life, and in pursuing one good you will sometimes inevitably do harm to other goods.

Under this line of reasoning, a lawyer may take a great many actions in aid of a client. But at least some important things are categorically ruled out as things a lawyer should not do. For example, suppose you file a colorable claim but do so with the purpose of inflicting damage to the other party, using the legal system as a sort of weapon to harm another. Note that the means you're using are entirely lawful and you are entitled as a lawyer to use them. The claim is itself valid on the merits. But you harbor an ultimate purpose or end to hurt another person. If the analysis I've suggested holds, this is a no-go. The lawyer should not pursue the end purpose of harming others, even if the means he uses are institutionally permitted. It is, I think, for exactly this reason that the common law long ago developed torts like abuse of process.

Consider as well the fugitive slave law example. What if an antebellum client sought your assistance to recover a fugitive, claiming he is merely asserting a property interest protected by law? To vindicate your client's property interest you must intentionally seek to place another person in chains. And you don't just foresee the fugitive's enslavement as a possibility, you intend it. It would, after all, frustrate your whole purpose in the case to see the fugitive slave remain a free person. Of course, we can hope that examples of such profoundly unjust laws are few and far between in a decent contemporary society. But we still might ask whether lawyers can be any more willfully blind to their possibility than Nazi field marshals.

Tonight, I have sought to suggest, at least as a starting point, that we have a duty to avoid taking actions for our clients that involve using means or ends that intentionally do harm to other persons or goods. This rule leaves considerable room for the lawyer to defend the client's interests thoroughly, to interpose alternative defenses, to conduct vigorous cross-examinations. But it does not leave lawyers morally blameless whenever their clients tell them to do something. Saying "the client made me do it" isn't a complete answer to the question of legal ethics. But if knowing this much might be a useful starting point, it's also reasonable for you to ask, Where is the end point? Beyond refraining from intentionally harming others, when should a lawyer decline to follow his or her client off the moral cliff?

This is surely an important question, and no doubt a comprehensive answer would require an even longer talk than the one you've already had to endure. But it might be enough for the moment to say I suspect that most of the answer to that question lies in lessons we probably learned a long time ago. The Golden Rule, tolerance, civility, and self-discipline come to mind as some of the cardinal virtues of the good lawyer as well as the good person. As Dean Hellman observed, when you enter this profession you are likely to encounter some who will encourage you to unlearn these old truths. But just because you have a law degree doesn't give you a license to forget what your grandmother taught you or what you learned in kindergarten. At the same time, I think it's important to admit that we all make mistakes and go awry. And, yes, that most assuredly includes us judges. No one is perfect and all of us in this profession are probably more in need of penance than praise when it comes to ethics; few of us can afford to live in glass houses. The truth is, the ethical virtues take hard work and constant practice, trial, and, yes, error. In fact, in law as in life it is usually our mistakes that are our best teachers and make us wise.

Aristotle recognized all this. He said that ethics involves a state of character that exhibits itself in actions. On this view, something that involves not just belief but repetition, reinforcement, success, and constant learning from failure. You remember the old saying: Watch your actions, they become habits; watch your habits, they become character; watch your character, for it becomes your destiny. It's not Aristotle but it's very Aristotelean. And let me assure you, you will have many chances for practice in our shared profession. The ethical challenges will surely come and so will the chance to learn from your mistakes. It's not possible to avoid either. But how you respond to them, what habits you develop over time, will make all the difference.

For me, a personal reminder of what I think we are all aspiring to as lawyers and judges lies in a scene from Robert Bolt's play *A Man for All Seasons* when Thomas More is betrayed by his protégé, Richard Rich. After Rich testifies falsely at the trial against More, More sees Rich wearing a new chain of office—one that signifies Rich has become attorney general for the relatively small principality of Wales. More asks, "Why, Richard, it profits a man nothing to give his soul for the whole world . . . But for Wales[?]" I think it can be helpful to keep that scene in mind and maybe ask yourself when an ethical challenge arises: My soul for a trial? An appeal? Or some lousy discovery motion? At the end of the day, after all, your personal integrity—your state of character, as Aristotle would have it—is among the most valuable things in your possession. Not the money or the clients, the wins or the losses. The reward of ethical practice is the ease of mind you feel when you go to sleep, when you tell your children about your career, when you retire with a clear conscience.

TEN THINGS TO DO IN YOUR FIRST TEN YEARS AFTER GRADUATION

Having now reached the point in life where others think I have lived long enough and made mistakes enough to give at least some useful life advice, I've delivered my share of commencement addresses. The one below I gave at the Florida State University College of Law during my time on the Tenth Circuit. In writing the speech, I tried to re-create a list of the "top ten" things I wish someone had told me to try in my early years out of school.

WHEN I WAS INVITED TO SPEAK WITH YOU, THE QUESTION arose: What fascinating legal topic would new law school graduates want to hear about? Maybe the fine points of the rule against perpetuities? Perhaps the thrilling opinions I've written lately? But then I thought: Why spoil such a beautiful spring day? So how about a little more practical advice? With a nod to David Letterman, here's a Top Ten List of Things You Should Do in Your First Ten Years After Graduation.

NUMBER 10:
GET IN THE GAME.

Some of you will become corporate or appellate or public policy lawyers. And those are great and rewarding careers. But if I had to guess, most of you came to law school with at least a twitch of a desire to try cases, perhaps inspired by *Boston Legal* or *Law & Order* . . . or maybe misled by them. Whatever your ultimate specialty, trying a case from soup to nuts is one of the great thrills of the practice of law. And know this: You can do it. Sure, you've spent three years reading a lot of appellate opinions and scholarly articles. And saying you learned how to win a jury trial in law school is sort of like saying you learned how to play baseball from George Will's book or Ken Burns's documentary. But a trial isn't rocket science. You don't need to be sixty years old to be effective. If you're willing to immerse yourself in the law and the facts of your case, and if you're willing to take guidance from those who've been in the trenches before, there's no reason why you can't be an effective trial lawyer right out of the gate.

One of my last trials in private practice was a $20 million fraud dispute. I asked a lawyer three months out of a clerkship to help, gave her witnesses and arguments. She did a brilliant job. . . . True, she didn't sleep for a month. . . . But she did do a brilliant job—and you can too.

Now, to be sure, standing up in court can be scary. I remember my first case in private practice. I was told to argue motions and prepare for trial an $80 million fraud claim. I had little idea what I was doing. Okay, no idea. But I had a great mentor and worked day and night. And when time came to go to court to argue this or that motion, I would often rent a car to drive the eighty miles to the county courthouse by myself. The other side would show up with a phalanx of lawyers. My knees were knocking.

NUMBER 9:
LEARN TO WIN—AND LOSE—GRACIOUSLY.

The first part is the easier part. We can all at least seem gracious when we're winning. The other part of the equation requires a lot more effort, and a sense of ethics. Ask the several prominent national lawyers who've been in the headlines recently for trying to bribe judges or pay off witnesses. They had glittering careers at the top of the profession, but their indictments for cutting ethical corners—being unwilling to lose graciously when the law required it—leave behind a stain on their careers that must be hard to bear. Cautionary tales for all of us.

What do I mean by ethics? Well, I do not mean the fill-in-the-bubble ethics from the professional ethics exam you will take. (You will hear the joke about that exam—the right answer seems always to be the second most ethical choice.) Instead, I mean what Aristotle meant by ethics—a state of character displayed in good, that is morally upright, actions.

You will face many ethical challenges in the practice of law. I guarantee it. If opposing counsel behaves inappropriately, you will be tempted to respond in kind. Your clients and colleagues may even encourage you to do so. And it's easy to fall into the trap. No one is perfect after all; we are all human. And neither is the practice of law supposed to be a game of tiddlywinks. It is an adversarial process and disagreements are the reason why our profession exists. But it is possible to disagree without losing sight of your soul.

Consider. Opposing counsel shades facts or case holdings in his or her brief. How tempting is it to respond by calling that a "lie" rather than simply pointing out that counsel erred and then citing the true facts and law to the court? Or opposing counsel won't produce basic materials in discovery, yet demands massive discovery from your client. Your client doesn't want to incur the expense of providing discovery without getting something in return. How easy is it to refuse production and engage in a game of tit for tat? But at the end of the day, your integrity is among the most valuable things in your possession. So be sure always to ask yourself: Would your grandmother approve of your behavior?

NUMBER 8:
TAKE A RISK.

I think you will find it mighty tempting to conform, to avoid saying or writing anything that might be controversial, and to stay in the same job forever. If you're headed into private practice with a large firm, you will find the golden handcuffs are real. And they get tighter over time, as your income increases and you take on responsibilities for feeding other people, both at home and at the office. Nothing is wrong with that. It is the nature of life, and we all have obligations to take care of those who depend on us. We lawyers are a risk-averse lot. That's why so many of us went to law school in the first place—because it was a "safe" option.

But don't *always* succumb to the most obvious and comfortable path. You don't want to find yourself headed into retirement wondering: What if you had run for office? Started your own law firm? Joined that nonprofit? Give those things a try. A law degree gives you a tremendous safety net, a marketability, even if your risk doesn't always pan out. When I left law school, I thought about joining an established firm. Then a new and very small litigation shop approached me, one that few had heard of at the time. I was intrigued by the opportunity the firm offered for a young person to get loads of experience. But I wondered: What if this little shop didn't make it? The answer I received from a good friend sticks with me: What's the worst-case scenario? Give it a try for two years and if the firm fails, one of those big places will probably still have you. Good advice then. Good advice now. Taking a risk may mean anxiety along the way, but it will make you wildly happy if it succeeds and wiser if it fails.

NUMBER 7:
SEE THE WORLD.

There are two great times in life to see the world: when you're a poor student and don't need the comforts, or when you retire and can afford them. In between, the demands of a busy career and even busier little ones running around make travel difficult. Ask any parent who has spent a long flight with a screaming child, trying to change a diaper while wedged into one of those airplane bathrooms.

If you haven't had an opportunity to see a bit of the world, now's your chance. Don't wait until you're sixty-five, or sixty-seven, or whatever it is. . . . Heck, by the time you retire, Social Security will probably have you working until you're eighty.

The simple fact is, most employers don't care whether you start work in August or December after your graduation in May. But those few months could generate some of your fondest memories and best experiences in life. I took some time off after law school to study in

England and wound up engaged to a British woman who is now my wife. The fortuity of a lifetime. Who knows where your travels might take you?

NUMBER 6:
WRITE SOMETHING SIGNIFICANT.

Lawyers are writers. The written word is the dominant tool we use to persuade judges or close a deal. Doctors have their stethoscopes and scalpels. Engineers have their calculators and cranes. For better or worse, we have our laptops and legal briefs.

You will experience a lot in this profession, become an expert in a field, and a good deal of wisdom will come to reside in your heads. Please take the time at some point along the way to write it down. There's no better way to share your learning with those who will follow you in the profession. And there's no better way to educate the generalist judges who do not operate in your specialized field every day.

I suspect you will also find the process of writing something significant to be a great reward. Yes, writing is hard. It forces you to focus exactingly on the logic of your argument and it is a solitary job. But it is a rewarding one too. Contributing to the development of a field of law, or to the solution of a contemporary social problem—you will be surprised by the influence your written word can have.

NUMBER 5:
PRO BONO IS *PRO BONO PUBLICO*—
AND *PRO BONO* FOR YOU TOO.

You will find it easy enough to sell every hour of your professional time to companies or millionaires. They have their troubles, need your help, and will pay you well for it. But find the time to take on other clients. You can eliminate your fee or work out some creative alternatives. You will find the time spent representing worthy individuals and nonprofits incredibly rewarding. From those seeking asylum in this country, to criminal defendants proceeding *pro se* on appeal, to litigation work for nonprofits operating on a shoestring budget, all need (often desperately) access to the skills you've learned in law school. And helping them will benefit you too. You will feel more grounded as a person, more a part of your community. And the psychic income is real: Most of these clients will be grateful for your help in ways that are maybe now hard even to imagine.

NUMBER 4:
RELISH YOUR FRIENDSHIPS DEVELOPED HERE IN LAW SCHOOL.

It's hard to pick out the best thing about law school—the professors, the time to think hard about new concepts and ideas, the opportunity to learn new skills. But maybe the best thing of all is your classmates. You're surrounded by an amazing group of people who will go on to do great things and who have much to teach you. Among those at law school with me, as it turns out, were a future solicitor general of the United States, loads of law professors and judges, the head of the Republican Party, and a president of the United States. Many of these people became real friends; others by chance (and regrettably) I didn't get to know as well; but what a collection of interesting people. So make the most of the chance to get to know your classmates while you have it and in the years to come relish your friendships from law school. They can become some of your most lasting treasures.

Now, I know you will respond: But I'm looking forward to having memories of law school fade away as quickly as possible! And fair enough. After all, some things are best forgotten. But don't forget your friends. You will enjoy watching them, their families, and their careers unfold almost as much as your own.

NUMBER 3:
FIND A PASSION OUTSIDE THE LAW.

We all hear the tales of the fantastic young lawyer who died of a heart attack at forty-four. He was super at what he did, but that's all he did. No sports, no hobbies, just a grind. Beware.

Now, I readily concede that hard work is inevitable in the profession you've chosen—especially if you want to be any good at it. He who works hardest often produces the best results. But at the same time, a life in the law doesn't mean your life has to be the law. You will enjoy your profession (not to mention your life) much more if you also pursue a passion outside the law. You may even be a more successful lawyer for it. Clients and jurors, after all, are real people and they relate to real and balanced people. Whether it's flying or fly-fishing, skiing or swimming, find something you love. If you already have a passion, don't forget it in the first few years of practice. Keep at it. If you don't have something you're wild about yet, it's hardly too late. But take up that new sport or activity now. Let me assure you, it doesn't get easier with age.

NUMBER 2:
A DON'T.

I've tried to focus on things you should consider doing—the "dos," if you will—rather than dwell on the negative, the things you shouldn't do. But let me mention just one here.

Please don't take yourself too seriously. Law school gives you many skills, but there are a lot of mighty smart people out there who didn't go to this esteemed law school, or any law school at all. Some of the wiliest trial lawyers I know went to law schools you probably turned down, and I have learned as much or more from them as I ever did from those with fancier degrees. Many of the most creative, entrepreneurial clients I represented also never went to graduate school or even college. Some dropped out of high school. Just because they don't speak our legal language doesn't mean they are any less able or interesting. Far from it.

NUMBER 1:
FINALLY . . .

And now, finally, the number one thing you should do during the first ten years after leaving law school: Remember why you came here in the first place.

Did you come to law school to make money or make a difference? I suspect it was to make a real difference in your community and the world around you. Don't forget that.

One of the great things about the legal profession is the many ways in which you can use your knowledge to make such a large and positive public contribution. Lawyers have shaped this country since its founding. Almost half of the signers of the Declaration of Independence were lawyers. Of course, public service isn't the road to riches or the sure path to celebrity. Those who put their names to the Declaration may be warmly remembered today, but in their own time many thought they were signing their own death warrant. The real value in service lies in the fact that, come what may, you will know that you've done your best with your time here, worrying not about satisfying your own needs and wants but working for a cause you recognize as something greater and more enduring than yourself. And public service is, I think you will find, the most rewarding thing you can do with your law degree. In my own life, I can tell you that 7:00 A.M. meetings at the Department of Justice were always easier for me to make than 10:00 A.M. depositions in private practice.

Finally, please don't forget to aim high. If you don't tackle the issues facing our country today—its debts, its wars, its social, legal, and environmental problems—somebody else will. And the risk is that it will be somebody less capable. So please don't worry only about making money and "check out" of civic society and our government. It is your republic—and up to you to keep it.

7.

FROM JUDGE
TO JUSTICE

As the process of my nomination and confirmation to the Supreme Court unfolded, it was an exercise in experiencing the unexpected. Every day brought a new surprise. Take the day when, shortly after my nomination, Louise got a voicemail from the milkman asking if, from now on, could he please make his deliveries during the daytime hours rather than follow his usual predawn schedule? Curious, Louise asked the marshals stationed outside our home if something had happened.

"There was an incident, ma'am," came the reply.

Louise didn't think much of it until she got a second voicemail. This one informed her that our familiar deliveryman would no longer bring the milk; someone else would now make the trip. Louise went back to the marshals and asked if by chance the "incident" with the milkman had been unpleasant.

"He ended in the prone position, ma'am, yes."

On further inquiry it came out that in the wee hours, something like four in the morning, a van came barreling around the corner of our quiet country road in Colorado and slammed to a stop in front of our house. A man jumped out and ran toward the house carrying a large package that made a clanging sound. Uncertain who the man was, it seems the marshals tackled him. For the marshals' diligence and care in protecting my family and all my judicial colleagues across the country, I am grateful every single day and beyond words. Still, the milkman was (understandably) shaken by the experience—and I'm not sure the apologies and chocolates Louise sent helped all that much.

That story is pretty emblematic of the whole confirmation process. Outside observers would sometimes say, boy, it's going smoothly. If they only knew! Former colleagues in private practice had to turn their law firm upside down to produce almost every document I had laid fingers on during my years there over a decade ago. A small army at the Department of Justice worked around the clock to find every email I had ever written during my tenure there years earlier. Neighbors and family members and old classmates were stopped outside their homes and questioned. Former clients were prodded for their opinions on my skills in everything from trying cases to skiing mogul runs. The priests at our church were cold-called by journalists who then showed up for services to talk with parishioners. My law school, college, high school, and (yes) grade school teachers were quizzed. So were parents at our kids' schools.

The amazing thing to me was how most people responded. I was embarrassed at the intrusion and inconvenience they had to endure. But instead of holding it against me, so many rallied to support my family. Some supported Louise when I was away in Washington meeting with senators. Others kept me company when I missed my family back West, made sure I had something to wear (I had left home without enough clothes), and helped fill out thick Senate questionnaires. Scores of friends and former colleagues volunteered to write their senators or testify at the hearing. Others made sure I was ready for the hearing, spending long evenings after work and over cold pizza preparing me. Former law students I had taught over the years and classmates from every period of my education stepped forward, volunteering to do whatever they could. An incredible number of friends and family flew in from distant parts of the country to support me before and during the hearings, all without being asked.

My law clerks, especially, were there every step of the way. Law clerks are young men and women who assist a federal judge, usually for just one year after law school before launching their own careers. By the time they leave, they have become part of the family and I am so proud of all they go on to do—working in government and for nonprofits, as parents, and now even as judges. The hardest part of every year is watching them go. When my former clerks heard I might be nominated, they rallied round immediately. Some quit their jobs or chose to end their maternity leave early; others picked up and moved overnight to Washington just to help out. I couldn't believe it. Many of these family, friends, and former clerks weren't "conservative" or "originalists" either; far from it. They just wanted to be there for my family and me.

In the middle of it all, I remember sitting on a flight leaving Colorado for Washington. By then, the confirmation process was in full swing and I was feeling more than a little unmoored. I wound up seated next to a young girl who couldn't have been more than six or so. She reminded me of my own daughters at that age. When the plane encountered some turbulence, the girl turned to me and asked if I wouldn't mind if she held my hand. Later, as the flight smoothed, she asked if I would like to draw with her. We spent the rest of the flight drawing pictures and coloring with her crayons and markers. She had no idea who I was; it was lovely to be anonymous for a moment and to forget about everything else. Once we got off the plane, her mother, who it turned out had been seated nearby, figured out who I was and not long after that I received a thank-you note from the young lady. It was a drawing of her and me holding hands in front of an airplane.

That experience turned out to be one of countless like it. After years of living happily anonymous as a lawyer and a judge, all of a sudden I found myself recognized nearly everywhere: in the airport, out jogging, even hiking in the Colorado mountains. It was unsettling at first; sometimes it still is. But with the loss of anonymity I came to learn I had received a gift in return I did not expect. Thousands of people stopped me or wrote to me during the confirmation process to wish me well. Some would come up to me and say: I didn't vote for the president who nominated you but I'm praying for you and your family. Others would nudge me in line at a coffee shop and tell me a joke to brighten my day. I got a pile of care packages too. One included a note saying the sender noticed on television that my socks appeared worn out, so she included a bundle of new ones. These encounters reminded me again and again of the goodness that runs deep in our collective heritage and sustains our republic.

This chapter collects some of the statements I made during and shortly after the nomination and confirmation process. In them, I tried to share the immense love of country I had witnessed from my friends, family, and countless others across America. I tried to explain my gratitude to the people and nation I am honored to serve. And I tried, too, to distill and explain some of the ideas I care about, and have written or spoken about over the years, as well as how I came to them—ideas about our Constitution, the separation of powers, the judge's proper role, and some of the challenges we face today when it comes to civics and civility.

THE EAST ROOM

In the moments leading up to the announcement of my nom-
ination, Louise and I met with the President. Secretly, each of
us was a bit disappointed with the plans for the evening,
which had her sitting in the audience rather than standing
with me at the podium in the East Room. But as we waited
for the designated time to arrive I could tell the President was
thinking something over. And then without a word to us he
directed a change in plans. Apparently, he could tell how
much Louise meant to me. When it all started, there she was,
standing next to me, as my nomination was announced.
These are the words I spoke that evening.

M R. PRESIDENT, MR. VICE PRESIDENT, YOU AND YOUR TEAM HAVE shown me great courtesy in this process, and you have entrusted me with a most solemn assignment. Standing here in a house of history, and acutely aware of my own imperfections, I pledge that if I am confirmed, I will do all my powers permit to be a faithful servant of the Constitution and laws of this great country.

For the last decade, I've worked as a federal judge in a court that spans six western states, serving about 20 percent of the continental United States and about eighteen million people. The men and women I've worked with at every level in our circuit are an inspiration to me. I've watched them fearlessly tending to the rule of law, enforcing the promises of our Constitution and living out daily their judicial oaths to administer justice equally to rich and poor alike, following the law as they find it and without respect to their personal political beliefs. I think of them tonight.

Of course, the Supreme Court's work is vital not just to a region of the country, but to the whole, vital to the protection of the people's liberties under law, and to the continuity of our Constitution— the greatest charter of human liberty the world has ever known.

The towering judges that have served in this particular seat of the Supreme Court, including Antonin Scalia and Robert Jackson, are much in my mind at this moment. Justice Scalia was a lion of the law. Agree or disagree with him, all of his colleagues on the bench benefited from his wisdom and enjoyed his humor. And like them, I miss him.

I began my legal career working for Byron White, the last Coloradan to serve on the Supreme Court—and the only justice to lead the NFL in rushing. He was one of the smartest and most courageous men I've ever known.

When Justice White retired, he gave me the chance to work for Justice Kennedy as well. Justice Kennedy was incredibly welcoming and gracious, and like Justice White, he taught me so much. I am forever grateful. And if you've ever met Judge David Sentelle, you'll know just how lucky I was to land a clerkship with him right out of school. Thank you. These judges brought me up in the law. Truly, I would not be here without them. Today is as much their day as it is mine.

In the balance of my professional life, I've had the privilege of working as a practicing lawyer and teacher. I've enjoyed wonderful colleagues whose support means so much to me at this moment—as it has year in and year out.

Practicing in the trial work trenches of the law, I saw, too, that when we judges don our robes, it doesn't make us any smarter, but it does serve as a reminder of what's expected of us: impartiality and independence, collegiality and courage.

As this process now moves to the Senate, I look forward to speaking with members from both sides of the aisle, to answering their questions and to hearing their concerns. I consider the United States Senate the greatest deliberative body in the world, and I respect the important role the Constitution affords it in the confirmation of our judges.

I respect, too, the fact that in our legal order, it is for Congress and not the courts to write new laws. It is the role of judges to apply, not alter, the work of the people's representatives. A judge who likes every outcome he reaches is very likely a bad judge, stretching for results he prefers rather than those the law demands.

I am so thankful tonight for my family, my friends, and my faith. These are the things that keep me grounded at life's peaks and have sustained me in its valleys. To Louise, my incredible wife and companion of twenty years, my cherished daughters—who are watching on TV—and all my family and friends, I cannot thank you enough for your love and for your prayers. I could not attempt this without you.

Mr. President, I am honored and I am humbled. Thank you very much.

THE SENATE
JUDICIARY COMMITTEE

———

As I was drafting my opening statement to the Senate Judiciary Committee, the men and women who brought me to that point in my life loomed large in my mind. I wanted to acknowledge their influence. I also was aware that for some watching it would be the first time they'd hear a judge speak about what judges do. I hoped to share, however imperfectly, a glimpse into what the judicial life looks like and some of the ideas that I had written about as a judge, and that are now found in this book.

M R. CHAIRMAN, SENATOR FEINSTEIN, MEMBERS OF THE COMMITTEE: I am honored and humbled to be here. Since coming to Washington, I have met with over seventy senators. You have offered a warm welcome and wise advice. Thank you. I also want to thank the President and Vice President. They and their teams have been very gracious to me and I thank them for this honor. I want to thank Senators Bennet and Gardner and General Katyal for their introductions. Reminding us that—long before we are Republicans or Democrats—we are Americans.

Sitting here I am acutely aware of my own imperfections. But I pledge to each of you and to the American people that, if confirmed, I will do all my powers permit to be a faithful servant of the Constitution and laws of our great nation.

I could not even attempt this without Louise, my wife of more than twenty years. The sacrifices she has made and her giving heart leave me in awe. I love you so much. We started off in a place very different from this one: a small apartment and little to show for it.

When Louise's mother first came to visit, she was concerned by the conditions. As I headed out the door to work, I will never forget her whispering to her daughter, in a voice just loud enough for me to hear: Are you sure he's really a lawyer?

To my teenage daughters watching out West. Bathing chickens for the county fair. Devising ways to keep our determined pet goat out of the garden. Building a semi-functional plyboard hovercraft for science fair. Driving eight hours through a Wyoming snowstorm with high school debaters in the back arguing the whole way. These are just a few of my favorite memories. I love you impossibly.

To my extended family across Colorado. When we gather, it's dozens of us. We hold different political and religious views, but we are united in love. Between the family pranks and the pack of children running rampant, whoever is hosting is usually left with at least one drywall repair.

To my parents and grandparents. They are no longer with us but there's no question on whose shoulders I stand. My mom was one of the first women graduates of the University of Colorado Law School. As the first female assistant district attorney in Denver, she helped start a program to pursue deadbeat dads. And her idea of daycare sometimes meant I got to spend the day wandering the halls or tagging behind police officers. She taught me that headlines are fleeting—courage lasts.

My dad taught me that success in life has little to do with success. Kindness, he showed me, is the great virtue. He showed me, too, that there are few places closer to God than walking in the wilderness or wading a trout stream. Even if it is an awfully long drive home with the family dog after he encounters a skunk.

To my grandparents. As a boy, I could ride my bike to their homes and they were huge influences. My mom's father, poor and Irish, started working to help support his family as a boy after losing his own dad. But the nuns made sure he got an education, and he became a doctor. Even after he passed away, I heard from grateful patients who recalled him kneeling by their bedsides to pray together. His wife, my grandmother, grew up in a Nebraska home where an icebox wasn't something you plugged into the wall but something you lowered into the ground. With seven children, she never stopped moving—or loving.

My dad's father made his way through college working on Denver's trolley cars. He practiced law through the Great Depression, and he taught me that lawyers exist to help people with their problems, not the other way around. His wife came from a family of pioneers. She loved to fish. And she taught me how to tie a fly.

I want to thank my friends. Liberals and conservatives and independents, from every kind of background and belief, many hundreds have written this committee on my behalf. They have been there for me always. Not least when we recently lost my uncle Jack, a hero of mine and a lifelong Episcopal priest. He gave the benediction when I took my oath as a judge eleven years ago. I confess I was hoping he might offer a similar prayer for me this year. As it is, I know he is smiling.

I want to thank my fellow judges across the country. Judging is sometimes a lonely and hard job. But I have seen how these men and women work with courage and collegiality, independence and integrity. Their work helps make the promises of our Constitution and laws real for us all.

I want to thank my legal heroes. Justice White, my mentor. A product of the West, he modeled for me judicial courage. He followed the law wherever it took him without fear or favor to anyone. War hero. Rhodes Scholar. And, yes, highest-paid NFL football player of his day. In Colorado today there is God and John Elway and Peyton Manning. In my childhood it was God and Byron White.

I also had the great fortune to clerk for Justice Kennedy. He showed me that judges can disagree without being disagreeable. That everyone who comes to court deserves respect. And that a legal case isn't just some number or a name but a life story.

Justice Scalia was a mentor too. He reminded us that words matter—that the judge's job is to follow the words that are in the law, not replace them with words that aren't. His colleagues cherished his great humor too. Now, we didn't agree about everything. The justice fished with the enthusiasm of a New Yorker. He thought the harder you slapped the line on the water, somehow the more the fish would love it.

Finally, there is Justice Jackson. He wrote clearly so everyone could understand his decisions. He never hid behind legal jargon.

And while he was a famously fierce advocate for his clients as a lawyer, he reminded us that, when you become a judge, you fiercely defend only one client: the law.

By their example, these judges taught me about the rule of law and the importance of an independent judiciary, how hard our forebearers worked to win these things, how easy they are to lose, and how every generation must either take its turn carrying the baton or watch it fall.

MR. CHAIRMAN, THESE DAYS we sometimes hear judges cynically described as politicians in robes. Seeking to enforce their own politics rather than striving to apply the law impartially. But I just don't think that's what a life in the law is about.

As a lawyer working for many years in the trial court trenches, I saw judges and juries—while human and imperfect—trying hard every day to decide fairly the cases I presented. As a judge now for more than a decade, I have watched my colleagues spend long days worrying over cases. Sometimes the answers we reach aren't ones we would personally prefer. Sometimes the answers follow us home and keep us up at night. But the answers we reach are always the ones we believe the law requires. For all its imperfections, the rule of law in this nation truly is a wonder—and it is no wonder that it is the envy of the world.

Once in a while, of course, we judges do disagree. But our disagreements are never about politics, only the law's demands. Let me offer an example. The first case I wrote as a judge to reach the Supreme Court divided 5 to 4. The Court affirmed my judgment with the support of Justices Thomas and Sotomayor, while Justices Stevens and Scalia dissented. Now that's a lineup some might think unusual. But actually it's exactly the sort of thing that happens, quietly, day in and day out, in the Supreme Court and in courts across our country. I wonder if people realize that Justices Thomas and Sotomayor agree about 60 percent of the time, or that Justices Scalia and Breyer agreed even more often than that. All in the toughest cases in our whole legal system.

Here's another example. Over the last decade, I've participated in over 2,700 appeals. Often these cases are hard too: only about 5 percent of all federal lawsuits make their way to decision in a court of appeals. I've served with judges appointed by President Obama all the way back to President Johnson. And in the Tenth Circuit we hear cases from six states, in two time zones, covering 20 percent of the continental United States. But in the West we listen to one another respectfully, we tolerate and cherish different points of view, and we seek consensus whenever we can. My law clerks tell me that 97 percent of the 2,700 cases I've decided were decided unanimously. And that I have been in the majority 99 percent of the time.

Of course, I make my share of mistakes. As my daughters never tire of reminding me, putting on a robe doesn't make me any smarter. I'll never forget my first day on the job. Carrying a pile of papers up steps to the bench, I tripped on my robe and everything just about went flying. But troublesome as it can be, the robe does mean something—and not just that I can hide coffee stains on my shirt. Putting on a robe reminds us that it's time to lose our egos and open our minds. It serves, too, as a reminder of the modest station we judges are meant to occupy in a democracy. In other countries, judges wear scarlet, silk, and ermine. Here, we judges buy our own plain black robes. And I can report that the standard choir outfit at the local uniform supply store is a pretty good deal. Ours is a judiciary of honest black polyester.

When I put on the robe, I am also reminded that under our Constitution, it is for this body, the people's representatives, to make new laws. For the executive to ensure that those laws are faithfully enforced. And for neutral and independent judges to apply the law in the people's disputes. If judges were just secret legislators, declaring not what the law is but what they would like it to be, the very idea of a government by the people and for the people would be at risk. And those who came to court would live in fear, never sure exactly what governs them except the judge's will. As Alexander Hamilton explained, "liberty can have nothing to fear from" judges who apply the law, but liberty "ha[s] every thing to fear" if judges try to legislate too.

In my decade on the bench, I have tried to treat all who come to court fairly and with respect. I have decided cases for Native Americans seeking to protect tribal lands, for class actions like one that ensured compensation for victims of nuclear waste pollution by corporations in Colorado. I have ruled for disabled students, prisoners, and workers alleging civil rights violations. Sometimes, I have ruled against such persons too. But my decisions have never reflected a judgment about the people before me—only my best judgment about the law and facts at issue in each particular case. For the truth is, a judge who likes every outcome he reaches is probably a pretty bad judge, stretching for the policy results he prefers rather than those the law compels.

As a student many years ago, I found myself walking through the Old Granary burial ground in Boston, where Paul Revere, John Hancock, and many of our founders are buried. I came across the tombstone of a lawyer and judge who today is largely forgotten, as we are all destined to be soon enough. His name was Increase Sumner. Written on his tombstone more than two hundred years ago was this description:

AS A LAWYER, HE WAS FAITHFUL AND ABLE;
AS A JUDGE, PATIENT, IMPARTIAL, AND DECISIVE. . . .
IN PRIVATE LIFE, HE WAS AFFECTIONATE AND MILD;
IN PUBLIC LIFE, HE WAS DIGNIFIED AND FIRM.
PARTY FEUDS WERE ALLAYED BY THE
CORRECTNESS OF HIS CONDUCT;
CALUMNY WAS SILENCED BY THE
WEIGHT OF HIS VIRTUES;
AND RANCOR SOFTENED BY THE AMENITY
OF HIS MANNERS.

These words stick with me. I keep them on my desk. They serve for me as a daily reminder of the law's integrity, that a useful life can be led in its service, of the hard work it takes, and an encouragement to good habits when I fail and falter. At the end of it all, I could hope for nothing more than to be described as he was. If confirmed, I pledge that I will do everything in my power to be that man.

THE FRONT PORCH

———

During my confirmation hearing, this question caught me off guard. It was a very personal one, but at the same time a very substantive one about all the subjects touched on in this book. It was a question about the front porch.

SENATOR SASSE: Let us engage in a little thought experiment. Thirty or forty years from now when you retire and hang up your robe, and you are out fishing or sitting on the front porch of your surely lovely home, and you look back over your career, how will you know if you were a good judge?

JUDGE GORSUCH: Senator, that is a question I ask my kids every semester when I teach ethics. I finish the semester by asking them to spend five minutes writing their obituary. They hate it. They think it is corny, and it might be a little corny. And then I ask them if they will volunteer to read some of them, and when they do, it always becomes clear people want to be remembered for the kindnesses they showed other people. And what I point out to them—what I try to point out—is that it is not how big your bank account balance is. Nobody ever puts that in their draft obituary, or that they billed the most hours, or that they won the most cases. It is how you treated other people along the way that matters. And for me, it is the words I read yesterday from Increase Sumner's tombstone [see page 321]. And that means as a person I would like to be remembered as a good dad, a good husband, kind and mild in private life, dignified and firm in public life. I have no illusions that I will be remembered for very long. If Byron White is nearly forgotten, as he is now and said he would be, I have no illusions I will last five minutes. That is as it should be.

SENATOR SASSE: So, when you distinguish between the rearview mirror of a justice later or a judge later in life looking back, and the rearview mirror of a senator, we have different callings. Unpack that for the American people. Help them understand how the retrospective look of a senator and her or his career is different than a judge's retrospective look.

JUDGE GORSUCH: I presume gingerly that you will look back on your career and say I accomplished this piece of legislation or that piece of legislation and changed the lives of the American people dramatically as a result. But as a judge looking back, the most you can hope for is you have done fairness to each person who has come before you, decided each case on the facts and the law, and that you have just carried on the tradition of a neutral, impartial judiciary. That is what we do. We just resolve cases and controversies. Lawyers are supposed to be fierce advocates, and I was once a fierce advocate for my clients. But a judge is supposed to listen courteously and rule impartially. So, frankly, my legacy should look and will look a lot smaller than yours, and that is the way it should be. That is the way the Constitution works.

ACKNOWLEDGMENTS

I WANT TO THANK THE MEN AND WOMEN OF THE FEDERAL JUDICIARY and especially my former colleagues on the Tenth Circuit with whom I worked closely for many years. Your work makes real the promises of our Constitution in the daily lives of millions of Americans and many of you inspired the reflections found in this book by your example.

I am grateful, too, for those who have supported my family and me through it all. Summit peaks are precarious spots and they are usually reached only after long and trying times through uncertain wilderness. But Louise and I have been graced with many guides and counselors, family and friends, law clerks and colleagues who have been there for us at every step. I do not know if I will ever have the words to convey the full measure of my thanks for your friendship and awe for your strength. I can only say that each of you has a place in my heart and Louise's, and always will.

I want to thank my students and former law clerks, too, for challenging, refining, and contributing to many of the ideas that appear in this book. Louise and I are so proud of you and grateful for your presence in our lives. Our law clerk family includes Mike Davis, Jessica Greenstone, Jamil Jaffer, Heather Kirby Lyions, Patrick Price, Mark Champoux, Ian Kellogg, Tim Meyer, Allison Jones Rushing, Theresa Wardon Benz, Jane Nitze, Matt Owen, Jonathan Papik, Leah Bressack, Josh Goodbaum, Michael McGinley, Lucas Walker, Katherine Crawford Yarger, Ben Strawn, Eric Tung, Stephen Yelderman, Tess Hand Bender, Dwight Carswell, Paul Dubbeling, Jason Murray, Sean Jackowitz, Jessica Livingston, Josh Parker, Jeff Quilici, Matthew Glover, Michael Kenneally, Leigh Llewelyn, Marissa Miller, Jerry Cedrone, David Feder, Hamilton Jordan, Jr., Collin White,

Alex Harris, Stefan Hasselblad, Jordan Moran, Allison Turbiville, Joe Celentino, Nathan Jack, Michael Qin, Dan Rauch, Ethan Davis, Alexander Kazam, Paul Mezzina, and Tobi Young.

Without Jane Nitze and David Feder, my collaborators, former clerks, and friends, this book simply would not have been possible. I am deeply grateful that they took time off before starting their new jobs to help assemble, develop, and refine the materials here. Their vision, insight, and enthusiasm always makes working with them a joy.

Twenty years later and I am indebted once more to Jessica Bartlow for her amazing editorial help and great friendship. Now, as well, I owe a happy new debt to Arielle Goldberg and Frances Lataif for their eagle eyes. Many of the pieces here I wrote with the help of my former judicial assistant, Holly Cody, who was and remains a cherished friend to me and mentor to my clerks.

Steve Benz, Ethan Davis, Jamil Jaffer, Greg Katsas, Alex Kazam, Ray Kethledge, Chris Mammen, Paul Mezzina, Tim Meyer, Jeff Quilici, Jeff Sutton, Grace and Michael Trent, Eric Tung, Tim Tymkovich, Steve Yelderman, and Tobi Young generously commented on pieces or the whole of early drafts. I am grateful not only for the many improvements they suggested but for the friendship their thoughtfulness represented. Mary Reynics and Tina Constable at Crown made the process of putting this book together fun and I am indebted for their wise advice along the way.

Finally, to Louise, Emma, and Belinda: Your love and support at life's peaks and through its wildernesses means more to me than I am able to express. You are the great blessings of my life.

A NOTE ON SOURCES

——

T HIS BOOK INCLUDES SPEECHES, ESSAYS, AND JUDICIAL OPINIONS written over the course of more than a decade. To make these pieces more accessible, I have revised and excerpted liberally and sometimes combined certain pieces with others, and I have done so without marking these alterations, additions, or deletions. Many of the pieces here have not been previously published and they contain no citations; others have been published with many citations and footnotes. To make the book more readable, I have omitted these citations and footnotes too. But many of the ideas discussed here are ancient and borrowed, sometimes from sources too long ingrained and dimly remembered to be faithfully recorded—but borrowed gratefully all the same. The reader interested in reference materials and notes may consult the following previously published speeches, essays, and opinions. I am grateful to the publishers of the speeches and essays for allowing them to be presented here.

SPEECHES AND ESSAYS

——

"Access to Affordable Justice," 100 Judicature 46 (2016)

"In Tribute: Justice Anthony M. Kennedy," 132 Harv. L. Rev. 1 (2018)

"Intention and the Allocation of Risk," in *Reason, Morality, and Law: The Philosophy of John Finnis,* ed. John Keown and Robert P. George (Oxford: Oxford University Press, 2013). Reprinted here under the title "Of Intentions and Consequences."

"Law's Irony," 37 Harv. J.L. & Pub. Pol'y 743 (2014)

"Of Lions and Bears," 66 Case W. Res. L. Rev. 905 (2016)

"On Precedent," adapted from Bryan Garner et al., *The Law of Judicial Precedent* (St. Paul, MN: Thomson Reuters, 2016). Reprinted with the permission of Thomson Reuters.

JUDICIAL OPINIONS

Alejandre-Gallegos v. Holder, 598 Fed. Appx. 604 (10th Cir. 2015)

A.M. v. Holmes, 830 F.3d 1123 (10th Cir. 2016)

American Atheists, Inc. v. Davenport, 637 F.3d 1095 (10th Cir. 2010)

Caring Hearts v. Burwell, 824 F.3d 968 (10th Cir. 2016)

Carpenter v. United States, 138 S.Ct. 2206 (2016)

Direct Marketing Association v. Brohl, 814 F.3d 1129 (10th Cir. 2016)

Gutierrez-Brizuela v. Lynch, 834 F.3d 1142 (10th Cir. 2016)

Henson v. Santander, 137 S.Ct. 1718 (2017)

Hester v. United States, 139 S.Ct. 509 (2019)

Mathis v. Shulkin, 137 S.Ct. 1994 (2017)

Sessions v. Dimaya, 138 S.Ct. 1204 (2018)

United States v. Carloss, 818 F.3d 988 (10th Cir. 2016)

United States v. Games-Perez, 695 F.3d 1104 (10th Cir. 2012)

United States v. Nichols, 784 F.3d 666 (10th Cir. 2015)

United States v. Rentz, 777 F.3d 1105 (10th Cir. 2015)

PHOTO CREDITS

———

INDEX

ABOUT THE AUTHOR

NEIL M. GORSUCH is an associate justice of the Supreme Court of the United States. A Colorado native, he served as a judge on the U.S. Court of Appeals for the Tenth Circuit, which is based in Denver and hears appeals from six western states, before his appointment to the Supreme Court in April 2017. He has also worked as a senior official at the U.S. Department of Justice, where he helped oversee its civil litigating divisions; as a partner at a law firm; as a law professor; and as a law clerk for Justices Byron White and Anthony Kennedy. He received his undergraduate degree from Columbia; his law degree from Harvard, where he studied as a Truman scholar; and a doctorate in legal philosophy from Oxford, where he studied as a Marshall scholar.